Praise for *In Silence*

"Well researched and insightful."
—*The Cleveland Plain Dealer*

"Donald Spoto takes us into an understanding of prayer
that enables us to live in the capacious light of God's
presence. A striking feature of the book is the way it offers insights about prayer in every faith tradition."
—Bishop Thomas J. Gumbleton, Founding President
of Pax Christi

"More than a survey or a review, for which some might
mistake it, *In Silence* is a challenging reminder about
why we MUST pray. It should be required reading."
—Father James Gardiner

IN SILENCE

Donald Spoto, who earned his Ph.D. in theology at Fordham University, is the author of nineteen books, including *The Hidden Jesus: A New Life* and *Reluctant Saint: The Life of Francis of Assisi*. Based in California, he lives mostly in Denmark.

Donald Spoto

In Silence

Why We
Pray

PENGUIN COMPASS

PENGUIN COMPASS
Published by the Penguin Group
Penguin Group (USA) Inc., 375 Hudson Street, New York, New York 10014, U.S.A.
Penguin Group (Canada), 90 Eglinton Avenue East, Suite 700, Toronto,
Ontario, Canada M4P 2Y3 (a division of Pearson Penguin Canada Inc.)
Penguin Books Ltd, 80 Strand, London WC2R 0RL, England
Penguin Ireland, 25 St Stephen's Green, Dublin 2, Ireland (a division of Penguin Books Ltd)
Penguin Group (Australia), 250 Camberwell Road, Camberwell,
Victoria 3124, Australia (a division of Pearson Australia Group Pty Ltd)
Penguin Books India Pvt Ltd, 11 Community Centre, Panchsheel Park,
New Delhi – 110 017, India
Penguin Group (NZ), cnr Airborne and Rosedale Roads, Albany,
Auckland 1310, New Zealand (a division of Pearson New Zealand Ltd)
Penguin Books (South Africa) (Pty) Ltd, 24 Sturdee Avenue,
Rosebank, Johannesburg 2196, South Africa

Penguin Books Ltd, Registered Offices:
80 Strand, London WC2R 0RL, England

First published in the United States of America by Viking Compass,
a member of Penguin Group (USA) Inc. 2004
Published in Penguin Compass 2005

1   3   5   7   9   10   8   6   4   2

The Scripture quotations contained herein are from the New Revised Standard
Version Bible. Copyright © 1989 by the Division of Christian Education of the
National Council of the Churches of Christ in the USA. Used by permission.

THE LIBRARY OF CONGRESS HAS CATALOGED THE HARDCOVER EDITION AS FOLLOWS:
Spoto, Donald, —
In silence : why we pray / Donald Spoto.
p.   cm.
Includes bibliographical references (p. 221) and index.
ISBN 0-670-03347-2 (hc.)
ISBN 0 14 21.9638 X (pbk.)
1. Prayer.   I. Title.
BV210.3.S765 2004
248.3'2—dc22   2004049614

Printed in the United States of America
Set in Aldus   Designed by Francesca Belanger

For the Ursuline Nuns
of the Convent of St. Teresa
in New Rochelle, New York

*Aquae multae non potuerunt
extinguere caritatem.*

Acknowledgments

For their friendly and efficient help, I am grateful to the personnel of the Beverly Hills Public Library; the Bibliothèque Nationale, Paris; the British Library; the Library of the General Theological Seminary, New York; the Los Angeles Public Library; the New York Public Library; the Santa Monica Public Library; and the libraries of the University of California at Los Angeles.

For various suggestions and contributions during the research and writing of this book, I owe thanks to Herbert Bard; Elizabeth Beaumont Bissell; Rev. John Chryssavgis; Bernard Dick; Philip Endean, SJ; David E. Green; and Bernard McGinn.

My literary agent, Elaine Markson, has been my primary advocate and dear friend for over twenty-five years, and no words can adequately express the extent of my gratitude. She and her colleague Gary Johnson provide invaluable counsel—as well as endlessly patient encouragement. Their constancy is my life support system.

At Viking, I am very fortunate indeed to have Richard P. Kot for editor. He has enthusiastically championed this book from the start and has been in every way a judicious guide, especially in the final preparation of *In Silence* for publication. This is our second book together, and Rick's kindness and friendship embolden me to look forward to our continuing collaboration. Rick's assistant, Alessandra Lusardi, provided cheerful help at every point. And in preparing the edited manuscript for printing, important critical comments and helpful contributions were offered by Beth

Greenfeld and by Timothy Meyer. I owe all these good people my thanks for their keen readings.

With enormous admiration and devotion, this book is offered in tribute to an extraordinary community of religious women, identified on the dedication page. I have enjoyed their friendship and collegiality for many decades, during which I have learned a great deal about the deepest meaning of prayer and its resonance in everyday life. I treasure their rich intelligence, their courage, good humor and profound humanity.

Los Angeles

August 20, 2003:

The Memorial of Bernard of Clairvaux, Abbot

Contents

Introduction

"Faith itself is the soul's true country, and prayer is its native language."

With those words I concluded a chapter of an earlier work, *The Hidden Jesus: A New Life*. That book considered certain specific questions about the ancient Hebrew notion of the mystery of God, and about the earliest Christian assertions concerning God's continuing activity in Jesus of Nazareth. The questions and the assertions, taken collectively, comprise the basis for Judeo-Christian faith.

Faith, I suggested in *The Hidden Jesus*, is primarily an attitude about reality—a refusal to admit that life has no meaning and that everything is doomed to extinction; faith then involves a willingness to wonder, to ask questions rather than simply to deny what the senses do not immediately validate. Faith goes further and more deeply than belief; I hope to make this the subject of a future book.

☙

The apparent problem of the hiddenness and silence of God runs like a motif through the entire range of the Jewish-Christian Scriptures; they very much concerned me in *The Hidden Jesus*. Hiddenness and silence do not imply nonexistence, absence or a sort of divine detachment. On the contrary: people have become aware, however dimly, of the reality of God, and have realized a relationship with Him, only in silence. Hiddenness and silence are not nothing, nor are they to be taken for God's remoteness; they are in fact the condition of our meeting with God in time, amid the chaos of the world.

If the silence and hiddenness of God are signs of His presence and the key to understanding the deepest meaning of our lives, then we may indeed listen for God, hear Him in His silence, and find Him as the ultimately real Reality precisely in that silence and hiddenness. In other words, communication with God may be not only possible but also necessary; indeed, it may be actual long before we realize it is as so. Hence the book you are now holding—an inquiry into the meaning, nature, history, quality, types and effects of prayer in human experience.

⁂

If one wishes to approach prayer as an intellectual construct, it can be studied as a psychological phenomenon, a theme in the history of world religions, a subject for academic theological discourse or simply in its most familiar form as written or spoken entreaties or formulas directed to a higher being. In this book I have chosen to examine the subject from a different perspective. My aim is not to present yet another history of religion, nor an analysis of the sociological aspects of certain forms of institutional religious life or formal worship. Likewise, I do not offer a history of mysticism: the rarefied language of many mystics is too idiosyncratic to be adequately treated in this book. But some mystics are more accessible than others, and because sometimes they have cogent and powerful things to say about prayer, their writings will be considered here.

I have elected to treat prayer as an expression of an individual's inner life as it develops within the contexts of several dimensions of human experience. Dialogue is one mode of discovery about oneself and others, and prayer may be spoken of as a profound sort of dialogue. Asking, needing and desiring in some ways characterize every life in its ordinariness, and this implicit sense of one's contingency relates directly to our sense of a relationship with God. Suffering often makes people turn to God, or at least wonder about His presence or absence, and a cry amid suffering is among the commonest kinds of prayers. Love, too, in all its guises and categories, makes us somehow aware of the inevitability of connection with another and others: this human experience cannot be separated from a sense of the divine. Reflection on our experience, on what we do or feel or endure or receive, forms what we call our inner life. That reflection is the first and basic kind of prayer.

The primal awareness of the Beyond is sketched in the first chapter, which offers selected moments in the spiritual history of humankind, but only insofar as they illuminate the interior mystery of prayer. In the chapters that follow, then, I try to trace our inclination to pray out of certain basic universal experiences, for I believe that it is in dialogue, petition, forgiveness, suffering, abandonment, serenity and loving that we not only act and endure but also reach the depths of being truly alive. Transformation—not just of our outlook but of our very selves—then occurs inevitably. At the level of everyday, common human experiences and in our very particularity, we meet the living God.

In a way, I am attempting a new understanding of the vocabulary, grammar and syntax of a universal language that we are, as individuals and as a species, always just beginning to fathom. Among the central motifs of this book is the notion that it may well be impossible to consider prayer apart from life as a whole. We are as we pray, and our prayer is always in a state of becoming. Prayer parallels and enriches the process by which we discover the depth and breadth of what it means to be human.

Any attempt to speak of prayer in the 21st century is likely to lead to a confrontation with a cluster of objections—the two most notable being that prayer is irrelevant in a sophisticated age of science and technology; and that prayer is primarily a solipsistic dialogue with the self. Both rest on a belief that prayer is by its nature psychologically suspect. But its critics, if they are intellectually honest, ought to ask themselves whether they can dismiss or deny profound interior experiences claimed by others merely because they themselves are strangers to those experiences.

We should not lose sight of the fact that psychology itself is a remarkably fluid and mysterious discipline, one that deals with all manner of highly variable conjectures and subjective interpretations. Various schools of analysis have emerged, and partisans often apply their own fixed systems as templates for interpreting each and every human life or dilemma. This methodology, however, tends to reduce the unique human person to a standard issue that can be "treated" by certain established principles. But good science does not proceed in so reductive a fashion.

Just so, it is helpful to recall that no less a figure than Albert Einstein observed that human awareness of the divine could not be summarily discounted, and that in fact (as he wrote) "science without religion is lame, religion without science is blind." Since Einstein's death a half-century ago, most scientists would agree that what we call "laws of nature" are best regarded as a series of probabilities in a universe that remains mysterious and open.

The idea that there are fixed laws of nature is in fact useful only as a way of assessing the current state of what is known about the material world: in other words, these so-called laws enable us to understand certain phenomena as they appear to us now, at our current stage of interpreting the world.

On the other hand, the realms of creative thought and art, the worlds of aesthetic and interior spiritual life, gain little from being subjected to a priori principles. In this regard, we can consider that when Aristotle contemplated the universe, when Mozart composed, when Monet painted and when Mendel experimented with plants and seeds, they were engaged in interior activities that were not ultimately comprehensible through merely rational methods.

Still, for some people prayer is fundamentally incompatible with a modern scientific worldview. What good is it, they ask, to pray for rain in the midst of a drought? After all, tomorrow's weather is determined by today's conditions—more accurately, it was determined by yesterday's. A similar argument might be made about the course of an illness. What use is it to pray once all the medical remedies have been applied? Nature, they conclude, has taken and will take its course, either in response to scientific protocols or despite them.

Two replies come to mind. First, we constantly alter the course of "nature" by expressions of our will and in light of evolving knowledge. We seed the clouds; we build breakwaters and construct complex irrigation equipment; we discover that a rare herb just might treat a grave illness. It is ridiculous to suggest that we can always know the circumstances under which a desired end might be accomplished. The second response is more abstract and yet more to the point. Scientists receptive to a mysterious and often unpredictable universe can, as we have seen, admit that the laws of nature have more to do with a current sense of probability than with anything like certainty.

As regards the criticism that prayer is an isolating and self-absorbed exercise, are we in fact merely deluding ourselves and avoiding life's demands when we pray? Ought we not to arise from our knees and take our place within social, political and economic institutions, the better to effect the improvement of life for ourselves and others, instead of indulging inner fancies? Escapism is, of course, always a danger in prayer, and no less an authority than the 16th-century Spanish religious reformer, Teresa of Ávila, warns against seeking prayerful solitude merely to avoid the tensions, disturbances and obligations of life. She was a sharp-eyed woman and a gifted psychologist, centuries before psychology became a unique discipline—and she never relied on theories to substantiate her observations on human nature or the interior life.

Today, the objection of escapism often rests on a false assumption—namely, that prayer necessarily avoids or is opposed to the requirements of serious life in the world. On the contrary, as we shall see, genuine prayer has everything to do with real life. Politics, economics, science and technology and even the laudable achievements of humanitarians are never permanent solutions for the problems of the world, if for no other reason than the fact that it is the accomplishments themselves that always reveal what more remains to be done on humankind's behalf. There is an arrogance in those who protest otherwise, for humility demands that we recognize that our efforts and attainments must always remain incomplete.

It is precisely the necessity of a serious and caring life in the world that exercised the Spanish philosopher and literary critic Miguel de Unamuno in the first third of the 20th century. Speaking for many in his time, he finally found himself forced to acknowledge that the very nature of involvement in the commonweal led to a consideration that we may not be alone in the universe; from there, it was a short route to reflect on the notion of God. Unamuno was not especially at home with the classical idea of existential causality, but he was struck by the truth of a universe that nurtured human personality, which must logically possess the hidden resources to account for that personality— in other words, the ground and basis of the universe itself cannot be impersonal. Unamuno leaned heavily toward the affirmation of an ultimately personal Reality, and he was, at the last, deeply uncomfortable with a rank denial of meaning and, finally, of God.

The German philosopher-theologian Paul Tillich did more than lean in the direction of affirmation. Denied the right to teach in Germany under Nazism, Tillich found a welcome in American universities, where, until his death in 1965, he wrote and taught with a sharp focus on the renewal of religion and modern culture. The depth and ground of all being is God, Tillich asserted. If the word "God" was off-putting for some, he recommended that one reflect on the depths of life, on one's ultimate concerns, on what one takes seriously without any reservation. "He who knows about depth," said Tillich, "knows about God."

~

But as Tillich and others have warned, there is a danger of infusing prayer with a self-centered, magical spirit that has nothing to do with the search for God; no one who believes in prayer is immune to the subtle contagion of this spirit of magic. Many well-meaning people pray in an effort to learn something about themselves or even to raise their self-esteem. Unfortunately, contemporary culture, perhaps taking its cue from some ideal of physical perfection, tends to see everything, prayer included, in terms of its value for self-improvement. As soon as prayer becomes a means to that end, the sense of transcendence vanishes, and with it the longing for God and the openness to His presence. Authentic prayer does not aim to become a comforting form of self-expression; it is about reaching within and beyond the imagined self to a greater purpose and power.

What of the objection that prayer is mere wish fulfillment or indulgence in narcissistic fantasies and daydreams? Anyone who seriously attempted to pray or who has known even a fleeting or rudimentary experience of a Beyond-in-the-midst can testify that this experience is inevitably characterized by a conviction of otherness—it is about response and contingency. However unclear or problematic the awareness may at times be, prayer is a consciousness that one has first of all been addressed. And for the most part, such encounters offer few immediate or facile emotional satisfactions.

The English scholar and mystic Evelyn Underhill, who contributed richly to the literature of spirituality in the 20th century, wrote that prayer "proceeds by way of much discipline, renunciation and suffering as it moves toward a total abandonment to God's purpose. . . . Experience of God is the greatest of the rights of man, and it should not be left to become the casual discovery of the few."

Even people who reject religion and would classify themselves as atheists often engage in concrete and very real forms of prayer as they seek to give of themselves, to transcend their own limitations, to work on behalf of human rights and to respond to the needs of others. Their dedication, their labors and their aspirations comprise their beliefs—and they can indeed be called beliefs. Thus, in a broad but true sense, they are involved in the enterprise of prayer.

⌘

The English verb "to pray" comes to us from the Old French *preier*, modernized as *prier*; this in turn can be traced back to the Latin *precari*. In its original sense, it means to beseech or to beg, either of a person or God. The phrase "I pray you," dating from the Renaissance, is a good example of how the word developed in English, when it denoted a simple appeal to someone. But to speak of prayer today—to say "I pray"—implies a transcendent address.

We begin to engage in this address and to know something of God through our experience, but language is ultimately inadequate to the task of articulating that experience. It is for

precisely that reason that all discourse about the divine is necessarily metaphorical and symbolic. We must take great care not
to consider our poor written and spoken attempts with anything
but an approximation of the Reality toward which they point.
And as for concepts or hypotheses about the nature of God, that
devout novelist C. S. Lewis was on the mark: "Every idea of Him
we form, He must in mercy shatter."

This statement is very much in the classic Judeo-Christian
tradition, which has long claimed that we know more accurately
what God is not than what He is. In the 4th century, Gregory of
Nyssa wrote compellingly of Moses' "meeting" with God in the
cloud atop Mount Sinai. From this image, Gregory developed a
notion that came to be called apophatic theology, which holds
that whatever we say about God, we must immediately qualify
by adding, "But He is not at all like that." Moses, we can state
with utmost reverence, knew very well that he did not know
much at all. In 14th-century England and 16th-century Spain,
respectively, the anonymous author of *The Cloud of Unknowing* and the mystic John of the Cross brought the richness and
advantages of this idea of "denial" to fruition.

Despite the impossibility of "knowing" God, and despite our
own intellectual limitations and spiritual poverty, we humans
have consistently felt compelled to write and speak of prayer
throughout history. Our experience of finding our way to God
has been so powerful or transforming that it has to be articulated, however inadequately. As Saint Augustine said in a sermon, "We are talking about God. What wonder is it that you do
not understand? If you do understand, then it is not God."

Among the great religions and philosophies in world history,
prayer has been the particular genius of the Judeo-Christian
continuum for more than four thousand years. It is not exclusive to these traditions, to be sure, but the phenomenon of personal prayer as a living dialogue and continuing relationship

with a personal God is found in no other tradition with the force and contemporaneity that it is in the lives and testimonies of Jews and Christians from classical times to today.

The Far East has given us the ethical genius of Confucius, the transforming meditations of Lao-tzu, the wisdom of the compassionate Buddha, the mystical techniques of the many branches of Zen and of Hinduism—all of which enrich and contribute to acts of prayer and continue to provide significant contributions to our collective spiritual life. But these do not have traditions of prayer to one personal and loving God.

That said, it should be stressed that the profound teachings of the East must not be considered abstractly. When considered in terms of direct experiences of the ineffable, it becomes clear that for all their clear differences, Eastern religions are engaged in the same human quest and struggle as those in the West. Buddhism, for example, focuses on liberation from suffering, which, in Christian faith, is the reality forever achieved in the death and Resurrection of Jesus. Both traditions stress the importance of silence; both stress the inadequacy of human comprehension and expression for matters of the spirit. The goal of Buddhism is to reach, through meditation, that genuine state that lies beyond the conscious ego; the goal of Christianity is union with God. Both traditions propose as an ideal the conversion, or ultimate transformation, of what we variously call mind, soul or heart. And in all traditions, formal or obligatory exercises, cultic laws, ritual incantations and similar customs have nourished countless millions of lives round the world, but they are ordinarily not the expression of free and spontaneous love—and that, finally, is at the heart of prayer.

᠅

Although I write from the perspective of a Catholic, as one who affirms the faith of the apostles and tries each day to discern anew its meaning, I have written this book with all people of goodwill in mind, with whatever backgrounds, affirmations, doubts or denials. I ask only of readers that they bring to this book the openness with which I myself have tried to approach this subject. *In Silence* seeks to prove nothing, nor is it a defense for a particular religious tradition. The paths to God are as many as there are people.

Because my concern here is with private prayer, there are only a few passing references to group prayer, or to corporate or liturgical worship, which by their nature are less than personal in expression. The forms of prayer composed for worship are notable for telling us what the particular tradition of a given faith proclaims—*lex orandi legem statuat credendi*, runs the ancient maxim: how we pray reveals what we believe. But those collective forms are ultimately meaningless unless we bring them to life within ourselves.

In Silence has been written in the same atmosphere it hopes to encourage: one of a dark and quiet interiority. If anything has become clarified for me in my seventh decade of life, it is that there is nothing simple or blind about faith, and there is nothing easy about prayer. And whatever I have to say must be inadequate.

Meister Eckhart, a sinewy medieval philosopher and mystic, proposed that there is nothing so like God as silence. I find much of his writing nearly incomprehensible, but in this case, I think he was bracingly clear. After a half-century of studying a dizzying array of books about prayer in various religious traditions, reading about the philosophy of prayer and investigating some rarefied mental states better left to the psychologist, I am at last left with the haunting simplicity of Eckhart: there is nothing so like God as silence, and there is no greater ambiance in which to encounter Him. Silence, after all, is not nothing.

ᘓ

But if Eckhart was on the mark, why not keep silence? Why another book on prayer? In my defense, I would say that the most valuable subjects to think and write about are those issues we can never fully comprehend or articulate, those things with which we have never finished. Prayer, after all, is linked to faith—as we have seen, an attitude about reality that (among other things) refuses to accept the final opacity of the universe, refuses to accept that life is meaningless, that the world makes no sense. This habit of being is also the foundation of an intuition that insists that love is better than hatred, that chaos is inferior to order, that compassion and respect are superior to vengeance and malice.

The French theologian Jean Daniélou once wrote, "To be occupied with God is the highest occupation. But this requires an apprenticeship." That training, I believe, begins again each day for us—however we describe our search, and however we express (or do not) the primary fact that God is first and always occupied with us, long before it occurs to us to give Him a thought.

This connection, this communion that tugs at us—this hunch that in the final analysis we may not be alone—is at the heart of prayer, and prayer is the most human response to our experience of that sensibility. In this regard, another recurring theme of this book is that prayer is not so much something we do as something God does, something we experience, something unbidden and uninvited, something heard but imperfectly sensed—it is, in other words, a voice and a calling that want to be heeded, despite our lassitude and tardiness in the face of it.

Prayer is an immense, enduring connective thread in human history, as it is in each human life and destiny. It is our surest link to a Beyond in the midst, a connection to what does not vanish, to what is not subject to our mood or whim; indeed, the Reality beyond prayer never fades as, so often, religious enthusiasm and high emotion fade like watercolors exposed to the sun. The astonishing fact of history is that everyone can pray—and perhaps, somehow, everyone at least makes an effort to do so. "The beginning is the more important part," according to Teresa of Ávila. "If a person takes only one step, the step will itself contain so much power that we will not have to fear losing it, nor will we fail to be very well paid."

Many women and men who have prayed over the centuries have written compellingly of their experiences of prayer, and I occasionally refer to them in this book. Sometimes they can be more or less amiable, wise guides as we try to understand our own understanding of Reality. But their language necessarily reflects *their* experience, and it is always conditioned and limited by their times, cultures and personalities (as is ours). These people can inspire us, they can hint and suggest directions we might take—but the journey must ultimately be our own. We need to discover our own language and our own silence. "A lively person prays one way," as a 4th-century desert monk said with remarkable psychological insight.

> A person brought down by the weight of gloom or despair prays another way. One prays another way still when the life of the spirit is flourishing, and another way when pushed down. One prays differently, depending on whether one is seeking the gift of some grace or the removal of sin. The prayer is different again when one is sorrowing . . . or when one is fired by hope . . . when one is in need or peril, in peace or tranquility; when one is flooded by the light of heavenly mysteries, or when one is hemmed in by aridity and staleness in one's thinking.

≈

To speak of a "history of prayer" would be to imply that there is some sort of logical development or discernible chronology in humanity's relationship with prayer—that we can trace it in an orderly fashion down through the ages, something like the stages of scientific thinking about the cosmos, for example. But the sort of "history" I draw upon here is more concerned with certain experiences and themes in life that are identified in the chapter titles.

Can a thematic survey of personal prayer, then—with special reference to the data of ordinary human experiences, like dialogue, suffering and love—take us beyond those ordinary experiences? I hope I have offered that possibility. Prayer derives from a conviction that God is indeed the Ultimacy toward which everything that is yearns, however imperfectly or unknowingly. This cannot be proven: it can only be experienced. And if we have not yet known it, we may still come to that unique awareness, to our everlasting surprise.

In a way, this book in fact explores our aptitude for deeper experience—a subjective inner experience, to be sure, but one that is discovered, not invented. And so *In Silence* also reflects on our ability to be astonished, which I take as a direct consequence of what Bernard of Clairvaux, in 12th-century France, called the universal capacity for God. That capacity is directly linked to the fact of prayer.

Persons who pray in light of that capacity, even vaguely perceived, experience what can only be called a sense of God, and they require no defense from an intellectual fortress. Indeed, the spontaneous and direct expression of an experience of the Beyond can take us—perhaps *must* take us—to a still, silent point where we begin to live as never before.

The "sense of God" is not a metaphor: it is a consciousness as sharp as love or pain, heat or light; it is like the homing instinct of birds, which can be neither explained nor denied. And to those who experience it, there is no doubt about its reality.

∽

When I was a first-year college student, I spoke one evening with a professor I much respected, who was also a kind of spiritual counselor to me. I do not recall the subject of our conversation, but at one point I put some question or other to him about the meaning of prayer. What seemed a long moment of silence intervened before he answered very quietly: "What can we do—what can any of us do—but throw ourselves into the arms of God?"

This book is offered in the spirit of that quietly overwhelming question.

In Silence

CHAPTER ONE

Of Time and Memory—
Some Historic Aspects of the Interior Life

Prayer as the Expression of Personal Religion

Considered independently of specific cultural forms, traditions, doctrines and rituals, religion in general may be described as the inner awareness of an ultimate Reality beyond the self and beyond the human. Once acknowledged, this perception, however dim and provisional, invites a personal response to and association with that Reality—a living and active relationship we may identify as prayer. As distinct from aesthetic or poetic feelings, which establish a link to the divine through art, prayer is essentially a relationship we have with God in this world.

When it is expressed communally or liturgically, prayer is authentic for the one who prays only when there is or has been a prior awareness of the divine presence in secret and in silence—in other words, a sense of the numinous evoked by an apprehension of what is subjectively holy or sacred.

Ideally, of course, such feelings should also be evoked by public acts of worship; that they so seldom do is one of the failures of contemporary religion, which often seems content with conveying a comfortable feeling of good fellowship or a pleasantly undemanding folksiness. A profound sense of the holy does not, of course, require grand panoply: the Quaker tradition of congregational silence can bring many participants to the threshold of profound reverence. Such a practice takes seriously the words of the biblical injunction, "Be still, and know that I am God."

Prayer has a quite personal and empirical character; as a habit of being and of becoming oneself in this life, it goes beyond intellectual analysis. Hence William James, the American philosopher and pioneer psychologist of religion, claimed that without prayer there can be no religious life. Found everywhere in human history, prayer expresses, with or without images or words, the experience of a mystery and of a presence beyond this world and above the human; as such, it is concerned not with thinking about God but with relating to Him.*

Prayer in Time and Memory

In his Gifford Lectures at Edinburgh University between 1902 and 1904, William James perhaps startled his academic audience by calmly stating, "Many reasons have been given why we should not pray, whilst others are given why we should. But in all this, very little is said of the reason why we do pray. The reason why we pray is simply that we cannot help praying."

Prayer also occurred, as James rightly presupposed, in archaic, prehistoric cultures: this is clear from modern studies of primeval clans and tribes that survived with their traditions relatively intact and uninfluenced by the encroachments of developed society.

Even a brief consideration of ancient history reveals that wherever there was a sense of wonder or awe in the face of the unknown, there was prayer; where there was gratitude for a successful hunt or a good harvest, there was prayer; where there

*Given the status of current English (and at the risk of disappointing some readers), I refer to God pronominally in this book by the traditional masculine form—but for the sake of simplicity only, since it is axiomatic that God has no gender. And for reverence, these pronouns are rendered uppercase.

was fear for life or safety, there was prayer. One might even say that prayer was natural for those living closer to nature. In the case of Native American tribes and of the peoples of the Far East, for example, this did not mean that prayer was always directed to a specific being or invisible spirit: often the address was made vaguely, to the spirit of a tree or a river, conceived as a foreign but vital "being" who shared the universe with the perceiver.

Centuries and perhaps millennia before there was anything like the separate department of life known as religion, there was what might be called a religious sensibility—a sense of the Beyond, that seems to have been as instinctive as breathing, sleeping and eating. Conscious of their connection to that Beyond and evidently aware that a relationship could be established with it, people expressed their needs, wishes and reverence. They did not require knowledge in order to understand.

The word "religion," as a matter of fact, never occurs in the Hebrew Scriptures, nor is it to be found in the gospels; there are a mere five references to it elsewhere in the New Testament. The idea that matters of faith have come to comprise but one discrete aspect of life among others—competing, as it were, for our time and attention—is unfortunate, for such a notion implies that faith centers only around ritual observances or subjects that are obviously "religious" (all of which are of human development and expression in any case). To think this way, as C. S. Lewis trenchantly observed, is to substitute navigation for arrival or courtship for marriage. What is infinite, after all, can have no standing as a department: either everything in life exists in its light, or faith itself is an illusion.

⌥

The precise origins of prayer itself we may never know. But the consensus of anthropological and ethnological studies should be noted: we can find at every point of human experience some idea of transcendence and an attempt to relate to it. An intuition about life beyond the grave is a significant corollary of this: "It is certain," wrote W. F. Albright, one of the great scholars of the ancient world, "that the belief in an after-life has a very long prehistory, going back in some form as far as the Neanderthal men of the Mousterian age. Just what physiological and psychological sources it had, we can hardly demonstrate."

Albright's studies in the origin of language support his insistence that what we now call primitive man (flourishing at about 5000 B.C.) was capable of abstraction: "The earliest known stages of the Egyptian, Sumerian and Semitic languages show that general qualities such as 'goodness, truth, purity' could be abstracted from the related adjectives and identified as abstractions by some linguistic device." By the 4th millennium B.C., humans had certainly developed a sense of a divine being—and they associated this being with creation and with characteristics their cultures held to be good. It is at least tenable, therefore (and probably quite correct), to say that the sense of the divine is an innate human perception—not an invented projection, but rather the acknowledgment of a primal certainty.

From Egypt to Rome

"It is difficult to imagine," wrote Mircea Eliade, "how the human mind could function without the conviction that there is something irreducibly *real* in the world." A prolific historian of religious ideas, Eliade demonstrated in more than fifty scholarly books the logic that our collective consciousness of a meaningful world is intimately connected with the discovery of the sacred: "Through experience of the sacred, the human mind has perceived the difference between what reveals itself as being real, powerful, rich and meaningful and what lacks these qualities—that is, the chaotic and dangerous flux of things."

In other words, the very idea of the sacred and our connection to it is an element in the structure of consciousness, and not merely a stage in its history. And notions about both the deity and life beyond the grave highlight the development of this "idea of the sacred" in almost every ancient culture about which we have any knowledge.

As it was in every ancient religion (including those of the Greeks, Romans and the Hebrews before the 8th century B.C.), polytheism was taken for granted in ancient Egypt, for which we have very extensive and detailed records. During the period from about 2700 to 2200 B.C., for example, the Egyptian kings themselves were worshipped as sons of the sun god. But from 2000 B.C., there is clear evidence of monotheism: Amon was regarded as the one supreme deity, and when one ruler addressed a spontaneous hymn to Amon, his prayer was set down in hieroglyphs: "Creator, Maker, Giver of breath—how manifold are your works, O sole God, whose powers no other possesses. You created the earth according to your heart." Egyptians also offered morning and evening prayer to Amon.

Along with the tendency toward monotheism, there was a conviction about the afterlife. *The Papyrus of Ani*, which can be dated to about 1250 B.C., is a major extant portion of the texts now collectively known as the Egyptian *Book of the Dead*; it contains hymns and invocations interred with the deceased and intended to guide them safely to the beyond. A typical prayer for mercy was addressed, for example, to "My Shining One, who dwells in the Mansion of Images . . . O Preeminent One . . . may you grant me life. . . . O my father, my brother, my mother— Isis! . . . I shall cross to the Mansion of him who finds faces, the collector of souls. . . . And I will not die again in God's domain . . . I give you praise, O Lord of the gods."

Perhaps nowhere are the traditions of prayerful acts discerned more clearly than in this ancient conviction that life endures beyond the grave, a conviction to which the pyramids remain a grand and silent witness. Within them all manner of provisions were made for the entombed rulers in the hereafter. The custom of sprinkling corpses with red ocher—as a substitute for blood and hence as a symbol of life—is found in Egypt and from northern Europe to as far south as Tasmania. More to the point, ancient peoples often buried their dead in a fetal position, which may indeed signify the hope of rebirth; the appearance of the dead in dreams seems also to have suggested the survival of the spirit. The 20th century discovery and translation of Egyptian invocations is precious witness to prayer in one of the most sophisticated ancient cultures.

From the 3rd millennium B.C. to the time of Jesus, forms of prayer changed little in Assyrian and Babylonian cultures. The Babylonian god Marduk was addressed by an unknown speaker in an intimate tone: "O Lord, great are my sins—do not cast your servant down, but remove my transgressions." Another supplicant expressed confidence in his prayer for protection from enemies: "I have prayed humbly, and I have been heard by my Father, my God." Equivalent sentiments are found in Cretan civilization of the same era.

From the Sumerians and Egyptians to the Central American natives, the terms "father" and "mother" are everywhere to be found as expressive of the affinity between the human and divine. About 2000 B.C., the Sumerians asked a Father-Mother God to "strip us of our many sins, which we wear like a garment." In ancient Egypt, Isis was "my father, my mother, my brother," and the Babylonians addressed Marduk, "as a father and mother, you dwell with your people." And at the end of the 2nd century A.D., the *Acts of St. Peter* (a nonbiblical account of early Christian traditions concerning that apostle) placed on the lips of the dying apostle a boldly confident address to God in Jesus: "You are a father and a mother to me—a brother, a friend, a servant. You are all that is, and all that is, is in You."

The true primitive spirit of prayer is not the expression of a savage or uncivilized nature, nor of atavistic fear or selfish desire. Nor does "primitive" connote a naïve stage of human development; rather, it describes a basic experience of human contingency. Those we call primitives often disclose not what we have outgrown or put aside but what is fundamental to our humanity.

⌁

Attributed to Homer in the 8th century B.C., the Greek epics, the *Iliad* and the *Odyssey*, contain both poetic prayer and ceremonial prayer. The former invokes a god, tries to justify a reason for a petition to be favorably heard, and then formulates the petition. The latter type follows a pattern of ritual washing, prayer, sacrifice and libations. Greek prayer reflected the tone of its mythology and hence presumed the reality of a feisty give-and-take between gods and mortals; the heroes are always aware of their dependence on the capricious power of preternatural (but not omnipotent) beings, of whom they beg favor and protection in time of need, and to whom they offer sacrifice and honor. *Do ut des*, as the Romans said later in Latin, was the working principle of reciprocity: "I give to you so that you might grant to me . . ."

The Greeks also knew their gods in an almost personal way—that is, the gods were comprehensible, even sometimes predictable in their emotional responses and their particular loyalties. Existing somehow in space but not omnipresent, the gods had to be summoned in prayer, but there was never a sense of intimacy or loving union between the supplicant and the deity. (The Judeo-Christian God, contrariwise, is both beyond space and time and intimately present within it: He does not have to be summoned, it is humans who are summoned by Him and to Him.)

The *Iliad* and *Odyssey* recount many petitions and prayers for safety, as well as curses hurled like Zeus's thunderbolts. The earliest extant prayer in Greek literature is probably that of the priest Chryses, in the *Iliad*, when he asks Apollo to avenge him: "I built your temple and burned sacrifice to you—so let your arrows make [my enemies] pay for my shed tears." One of the most touching examples of a personal prayer is found in the *Odyssey*. Penelope, faithful wife of Odysseus, has waited patiently twenty years for his return. Weary of temporizing with increasingly insistent suitors, she begs heaven to end her life: "Great goddess Artemis, let some whirlwind snatch me up and drop me into the ocean: I wish that the gods who live in heaven would hide me from mortal sight, or that you, fair Diana, might strike me. I would rather go beneath the sad earth awaiting Odysseus, without having to yield myself to a man so much less than he was."

By the 5th century B.C. and later, Greek prayer became more refined, as can be seen in the tragedies of Aeschylus and Sophocles, the poems of Pindar, the histories of Xenophon and the philosophical dialogues of Plato. There was now a greater concern for the spiritual efficacy of honor and reverence for the gods, and prayers for revenge are softened to entreaties for justice.

"Without thee, no mortal shall have strength to achieve or prevail," the Chorus prays to Zeus in Aeschylus's *Suppliants*; that sense of dependence has moral consequences. Timaeus, in the eponymous dialogue by Plato, observes that "all who possess even a modicum of wisdom, everywhere and always, at the beginning of every work, important or unimportant, call upon God." Elsewhere, Plato includes entreaties to the gods for the forgiveness of moral guilt. Xenophon and Sophocles also bear witness to the customs of daily prayer at sunrise, sunset and before meals.

It must be stressed, however, that Hellenic prayer was entirely focused on the needs of contingent mortals in this world: ecstatic or contemplative prayer—that is, the sort of prayer aimed at achieving an intimate life with a god—was unknown. *Timaeus* may have come closest to an intuition about mystical prayer, with its germ of a notion about humanity's almost existential relation to the Creator-Demiurge.

While Hebrews and, later, Christians employed a variety of postures for public and private prayer (kneeling, standing, sitting, bowing, crouching), the Greeks and Romans almost invariably seem to have stood while praying, extending both arms upward and bringing their hands together with the palms open; medals struck during the Roman Empire indicate that the arms were thrown wide apart.

To this day, Jews, Christians and Muslims extend arms or lift up hands in the act of prayer, much as a needy child does toward a parent. Prostration, bending, striking one's breast, bowing and kneeling, touching the forehead to the ground, bringing together upraised palms, folding the hands and interlacing the fingers—these are remnants of ancient gestures of greeting and petition and require no academic interpretation.

The most common form of Roman prayer, it must be noted, was to flatter or even to bribe a god—and it was critical to invoke the correct god for one's cause: "Help me, Jupiter, because it is in your power. . . . Cure me and I'll give you an offering. . . . Make me richer than my neighbor." In exchange for divine favor, a person might make a *votum* or vow to offer a sacrifice, to build a temple or even to bind oneself to the god forever. Two millennia later, this kind of bargaining quid pro quo still characterizes some naïve notions in just about every tradition of prayer.

The custom of offering spontaneous prayers to nature gods in the temples of Mayan, Aztec and Incan civilizations is well attested; here as in Egypt, religious iconography included colorful representations of the sun, and the practice of mummifying dead kings was well established. Although there is no certain record of the content of spoken prayer, the existence of Central and South American temples and of a priestly class certainly implies a tradition of public worship, which in turn presupposes formulas of prayer.

The early 6th-century-B.C. Persian prophet Zarathustra, or Zoroaster, named the Supreme Being "Ahura Mazda." Surviving prayers attributed to Zoroaster seem remarkably modern in their warmth and in their ethical principles; more to the point, his prayers presume a benevolent divine will that evokes a serene dependence.

> With outstretched arms, open mind and my whole heart, I greet you, Ahura Mazda, in spirit. Turn your countenance toward me, dear Lord, and make my face happy and radiant. My heart yearns for you with a yearning which is never stilled. You are my most precious possession. My joy is in you, my refuge is in you. Let me live before you and with you and in your sight, I humbly pray. . . . Everything that my eyes rest upon reveals your glory. . . . Help me to cultivate the habit of prayer, to know your will, and to conform my impulses to its demands . . . I will pray to you in silence, for you hear my prayers even in my thought.

At about the same time, the Pygmy of Gabon, in Central Africa, were developing a similar prayer of simple thanksgiving, addressed to the god Waka: "You gave me this buffalo, this honey, this wine." Their orations were as intimate as Zoroaster's. To this day, the Ovambo tribe of Africa greets the dawn with a cry of desire, and the Bantu express their social sympathies in a language of humble gratitude and religious intercession at dawn and nightfall. In these cases, there is no evidence of syncretism—no influence, for example, from the Judeo-Christian tradition, which also has an ancient practice of prayer at sunrise and sunset.

To put the matter briefly: primitive peoples had an ineradicable sense of awe, of transcendent power. Later, these feelings were ritualized and formalized, but originally, they seem to have been spontaneous and improvised in simple sounds like tongue-clicking, loud breathing, deep lamentation or even whistling.

North American natives still routinely withdraw into solitude to pray. The Osage, for example, seem always to have withdrawn from the community, from family and companions, for acts of morning reverence. Similar cases abound, reflecting a wide variety of impulses and motives, including expressions of awe, complaint and petition; all of these seem to have paralleled or even preceded the more developed forms of ritual and sacrifice.

∽

"O God, you are my Lord, my father and mother, Lord of the mountains and the valleys," prayed the Kekchi Indian. "What have I done?" asked the Khoi-Khoi, "that I am so severely punished?" The Melanesians to this day have an ancient form of supplication when they are in a storm at sea: "Save us in the deep, O dear divinity—save us from the storm and bring us to land!" The Amazalu still ask of their tribal deity, "Give us what is good and watch over us," and the Khonds of Orissa go one step farther: "We know not what is good or for what we ought to pray. You do. Give that to us."

The Watje of the Caribbean prayed daily, "O God, I know You not, but You know me. I need You!" And with remarkable tenderness (and theological sophistication), the North African Galla stood alone in the desert, facing the sky for an evening prayer: "In Your hand I pass the day, in Your hand I pass the night—You Who are my mother and my father."

Similarly, the evolution of Hindu prayer, which is not doctrinally rigid, allows multiple gods to be invoked while many people have one favorite. But recently, deeper study of Hindu texts and more respectful dialogue with Hindu sages have made it clear that Hinduism ought not to be regarded as naïvely polytheistic.

Although it is true to say there are as many approaches to Hinduism as there are Hindus, Hinduism may be regarded as essentially monotheistic: in this light, all its gods are aspects of a single universal Reality which is the only Reality; the world itself, for the Hindu, is the Unreal. In this regard, Ramakrishna, Gandhi, Tagore and Aurobindo—all of them profoundly mystical Hindus—prayed to God in terms no Jew or Christian would have to reject. At the heart of their prayer is a conviction that informs all Asian prayer and the best of Western prayer: we are one with God and we are not one with God. Real prayer does not reject the language of paradox but embraces it.

In Hindu private prayer, great stress is placed on proper sounds and chants, and the repeated mantras are credited with almost magical power. Purification of the mind and inner transformation not only realize the deepest inclinations of the self but also bring one closer to one's God.

❧

In China, remarkable contributions were made not to the concept or practice of prayer or matters of religion as commonly understood, but to the notion and nature of ethics. Confucius, who was probably born in 551 B.C. and died about 479 B.C., had no interest in what we call God or the gods, nor was he concerned about an afterlife. "Why do you ask me about death when you do not know how to live?" he was reputed to have asked. Orphaned and poverty-stricken, he became a self-educated public servant, urging the reform of oppressive taxes that were ruining the lives of countless Chinese.

A living embodiment of the most worthy social ideals and an advocate for just government, he was unsuccessful as a politician but brilliant as a teacher. Confucius insisted that the truly superior man is benevolent and that a moral existence lived in harmony with the universe is the highest achievement. The realization of that goal was to be found in a government that existed only for the benefit of all the people.

Eventually, the ideals of Confucius (preserved only in fragmentary documents) were absorbed into a variety of popular religions, some of which, as they evolved, made room for various kinds of deities. One especially noteworthy outgrowth of these became known as Taoism, which can be traced to the writings of the mysterious Lao-tzu, who lived sometime between the 6th and 4th centuries B.C.

In the *Tao-te Ching (The Book of the Way and Its Virtue)*, attributed to Lao-tzu, there is mention of an infinite mystery that can be neither named nor described in human language. Lao-tzu claimed that "the Tao that can be told is not the eternal Tao. The name that can be named is not the eternal name." He spoke of moving beyond thinking and encouraged entrance into a dark emptiness that was not nothingness but a state beyond multiplicity, and he understood that what we call the truth is nothing like an absolute.

There may be no analogue in Chinese thought for the idea of a Creator as we often use that word in the West, but a potential symbiosis should be appreciated. The Eastern intuition about the power of natural forces in the universe and the Eastern insistence on ethical responsibility are two notions consistent with the invitation extended to Adam by God, Who invites us to collaborate with Him in the management of this mysterious, created world, and to live and act in solidarity with others.

This is one of the astonishing, unique characteristics of Hebrew faith: that the world is the setting for God's continuing and effective dialogue with humanity. But how is it possible to speak of a dialogue with God?

CHAPTER TWO

Prayer as Dialogue (I)—
The Experience of Israel

The Hebrew Scriptures: Foundation and Historic Impact

"Judaism," as the rabbinic editors of a history of Jewish worship have noted, "is unimaginable without prayer." Indeed, if one were to distill the richness of that tradition to a single idea, it would be that Jewish liturgy is the best kind of prayer. But public worship presumes and is preceded by a personal life of prayer, and the Old Testament is in large part a record of God's primal dialogue first with individuals.

For Jews, prayer has always been a living response to the divine initiative—an opening of self to life in the presence of God. In light of the long recorded odyssey of this extraordinarily resilient people, the evidence is clear: Jewish faith proclaims that God is indeed present everywhere and to every person, even when we ignore or think we can avoid Him. "Do not be frightened or dismayed, for the Lord your God is with you wherever you go." So begins the Book of Joshua; the resulting sense of awe is one of the major motifs in the Hebrew Scriptures.

God's self-disclosure, His everlasting dialogue with this nomadic Near Eastern tribe, is presented as progressive and gradual, and so it must be for everyone. How could it be otherwise when humanity is invited to intimacy with the Absolute and the Eternal? The Hebrews did not, for example, affirm the existence of only one God from the very beginning of their history: the God of Abraham, Isaac and Jacob, the God of the Torah, was *their*

God, but the validity of the gods of the nations, the deities of the gentiles, was not denied. The unambiguous awareness and proclamation of monotheism seem to have occurred for the first time in the 7th or 6th century B.C., in additions to the Book of Isaiah.

Persistently told by their patriarchs and prophets that they were a Chosen People, the Hebrews had also to be constantly summoned to renewal and conversion—to turn back to Yahweh, to resume their intimate communication with Him. He alone is faithful to His promises, even when His people stray, even when they worship false gods, even when they murder His prophets. The choice, they had to be reminded, was no cause for triumphalism, however, for they were chosen and called to serve the world by the model of their faith.

The Hebrew Scriptures chronicle a long history of intimate conversation between the Lord and His people. With disarming directness, the editors of the Bible present prayers in expressions of wonder, petition, complaint, lament and adoration. But it is, of course, God Who first speaks, inviting Adam (which means "mankind" or "all people") to collaborate in stewardship over creation, then warning him against the consequences of disobedience. God also promises Noah that He will never again destroy the earth by flood.

The history, however, begins properly after the curtain-raiser of the first eleven chapters of Genesis, which are a dramatic counterstatement to ancient Babylonian and Persian myths. "Now the Lord said to Abram, 'Go from your country and your kindred and your father's house to the land that I will show you.' " Those opening words of Genesis 12 mark a definitive turning point in Hebrew history, and indeed, of the religious history of the world. God acted out of unimaginable mercy to bring order out of chaos, to save and embrace humanity within the setting of a broken, divided world—such is the collective significance of the sin of Adam, the devastating flood, Cain's hatred of his brother Abel and the disorder of Babel.

"Now the Lord said to Abram. . . ." Many people today find such passages incredible: after all, how did God "speak" to a man? The tradition was perhaps not so naïve as to think that the sound of a voice was literally heard. The Bible often refers to the word of the Lord's being heard "in a vision," or "in a dream," which is a wonderful device, for the hearing and the seeing are a matter of interior revelation. But that being said, faith certainly accepts that extraordinary things may occur.

The invitations and the conversations record the subsequent Jewish doctrine that God had *acted* in summoning Abram and naming His chosen people—and not for the Jews alone, but on behalf of all humanity. "In you, all the families of the earth shall be blessed," God adds: as the prophets insisted, the gentiles are called and included because Abram and his progeny are summoned to serve, to be an example, to become a light to all nations.

God summoned, and Abram responded by obedient action—that, after all, is the meaning of living faith. "So Abram went, as the Lord had told him." His prayer, in other words, was expressed in deeds: he went forth, he built an altar "and he journeyed on by stages." There may be no better expression of the voyage and the process that constitutes the life of prayer and faith: like Abram, we journey on by stages.

"Do not be afraid," the Lord then told him after promising a great progeny; "I am your shield." And then, for the first time, Abram prayed in words boldly expressing his incomprehension of so great a destiny: "O Lord God, what will you give me, for I continue childless? . . . You have given me no offspring." The Lord then indicated the night sky: "Count the stars, if you can—so shall your descendants be." Abram believed, his friendship with God was sealed, and his name was changed: Abram ("exalted ancestor") was thenceforth Abraham ("ancestor of a multitude").

٭

The dialogue between God and Moses is presented as equally close and direct. While guarding his father-in-law's flock of sheep, Moses saw a desert bush—all afire, but unconsumed by its flames. God called the name of Moses, and he replied, "Here I am!" God then identified Himself as the God of his ancestors. From reverent fear, "Moses hid his face." But almost at once, the relationship between Moses and the Lord was seen to have been astonishingly intimate: "The Lord used to speak to Moses face to face, as one speaks to a friend."

The words are of course poetic, but they express a conviction that the salvific events of Moses' lifetime (the delivery of Hebrew slaves from Egypt, their Passover from death to life, their amalgamation into a new people at Sinai, the giving of the Law) were a continuation of the "conversation" between the Lord and His people.

Moses could, in his intimacy with God, rail against the ingratitude of the Hebrews and the ineffectiveness of his own leadership: "Did I conceive all these people?" he cries, comparing himself to a mother. "Did I give birth to them, that You should say to me, 'Carry them in Your bosom, as a nurse carries a sucking child,' to the land that You promised on oath to their ancestors? . . . I am not able to carry this people alone, for they are too heavy for me." And the answer came: "Is the Lord's power limited? Now you will see whether My word will come true for you or not." And with that, God defends Moses against all adversaries.

Hannah—the favorite wife of a man named Elkanah—apparently felt she could complain and say what she felt to the

Lord in the secrecy of her heart. Grieving over her infertility, "she was praying silently; only her lips moved, but her voice was not heard." Her prayer for maternity was then granted, and she bore the prophet Samuel, who, even in childhood, was alert for a divine summons. "The Lord called, 'Samuel! Samuel!' And Samuel said, 'Speak, for your servant is listening!'" And the boy, according to the account, "grew up in the presence of the Lord."

Attentive for God, waiting for God, eager for the word and touch of God—such expressions all point to the meaning of dialogue, of living "in the presence of the Lord." And that divine presence ultimately freed people from any undue preoccupation with only physical needs, and from an obsession with being protected from enemies. Vigilance, goodwill, trust, generosity of spirit: such was the Hebrew experience of prayer, and it lost none of its relevance for succeeding generations. Thus hearing, taking to heart and responding in word and action were the prophet's foundation for securing his inner life and his destiny.

Personal prayer in the Hebrew Scriptures, then, is not a matter of a special prescription or arcane technique; nor does it depend on the intellectually refined quality of a person's spirituality. It is simple conversation with the living God. The intimacy of prayer is possible because God has revealed Himself and His loving plan for His people, and the rhythm of prayer includes action on the part of both.

∽

Many centuries after Abraham, Isaiah leaped to the task of prophecy, which meant not fortune-telling but a vocation to call the Israelites back to a life of faith in their God. "Here am I!" cried Isaiah when he became aware of the Lord's invitation. "Send me!" Similarly, Jeremiah—called to proclaim both judgment on the people's infidelity to God and a promise of enduring friendship with Him—at first objected to the summons: "Ah, Lord God! Truly, I do not know how to speak, for I am only a boy." But God had His own purposes: "Do not say, 'I am only a boy,' for you shall go to all to whom I send you. Do not be afraid of them, for I am with you to deliver you."

The Book of Jeremiah, which was probably compiled in the 6th century B.C., represents a major development in Hebrew prayer. This prophet uttered six personal laments to God about his outcast fate as an unheeded prophet and as the object of an assassination plot. "I was like a gentle lamb led to the slaughter . . . but You, O Lord, judge righteously . . . for to You I have committed my cause." His prayers reveal a confident access to God: "Why do all who are treacherous thrive?" he longed to know. Even in the midst of persecution from a mostly faithless generation, Jeremiah believed: "O Lord, You know—remember me and visit me. . . . On your account, I suffer insult." Came the reply: "I am with you, to save and deliver you." From Abraham through the lives of the prophets—a history spanning more than two millennia—Hebrew prayer always began with the experiences of individuals.

ᴈ

The Book of Psalms, composed by many hearts over the course of several centuries, is a collection of prayers reflecting the Jewish people's experience—expressions of lament, exclamations of trust, appeals and petitions. Compiled after several centuries of collective suffering, the Psalms articulate individual and group experiences of triumph and failure, of piety and iniquity. The Psalms are still often prayed in private today, for almost all are suitable for individuals just as they are for communities gathering for the formal liturgies of both Jews and Christians. The Psalms embrace all human history, longing and emotion, and their sentiments are invariably linked to a sense of praise—

hence the title of the album as it has come to us: Psalms, which means "The Praises."

Most of all, however, these extraordinary prayers meet us in our disarray, and (as one contemplative has suggested), "they can make great sense as chaotic prayer. They are full of darkness and conflict as well as joy in God's presence [and] they are often ugly with vengeance, hatred and smugness. . . . [Nothing] is hidden from God or felt to be unmentionable in His presence."

Indeed, a major theme of the Psalms is the omnipresence of God:

> Where can I go from Your spirit, or where can I flee from Your presence? If I ascend to the heavens, You are there; if I make my bed in the grave, you are there. If I take the wings of the morning and settle at the farthest limits of the sea, even there Your hand shall lead me. . . . If I say, "Surely the darkness shall cover me, and the light around me become night," even the darkness is not dark to You; the night is bright as the day, for darkness is as light to You.

The ubiquity of God is comforting rather than threatening, because of the confidence in God's fidelity. "You, O Lord, are good and forgiving, abounding in steadfast love and faithfulness—a God merciful and gracious." This is the unshakable conviction underlying each Psalm—a trust that is as ancient as the Book of Exodus: "The Lord is merciful and gracious, slow to anger and abounding in steadfast love and faithfulness, keeping steadfast love for the thousandth generation, forgiving iniquity and transgression and sin." God's "steadfast love"—in Hebrew, *hesed*— endures despite human folly; referring to God's loyalty to His people, *hesed* occurs no fewer than 172 times in the Hebrew Scriptures, of which 109 are in the Book of Psalms.

Confidence in God has an effect: "This I know, that God is for me"—that He acts out of unfailing benevolence even when His ways are incomprehensible. To express their longing for God and to be reminded of their need for Him, this desert people had a tangible sign—the constant necessity of fresh water. With this image in mind, those who prayed soared poetically: "As a deer longs for flowing streams, so my soul longs for You, O God. My soul thirsts for God, for the living God. When shall I come and behold the face of God?" Again: "O God, You are my God—I seek You. My soul thirsts for You, my flesh faints for You, as in a dry and weary land where there is no water."

The brilliant conjunction of the personal and the public in the Book of Psalms resolved an ancient question about prayer in the life of Jewish people, but the question is still relevant today: Is prayer primarily a personal or a communal act? The answer may seem self-evident: One can hardly worship within the context of a group if one has not been led there by an inner impulse, an act in the direction of prayer beforehand. This prior inclination toward private prayer is termed by the rabbinic tradition "the service that takes place in the heart . . . something that a person *feels* like doing or is *moved to do*" from within, as one Jewish scholar has written. To put this in biblical terms: the inward response of personal and private devotion is presumed as necessary by virtue of the commandment "to love the Lord your God with all your heart [=mind and will], and with all your soul [=self], and with all your might [=full measure of devotion]." In the history of postbiblical Judaism, however, personal prayer takes second place to the devout communal consideration of the requirements of the Law. Personal piety, in other words, must invariably lead to ritual; hence, the focus of all Jewish prayer became temple worship.

It is not hard to understand this development, given that one of the remarkable aspects of the Hebrew tradition is its insistence on the eternal love and fidelity of God. Its corollary was an acute sense of human frailty: the Scriptures are in effect a long chronicle of human indifference compared to divine ardor—of the downright failure of every generation to respond to the covenant bond that God neither forgets nor withdraws. Such is the single great theme of the Psalms and the prophetic literature.

The practical effect, in the last five centuries B.C., was to stabilize and codify prayer in light of the majesty of Yahweh, whose very name was not to be uttered in prayer. Angels, borrowed from the imagery of the Eastern potentate's court, were set forth as intermediaries between God and mortals—and, inevitably, a meticulous legalism began to hinder the development of the personal spiritual life.

Even the once free and private times of prayer (thrice daily and at mealtimes, for example) became ritualized—a necessary defense (it was thought) against lethargy, distraction and irreverence. When temple worship was impossible because of distance or exile, then one prayed the assigned formulas as best one could in private.

"Christian guides to prayer are likely to place it in the wider context of living and communing with God," as a Cambridge University Jewish rabbinic scholar has noted. "Their Jewish counterparts, on the other hand, tend to deal with private prayer in a few pages, en route to their real preoccupation: formal liturgy for organised public worship. Though not actively discouraged from praying in their own words, Jews are constantly reminded of the superiority of public worship."

But the need for private prayer remains inevitable if one leads any sort of life in communion with God. The importance of dialogue—as relationship and method—is rooted in the Hebrew Scriptures. Its significance cannot be exaggerated, nor can its impact on the history of prayer.

Meeting God

People often speak and write about prayer as if there were a best way to do it: what is the correct method, the proper technique, the system that will ensure success? Consequently, they are often astonished to discover that prayer does not involve going through a routine, in the way one approaches exercise machines. Nor does it demand composing a touching and poetic soliloquy to recite before God—arranging words that would in fact be primarily comforting to oneself, a balm for the ego. Prayer is, to the contrary, an encounter, a dialogue with One Who has first addressed me; hence it begins with attentive listening.

The vague stirring in my heart, suggesting that I am being touched by something outside myself; the beauty I behold in the world, in art and in the kindness of others; the sense that I am not abandoned or alone; the presentiment that there is finally a meaning for my existence, and that I can seek for it and work toward it—all these occurrences in ordinary life set the foundation for prayer. Paying attention and being aware, I then move outward toward a frame of reference beyond my own immediate experience and limitations—and I move inward, to consider what I have been told or what I have been shown.

Dialogue is not primarily about speech: it is about a rhythm of alertness, of taking experience seriously the way we take others seriously and want to be taken ourselves. Just as our ordinary lives comprise a dialogue with the outside world as we alternate between thought and action, reflection and deed, so prayer is a cycle of engagement and withdrawal, of listening and response, of attention and performance. God, in me and through what He has made, addresses me; in and through my experience, through everything that I am and everything that happens, God somehow speaks.

This happens, almost inevitably, very gently and mysteriously, and sometimes painfully, too—and part of the pain is a result of the kind of self-knowledge that attends prayer. That self-knowledge should bring about some unpleasant (even humiliating) realizations is fundamental to every spiritual teaching in every tradition. "It is absurd," wrote Teresa of Ávila with her usual psychological acuity, "to think that we can go to God without first entering our own souls, without getting to know ourselves, and reflecting on the poverty of our nature and what we owe to God."

It is always tempting to consider any encounter with "spiritual things" as somehow exalted and otherworldly, and so to see them as from a distance. Once that happens, however, prayer becomes wholly unreal and irrelevant, which enables us to excuse ourselves and return to "real life." But as soon as we presume that there is a wide gulf between this world and God the results are all too evident: religious institutions that ignore human suffering and hardship, and political institutions that pay lip service to God but would much prefer that His mercy and compassion not be extended to everyone indiscriminately.

Real prayer makes such dichotomies impossible because it takes very seriously the principle of the world as the forum for God's primary speech to us and because it is the place where prayer becomes a dialogue. "Prayer is encountering God," wrote an anonymous 6th-century Syrian. His brief descriptive definition may have said it for all time. But let us be clear: prayer is about encountering God and not an *idea about God*. It means being open to a God of unimaginable mercy and infinite possibility, Who acts freely on our behalf. Authentic prayer requires us to admit that God may, after all, act like God; we may not presume to limit the divine ingenuity, nor may we presume that there may be constraints or limitations on Him.

Prayer is a matter of listening; we are not looking for God—

it is He Who has found us. Our forebears were not looking, either. Apparently to his great astonishment, Abraham was found and addressed, as were Moses and Hannah, Ruth and Judith, Isaiah, Jeremiah and the prophets, the disciples of Jesus and Saul of Tarsus. The history of encounter is in fact a history of surprise. No one set out in search of God and then spoke with Him: it is God Who breaks the clouds of oblivion and first speaks.

ॐ

But is there a paradox here? We speak of an encounter and of being addressed, and want to enter into the great dialogue with God. Is God, then, a person, a distinct Being among other beings with Whom we may converse? If we pose the question that way, of course, the reply must be no: God is not a person because God is not an individual among other individuals—to assert the contrary would be to reduce Infinity to particularity, to limit the Absolute to something specific and identifiable (in other words, to the limitations of creaturehood). However, if we predicate personality to God analogically, the emphasis shifts. God may be said to have qualities or attributes we normally ascribe to humans, whom we understand as expressing intelligence, faithfulness, compassion, wisdom and the capacity for a personal commitment to relationship.

When we attempt to speak of God, we must certainly intend such qualities, and so it is better to attribute "personality" to God, knowing that this is an analogy, rather than to regard Him as some sort of cosmic force, principle of energy or evolutionary spiral—notions that do not encourage dialogue, much less invite a loving response. Neither the faithful God of the Hebrew Scriptures nor the saving God of Jesus is an impersonal, distant Being or a construct of philosophy or metaphysics. He is, by analogy, "a Person" with whom we intimately relate now and forever.

Faith in God's friendship—the consequence of His presence—

is a prerequisite for a prayerful response; only in light of this friendship may we dare to think of God as embodying personality. For Christians, God's self-disclosure in Jesus Christ enables us once and for all to attribute personality to God, for nowhere else is His love, compassion, fidelity and capacity for relationship more obvious or fully expressed. Thus Jesus is described as God's Word, through whom He speaks and with whom His activity is identified.

For both Jews and Christians, it is not only proper but also necessary to affirm that God has spoken in history—and, more to the point, that God continues to speak today. The only kind of God Who makes sense, after all, is a God Who is living, Who continues to relate to us in the specifics of our time and our individual lives. The past, then, becomes guide and model for the present: "The Lord our God made a covenant with us," Moses tells the Israelites—and then, immediately and significantly, he shifts to the present tense: "Not with our ancestors did the Lord make this covenant, but with us, who are all of us here alive today."

The covenant bond, with ritual sacrifice expressing the alliance between the Lord and His people and a ritual meal the profound union, was not held to represent a thing of the past involving a distant generation: it was and remains a living and active friendship "with us, who are all of us here alive today." Cynics of the French Enlightenment were quite right about at least one matter: there is no sense in believing in a God Who once spoke to Abraham and who now speaks no longer. We can take this sentiment further and assert that that sort of silent God is no God at all.

Dialogue is more than conversation, of course: it is first of all a condition of openness, of receptivity, which is the prerequisite of communication. Yet many people come to prayer presuming that it is the time for God to listen to our needs. "Yet it is just the reverse," as the Danish philosopher Søren Kierkegaard wrote not long before his death at forty-two, in 1855. "The true relation in prayer is not when God hears what is prayed for, but when the person praying hears what God wills. The true man of prayer only attends." The story of attending to God is at the heart of the Hebrew Bible.

CHAPTER THREE

Prayer as Dialogue (II)—
The Experience of Christianity and Islam

Jesus on Prayer

Devout Jew that he was, Jesus of Nazareth observed the tradition of temple worship when he was in Jerusalem and of synagogue meetings outside the holy city. He and his disciples also followed the customs and prescriptions of Jewish law, but a major thread of his teaching went against the complicated religious requirements of his time: he resolutely placed human need above legalism. Mere man-made religious laws, taboos and cultic practices, he taught, had to be set aside when people were hungry or ill, poor or outcast—or were simply sinners in need of correction and conversion. The abandoned, the sick, the emotionally and psychologically wounded, criminals and the wicked, those who were for whatever reason outcasts: these he especially sought out and made the object of his attention and compassion.

Jesus deepened and broadened the existing methods, content and teaching about prayer; in doing so, he freed it from ritualistic constraint and restored it, in its pristine simplicity, as the great gift of divine revelation to humanity. His attitude toward everyone and everything was prayerful; thus his individual acts, his teaching, his ministry of healing—all these were both subsidiary to and the inevitable consequence of prayer.

In the gospels, we seldom read about Jesus eating or sleeping, but very often we are told that Jesus prayed—not only in accordance with Jewish custom, but in solitude, as well. "In the morning, while it was still dark, he got up and went out to a deserted place, and there he prayed. . . . After saying farewell to them, he went up on the mountain to pray. . . . After he dismissed the crowds, he went away by himself to pray. . . . He withdrew to deserted places to pray. . . . He spent the night in prayer to God."

The verb "to pray" (in New Testament Greek, προσεύχομαι, pronounced "proseuchomai") occurs forty-four times in the first three gospels alone, where it characterizes every stage of Jesus' life and ministry. His counsel and teaching about prayer were both a reflection of his own practice and a strong corrective to the dangers of public display:

> Beware of practicing your piety before others in order to be seen by them. Whenever you pray, do not be like the hypocrites, for they love to stand and pray in the synagogues and at the street corners, so that they may be seen by others, Truly, I tell you, they have received their reward. But whenever you pray, go into your room and shut the door and pray to your Father who is in secret—and your Father who sees in secret will reward you. When you are praying, do not heap up empty phrases as the gentiles do, for they think that they will be heard because of their many words. Do not be like them, for your Father knows what you need before you ask Him.

It must have come as something of a surprise for the audience and for later readers of this sermon to learn of the command to be brief, for prayers at that time were astonishingly protracted: the impression was that quantity meant quality. But prayer is for our benefit, not God's: the Father "knows what you need before you ask Him."

His contemporaries could only have understood Jesus' injunction to enter one's own room and shut the door as meaning solitary prayer: almost no one but emperors, noblemen or the very rich had anything but a one-room residence. It was, on the other hand, the understanding of early Christians that Jesus referred to the "room" symbolically as a kind of private withdrawal, the prayerful solitude on which his own interior life was based. "We pray in our rooms," observed a 4th-century teacher, "when we withdraw our hearts completely from the tumult and noise of our thoughts and our worries and secretly and intimately offer our prayer to the Lord. We pray with the door shut when, without opening our mouths and in perfect silence, we offer our petitions to the one who pays no attention to words but who looks hard at our hearts." The place and particular space were secondary: what mattered was that solitude and stillness were available.

But there may be a second allusion in Jesus' direction—to the small storeroom often attached to a one-room dwelling, accessible only from the room and without doorway access to the outside. By Jesus' time, this storeroom had an almost proverbial resonance, meaning a place where one could not be seen. In any case, the reference is to private, wholehearted prayer without concern for appearance or convenience—prayer in an ordinary place. Hence, Jesus refers to the necessity of abandoning the tangle of our activities, plans, anxieties and relationships simply to spend time in our "room," that inmost part of our being where we belong to God and make time to be with Him.

ॐ

The gospels reiterate that, to the outrage of many contemporary religious leaders, Jesus constantly criticized public displays of piety by those "who like to walk around in long robes, and to be greeted with respect in the marketplaces, and to have the best seats in the synagogues [which faced the congregation] and places of honor at banquets. They devour widows' houses [with their demands for tithes] and, for the sake of appearance, say long prayers. They will receive the greater condemnation"—as, he adds, will those who refuse to forgive others' offenses. The revolutionary nature of this proclamation cannot be overstated.

Jesus sets a choice before his hearers: to take God seriously or not. He taught and worked against a background of intolerable religious legalism, which, while a constant threat in all traditions, was especially understandable in his time given the beleaguered condition of Palestinian Jews trying to maintain their faith and identity under Roman occupation. In this milieu, Jesus proclaimed the single, essential, transforming reality: *God really is, and He is here, near and within.*

That recognition alone, that apprehension, that sense of the divine presence (however fleeting) arouses at least a longing for prayer, and the longing itself is the beginning of prayer. "I am as sure as I am alive," said Meister Eckhart in a sermon, "that nothing is so near to me as God. God is nearer to me than I am to myself; my existence depends on the nearness and presence of God . . . God is always ready, but we are very unready. God is near us, but we are far from Him. God is within, and we are without. God is friendly; we are estranged." This is dialogue at its deepest level—awareness of being beheld.

As for the life of early Jewish Christians, it is clear from the contemporaneous literature (the letters of Paul, for example) that private prayer always complemented its corporate counterpart, whether in synagogue, in temple or in the celebration of the Eucharistic meal. Paul often broke into spontaneous songs of praise: "Blessed be the God and Father of our Lord Jesus Christ, the Father of mercies and the God of all consolation, Who comforts us in all our affliction." He also reminded the recipients of his letters that they were constantly in his private prayer, and this is a vital clue to the early belief that prayer for others was presumed to be efficacious on their behalf: "I remember you always in my prayers, asking that by God's will I may somehow at last succeed in coming to you. . . . I keep asking God to give you a spirit of wisdom and revelation, so that you may know Him better. . . . We have not stopped praying for you and asking God to fill you with knowledge of His will."

Paul's fundamental idea of prayer—not by means of the recitation of formulas or words, but as living a life open to God—was expressed in his instruction to the Thessalonians to "pray without ceasing," words that conclude the earliest New Testament document. His own busy life (not to mention his adherence to the tradition of Jesus' teaching on prayer) served as the model for the kind of spiritual alertness that results in a lifelong inclination to prayer, much as one might say, "Always remember . . ." It is, therefore, unnecessary to torture the verse into an unrealistic demand that one ought to be constantly "at prayer" or saying prayers at every moment.

That there must be a connective bond linking prayer and one's life outside the time of formal prayer is well established in early Christian thought. The great spiritual writer Origen, who died about A.D. 254, wrote that "those who pray as well as work at the tasks they have to do, and combine their prayer with suitable activity, will be praying always." His contemporary, the teacher and theologian Clement of Alexandria, claimed that a prayerful spirit made life itself an uninterrupted celebration of the presence of God in our midst. Such an awareness continues through the centuries: "Prayer is not an occupation for a certain time, but a permanent state of the spirit," according to the 19th-century Russian Orthodox bishop and spiritual writer Theophan the Recluse.

That state was the goal of Theophan's private attachment to the so-called Jesus Prayer, which developed during the era of the desert monks in the 4th and 5th centuries and was finally codified in *The Way of a Pilgrim.* Actually an ancient technique aimed at eliciting a constant awareness of God's presence, the prayer recommends the silent repetition (as often as possible, like a mantra) of the name of Jesus.

Whether or not one considers this sort of private practice congenial—and many in the modern world often find it impractical—the so-called Jesus Prayer has a noble goal: the practice of acknowledging the presence of God. There is always, however, the danger that this kind of prayer will come to be seen primarily as an "exercise"—a reliance on rote formulas to achieve a desired result. Paul's reminder to pray always, on the other hand, calls attention to prayer as a habit of being—or, in the appealing language of medieval theology, as the summons to a state of grace.

⚓

All these themes—the omnipresence of God, our dependence on Him for every breath, His constant drawing of us to Himself— are summarized in the New Testament's Acts of the Apostles, in an important speech attributed to Paul at Athens. God has enabled all people to look for and find Him, Paul explains, "though indeed He is not far from each one of us—for 'by Him we live and move and are,' and, as even some of your own poets have said, 'we, too, are His offspring.' "

The first citation ("by Him we live . . .") is usually ascribed to Epimenides, the Greek philosopher-poet of the 6th century B.C.; the second ("we, too . . .") is certainly from the Stoic poet Aratus (born about 310 B.C.), whose long meditation on astronomy, *Phaenomena*, describes humanity's relationship to Zeus.

These allusions to Greek poetry by the author of Acts are not mere literary window dressings; to the contrary, the text insists that because we are given life *by* God, we find our life *in* God. Dependence, in other words, is not merely functional but ontological: the emphasis on our contingency reminds us that we come from and live within the Ultimate Reality, God Himself.

Hence prayer is not an exercise in long-distance communication: it is an awareness of our condition at every moment. Our being itself and our connection to God comprise the condition of dialogue.

Islamic Prayer

The sense of God's omnipresence summarizes the spirit of Muhammad (who died in A.D. 632) and of Islam, which may be traced to his prophetic ministry: "It is glory enough for me that I should be Your servant—it is grace enough for me that You should be my Lord." The word "Islam" means "submission" to the mysterious will of *Allah*: the One God, in Arabic. Its faith looks reverently to the Abrahamic covenant with Israel and beyond, to Muhammad as the sole great prophet. Islam, it must be noted, also includes a deep veneration for Moses and Jesus.

Muslim prayers are of two kinds—*salat* and *du'a*. The ritual *salat* consists of standard formulas to be recited five times daily (dawn, midday, midafternoon, sunset, and nightfall) while turning toward Mecca in Saudi Arabia. It is not required that a Muslim be in a mosque to fulfill his duty; a portable prayer mat is sufficient if the prayers are recited in private. The times of prayer are announced by a call from a mosque tower, preceded by ritual cleansing, and include prescribed moments of standing, bowing, prostrating and sitting. *Salat* always begins with the basic proclamation of Islamic faith: "In the name of Allah, boundlessly merciful and compassionate . . ."

Du'a refers to personal supplications; this practice, too, is among the constitutive elements of Islamic faith, although (as in Judaism) private prayer is ranked below formal worship. But awareness of God's presence everywhere "is the hallmark of the true Muslim," as one Islamic scholar has written. "Once the presence of God has dawned upon a person's life . . . then every aspect of that life is touched and changed." In light of that presence, prayer is "any thought, word or action done with God in mind, and the true Muslim—who is aware of God constantly—really spends every waking moment of his or her life in a state of prayer."

Muhammad himself recommended three positions for private prayer. When making a petition, hands should be raised above the shoulders; when asking forgiveness, one finger should be pointed upward; and when making a particularly earnest supplication, both hands should be spread out in front of the chest.

Islam does not insist, however—just as Judaism or Christianity do not—upon a slavish adherence to the primacy of rigid schedules, postures or the recitation of formulas: Islamic prayer places highest value on a turning of the heart toward God and the direction of one's *niyyah* (intention) toward Him. Nor are words always essential. The 13th-century Islamic mystical poet Rumi told the ancient tale of a man hurrying to the mosque on Friday evening to hear Muhammad. But when he arrived, the congregation was departing, having just been dismissed with the prophet's blessing. The poor man sighed in deep frustration, and a passerby was so moved that he said he would exchange all his own formal prayer for the merit of that man's one deep sigh. As the man who accepted the sigh slept that evening, he heard a voice: "You have bought the water of life and healing: to honor your choice, I have accepted the ritual prayer of all my people."

Much the same conviction as that in Acts was expressed by Rabi'a al-'Adawiyya, an Iraqi Muslim from Basra who died about A.D. 801. Orphaned in childhood, she spent years in slavery before being permitted to pursue a life of solitude and intense personal prayer; her reputation for wisdom, however, drew the devout to her doorstep for counsel and explains her well-documented place in Islamic history. "I exist in God and am altogether His," Rabi'a said when asked about the focus of her life. In the 14th century, Julian of Norwich (the first woman to write in English) expressed the same sensibility: "From God we come, in Him we are enfolded, to Him we return."

Setting down some of her own private prayers, remarkable for their serenity and the intensity of their love, Rabi'a al-'Adawiyya prayed one night: "My God, the stars have set; eyes are closed in sleep; kings have barred their gates. But Your gate is open. Every lover is alone with his beloved, and this is my place, in Your presence." In the morning, she prayed: "O God, this night has slipped away and this day has unveiled itself. By Your power I persevere and by Your eternal tirelessness You give me staying power. Let nothing but Your generosity and bounty descend upon my heart."

Nothing but His generosity and bounty: this is the desire of anyone who has known even one or two moments of authentic prayer. In their solitude, simplicity and silence, people like al-'Adawiyya remind us that prayer must not be approached as if it were a means to change anything. It is we who are to be changed, and this occurs because we are addressed by God, because we behold Him and our existence is linked to His.

This spiritual sensibility, perhaps more than any other, links Judaism, Christianity and Islam. In this regard, a noteworthy French Catholic named Henri Le Saux adopted a Hindu monastic lifestyle without abandoning Catholicism. He died in 1973, after spending the last twenty-five years of his life in India, where he assumed the more elaborate Sanskrit name Abhishiktananda, under which his writings were published. We do not, he said, first think of the air around us and then draw breath; we breathe in order to remain alive. "So it is with the divine Presence, which is still more essential to our life and to our very being than is the air to our bodies."

CHAPTER FOUR

Prayer as Dialogue (III)—
The Living God Speaks

The Premise

God really is, and He is here, near and within. He speaks, and we have only to listen, to allow the dialogue to begin. But in doing so, we must confront a hard question: How can we know it is God Who speaks?

In Judaism, Christianity and Islam, there has been a long history of individuals who have claimed to hear voices and see visions. Joan of Arc is a classic (and romantic) example. A teenager of uncommon courage and integrity, she died at the merciless hands of scheming churchmen and cowardly royals, precisely those she tried to serve. Rather than betray her solid faith that God had addressed her through the "voices" of certain saints, she went to her death—but not without cold dread and only after a fierce fight to defend herself. The transcript of her trial, preserved to this day, is both terrifying and heartbreaking; with savage inevitability, the account leads to one of the most egregious miscarriages of civil justice when, at the age of nineteen, Joan was taken to the town square at Rouen and burned at the stake in 1431.

Playwrights, historians, poets, composers, filmmakers, sculptors, theologians and painters—those who shared her orthodoxy and those who thought little of it—have been unable to shake off Joan's mysterious but firm grip on our collective imagination; some modern scholars even see her as a heroic and ideal androgyne, victimized by fatuous men of both Church and State. The deepest reason for our fascination, however, may be her insistence on her "voices." How are we to understand her, and the countless others like her, who claim that they heard a clear message from beyond? How do we know it is God Who speaks, and not just some projection of ourselves, eager to have an endorsement for our own wishes and fantasies?

The best approach may be the most obvious—and the most helpful to us as we listen for God. He communicates with us as He did with them—in our intuitions, the lights that go on sometimes dimly, sometimes brightly. In these quiet hunches, He directs us to deeper thoughts, concerns and actions than we have yet considered.

Today, the choice of spiritual claims (whether termed inner voices or not) as the basis for a life motif is widely held suspect. Things were not so different in the hostile time of the Spanish soldier and religious genius Ignatius of Loyola, who died in 1556 after founding the Society of Jesus (Jesuits). While recuperating from a battle wound at thirty, he indulged all sorts of fantasies about ideal women. But when he looked around for romantic literature to prop up his daydreams, only books about the life of Christ and the saints were available. Perusing these, he had even more grandiose daydreams about the pursuit of saintly valor, and these he entertained as often as his knightly and courtly aspirations.

Over time, however, Ignatius (as William Barry has written) "came to believe that God used one set of such daydreams to draw him towards a new way of life." Ignatius was not praying when this realization occurred to him: he was daydreaming. But when he attended to his emotional reactions during and after the different daydreams, Ignatius noticed that the romantic-courtly fantasies had left him forlorn, while the idea of dedicating himself to Jesus left him elated. "Because of experiences like these," Barry added, "Ignatius came to believe that God is always communicating [with] us, that every experience has a touch of God in it. It is almost a motto of Ignatian spirituality that God can be found in all things. The only question is whether we will be aware of God's presence or not."

The daydreams of Ignatius are, then, directly connected to our inquiry about how God "speaks" to us, and one way is through our emotional responses to inner experiences and hunches. Once we are familiar with the general pattern or orientation of our lives—are we really on the alert for God, or would we rather remain, as it were, "on holiday" from God?— then we can trust our inner reactions to be a way in which God truly speaks.

The *Spiritual Exercises*, formulated by Ignatius and completed by 1541, consist of a structured program of meditations on the life, death and Resurrection of Jesus, all designed with the goal of moving one forward in life. Ignatian prayer depends heavily on the vivid use of the imagination in "compositions" of place, time and event, but the system is no mere reverie. One's emotions, fantasies, memories, reason and will are all brought into the scheme in order to make the spiritual life concrete and efficient. Some might consider this prayer too schematic, but it has withstood the test of time and still speaks to the needs of many.

᷼

There are other modes of dialogue in prayer, of course, and Teresa of Ávila, a contemporary of Ignatius, discussed them at length. By the 16th century, the custom of *lectio divina* was well known, and Teresa used and developed it; the phrase means simply a pious reading or attention to Scripture.

As a method of prayer, *lectio divina* developed naturally from the Jewish custom of reading and praying over the Torah,

a practice certainly known to the earliest Christians. It was familiar to Benedict, the patriarch of Western monasticism, who
died about A.D. 550, and was certainly practiced by the desert
hermits of the two centuries before him. In his *Rule*, composed
for a community of laymen, Benedict enjoined this kind of
prayer, along with study and work, on all who would seek God in
community.

A thousand years later, Teresa of Ávila detailed the fine
points of something very like *lectio* in her treatment of the
stages of prayer. Shrewd, practical, emotionally balanced and
psychologically perceptive about human nature, Teresa was (after a series of conversion experiences in her forties) tireless in
her efforts to reform lax Carmelite convents and monasteries
throughout Spain. But her travels did not prevent her from dic-
tating and writing an enormous amount, much of which is
structurally chaotic and most of which is deeply moving and remarkably personal. Teresa's admirable blend of mystic insight
and ceaseless activity in and outside her convents witness the
fact that a profoundly contemplative life is entirely compatible
with secular achievement.

In her colorful and frank autobiography, for example, she set
down some of the troubles encountered by those beginning to
pray—especially the difficulty of trying to calm one's senses,
imagination and feelings in order to be quiet in God's presence.
Comparing this effort to the onerous task of drawing water
from a well in order to irrigate a garden, Teresa advised: "Speak
with God as you would with a father, or a brother, or a lord, or a
spouse—sometimes in one way, sometimes in another. He will
teach you what you must do." This effort "is called recollection,
because the soul collects its faculties together and enters within
itself to be with its God." A great deal of effort and discipline is
required at this stage, but, as she had said, one will finally be well
paid.

Great spiritual mentors through the centuries have fore-
stalled the kind of disappointment that is unavoidable when we
are beset by distractions and rambling thoughts during these
times of recollection. To counter these, one is encouraged simply
to return to the verses at hand when one becomes aware of the
distraction—to return to the hints, inclinations and feelings
aroused by the text. We would not, after all, have stopped by the
side of the road if something did not beckon to us: hence we find
something of ourselves, something of what God has placed
within us that responds to His primary speech.

Very like the gradual deepening of a relationship with one
who becomes a friend through conversation and correspondence, *lectio* is not so much a method as an abandonment of
method in order to be open to the Spirit of God. Teresa recommended going to a quiet place, banishing noise and distraction
as much as possible and considering a portion of the Bible
silently—as few or as many verses, until something is stirred
within. From perhaps a visualization of a scene in Scripture or
awareness of a feeling about the text, one is moved to explore
their impact more deeply.

Passages of Scripture, it must be emphasized, are not to be
read as specific directions on how one is to conduct one's life on
any given day. Our task is to establish ourselves in stillness
through a gentle concentration—a focusing or centering on self,
not on ideas, concepts or images. God comes to meet us in our
stillness and attention to Him, and the consequences and effects
of this meeting become clear only with time and patience. It is
tempting to look for answers and concrete results in our prayer,
but it is not some *thing* we should seek to take away from it. It
is God Himself Whom we wish to meet and by Whom we are
embraced.

The *lectio*, therefore, is more than mere reading for a purpose. It is a means to discovery of who we are, of what God
summons us to be. And in this process, our unbidden intuitions

are not to be discounted. Hence prayer begins each time we try to be tranquil and alert, each time we listen without presumption, without expectation that we know "what is coming." It is a matter, first of all, of knowing Who is coming.

God's messages can be conveyed to us, Teresa reminded, "through the conversations of good people, or from sermons, or through the reading of good books—or through sicknesses and trials, or by means of truths which God teaches us at times of prayer, however feeble such prayers may be." For Teresa as for Ignatius, the entire world is God's, and He can use apparently small things and situations as means to speak to us. "Since He is Lord, He is free to do what He wants," Teresa wrote with typical candor, "and since He loves us, He adapts Himself to our size."

⁓

As for our response, the history of prayer offers a clear answer and was neatly summarized by Martin Luther: "The fewer the words, the better the prayer; the more words, the worse prayer." This should be taken as counsel rather than command, of course, for a person given to long and wordy prayers may in her own way be following where God leads, however much the prayer seems to become less a dialogue and more a soliloquy.

Religious people who spoke to Teresa of Ávila about their beautifully extensive prayers were caught short by her blunt common sense in response: after listening to their rhapsodies, she asked, "That's all very well, but can you still sweep the floor?" She offered equally brisk counsel to those who were pleased with their prayers in the same way that she advised those who were not: "It is very important for you to consult people of experience"—a recommendation based, no doubt, on the guidance she had received from her friend and fellow religious reformer, John of the Cross (who was twenty-seven years her junior).

In contrast to solemn monologuists with their protracted

speech-prayers, the cries of the truly great prophetic voices in Judaism, Christianity and Islam are terse calls for mercy or protection. The Psalmist, for example, cries in abandonment to God. "Have mercy on me. . . . Whom have I but You? . . . In You alone is my trust. . . ."

There are as many such brief phrases or motions of the heart as there are people who pray, and their experience is a common one: all the tangled untidiness within them clears for a moment when they pray with so few words. The critical issue in prayer is never what we say or seek but rather our attitude toward God. A mere glance or a very few words between friends or lovers is sufficient communication, and deepens a relationship: how much more must this be so in our being with God. The use of just a few words in prayer, frequently throughout the day, continues the dialogue—they give us something to hold on to, because they are, after all, our response to God Who has stirred our hearts, has first addressed us and turned us toward Himself.

That all prayer is response may at first sound odd. Self-reliance and ambition (not to say a healthy appreciation of our own talents) are so highly praised in our time that many people are astonished to discover that prayer is primarily not about what we do, but rather about what God does—to make us aware of His presence. "It is all His doing" is a biblical principle from first page to last. "God gives the growth," as Saint Paul said pithily of anything in the life of the spirit. Hence, we are always the recipients; the work is God's. Down through the centuries, this is the single major theme of those who have known true prayer.

Nicholas Herman, Francis de Sales and Jeanne de Chantal

The understanding that one is always the beneficiary of God's address was, for example, particularly well articulated by a 17th-century French soldier named Nicholas Herman. Eventually he became a monk and, known as Brother Lawrence, was given the unglamorous assignment of tending the scullery. His notes and letters, never intended for publication, were compiled after his death, and today they are known under the title *The Practice of the Presence of God*.

For Lawrence, prayer begins when we become aware of God. "Simple attentiveness," he said, enabled him to realize "that God protects me . . . and so I hold fast to Him as much as I can." But he recognized the difficulties of maintaining this degree of focus: "A persistent effort is needed to form the habit [of attentiveness to God]."

In 1611, the year Nicholas Herman was born, an exceptional manuscript was in process, by a bishop in the independent duchy of Savoy, near what is today Geneva. The churchman was Francis de Sales, and the book, *On the Love of God*, followed his immensely successful earlier work, *Introduction to the Devout Life*, the first popular treatise on spirituality written for ordinary people at work in the world.

The son of a minor nobleman, Francis was raised sternly in preparation for a military career. At fifteen, he attended the University of Paris, where he excelled; at the same time, he shone in all those qualities that defined the *honnête homme* of his day— gentlemanliness, style, prudence and a social grace that balanced courtliness with a sense of politics. Although accepted by fashionable society, he preferred his studies, and before he was twenty had developed notable skills as a writer and debater— qualities his father intended to be put to good use when the young man became either a general or a lawyer.

But Francis was turning more and more to religious matters, a subject occasioned by a psychological crisis. Since his early teens, he had been tortured by a notion then much argued by Catholics and Calvinists: whether and to what extent God's infinite knowledge "predestined" some people for salvation (in heaven) and others for damnation (in hell). If this was the case, he wondered, then why should some be born at all, and what good was it to speak of free will? Francis emerged from an apparent nervous breakdown over this matter by taking refuge not in academic discourse but in simple abandonment of himself to the love of God, to Whom he entrusted all matters regarding eternal life.

Directed by his father to a career in law, Francis won his degree brilliantly at twenty-four, at the great University of Padua. His father soon found a socially suitable candidate to be Francis's wife, but by this time the young man found his voice: he summoned the courage to announce that he wanted to serve all classes of society in the priesthood—a decision his parent accepted only because a family friend reckoned Francis would be the youngest bishop in Europe.

One of the most appealing among canonized saints, Francis pursued a life of astonishing literary productivity, balanced by constant attention to the spiritual needs of anyone who sought his counsel. He insisted that God invites people of all social classes, careers and backgrounds to a life of intimate dialogue with Him—a deep and joyful prayer life was not, he reminded, restricted to a few rarefied souls. No great austerities or penances were necessary, and no withdrawal from the world; instead, a recollection of God's presence by short prayers, a passage from the Bible or a reading from an edifying book during the course of the day could be the foundation for a deeply meditative life.

In all cases, "We must hold it an absolute fact that men do more through love and charity than through severity and harshness." This notion alone was a revolutionary idea in the Counter-Reformation Church of de Sales's day. Although it leaps from the pages of the New Testament and characterized the spirit of early Christians, the principle had been lost for centuries in an accumulation of moralistic detail that stressed sin and evil and made the cloistered monastic vocation the standard by which ordinary devout life was to be assessed.

The engaging mildness of Francis, his benevolent political skills in brokering accommodations between kings, regents and churchmen, his tireless work for people in all stations of life, the outreach he made to those of all denominations—all this made him something of an anomaly, and his writings became immediate best-sellers in France, Germany, Poland and England, where King James I was among Francis's ardent admirers.

At a time of dark suspicion about any category of loving relationship, Francis's deep and affective friendship with the young widow, the baroness Jeanne de Chantal, was also notable—indeed, this friendship is central to understanding the legacy of both these remarkable people.

In 1604, when he was thirty-seven and she thirty-two, Francis undertook the spiritual direction of Jeanne Françoise Frémyot, who at twenty had married Christophe de Rabutin, the baron de Chantal. For nine years, she skillfully managed her husband's estate. Her first three children died in infancy, and although the next three survived, the family was struck by tragedy. In 1601, her husband was accidentally shot during a hunting excursion, and Jeanne was left a widow at twenty-nine. She raised her children lovingly and sensibly, but was pitched into a terrible darkness that threatened faith itself, until she happened to hear Francis de Sales preach one Sunday in Dijon and sought his spiritual guidance.

Francis encouraged her simply to continue as she was: to be a good mother and member of society, to pray no matter how arid she felt and, when household duties permitted, to visit the poor, the sick and the dying in her neighborhood. Observing her leadership qualities, her attractive personality and her natural

charm, he also suggested that they might together institute
something quite new in the religious life of laypeople: a congregation of women who would live and pray together and, without
vows as nuns, serve others freely in the world. In 1610, they
gathered a community at Annecy for just that purpose. Because
their mission was to visit the needy, they took for the name of
their community the Sisters of the Visitation.

Alas, their goal was quickly sabotaged by the Vatican. The
Council of Trent, which concluded in 1563, had legislated that
religious women in formation as a group must be enclosed in a
cloister and pronounce solemn vows as nuns. To this stipulation
they had to conform and, once cloistered, the "Visitation" became one of laywomen coming to the convent, rather than vice
versa, as had been intended. But somehow Mother de Chantal
managed to continue to attend the needs of her own family even
as she founded more than eighty-five convents during her lifetime, places where visitors were always welcome even as the
nuns dedicated themselves to a contemplative life. The Visitation nuns may be found in many countries to this day.

Jeanne was much admired everywhere—the great minister
to the poor, Saint Vincent de Paul, was among the most ardent
admirers of her common sense and profound dedication. Few
knew that her own inner life was plagued with doubts, for her
correspondence and her talks all over France were marked by a
deep sense of trust in God and simplicity, even amid her many
demands and the frequent darkness that threatened her, and to
which she responded with a free and calm abandonment. Her
letters—direct, honest (even blunt), unautocratic and witty—
reflect a woman with a strong sense of self and even (though she
herself would not even have thought it) of feminine parity. To a
busy priest, for example, she wrote:

Well, I see you have fallen into the condition I've always
feared your fervor would lead you. Don't try to spend four or

five hours on your knees in prayer—try brief periods throughout the day instead. And for the love of God, get enough rest and plenty of good, nourishing food!

And to the French ambassador to Spain, she wrote:

Try to remain calm amid this warfare of distractions, and spend your prayer time quietly and peacefully. Just remain in God's presence—be there, without trying to feel anything or make an act of devotion unless you can do so easily. Sit there in inner and outer tranquility, and be convinced that patience itself is a powerful prayer. To sum it all up: we must be satisfied to be powerless, idle and still before God—even dried up and barren when He permits it. The whole matter of our union with God consists in being content with either pleasant or arid feelings.

The age of Francis and Jeanne was one of almost electric tension, as Christians of every persuasion saw danger from heretics everywhere and were only too ready to deal with them by inflicting condemnation or torture or both. European culture of the time was steeped in a paralyzing rigor, and people everywhere were poised for political and ecclesiastical battles, using doctrinal arguments like bludgeons in their endless religious skirmishes. In many cities, towns and duchies, one might say that Catholics could be found on one side of any given issue, Protestants on the other—but not a Christian among the lot.

It was also a period of strained, tense and mostly unhealthy piety, which stressed humankind's sinfulness and unworthiness—not, perhaps, an attitude to draw people to confident prayer. Against such attitudes, Francis de Sales and Jeanne de Chantal were adamant: "The uneasiness you feel at prayer is useless anxiety and can only result in weariness of mind," Francis wrote to a troubled young woman.

I think you would gain a great deal if you could keep from being so anxious, for that is a great obstacle. Anxiety pretends to incite us to good, but all it does is to make us run away. Remind yourself that the benefits of prayer are not produced by our efforts. We simply place ourselves in His presence. Remember, God will look with favor on our silence. When you come before the Lord, talk to Him if you can; if you can't, just stay there—let yourself be seen, and don't try too hard to do anything else. I don't know if it will work, but I'm not worried about that, for better advice than mine is available to you.

This sort of counsel remains a rare kind of spiritual sanity. The persistent kindness and devout humanism of Francis and Jeanne remind us of what we know beginning with Abraham: that God speaks only in the language of mercy and compassion, and that He wills us no anxiety. Our dialogue with Him becomes ever deeper as we learn the primacy of that vocabulary.

CHAPTER FIVE

Prayer as Petition

Whether we use words or raise our hearts in silence, prayer is a dialogue rooted in an awareness of our contingency—the conviction that we always stand in need before God, that our being is completely reliant on His. Because of this existential dependence, Augustine of Hippo, writing sixteen hundred years ago, noted, prayer always takes the form of petition, regardless of its specific tone or content, whether we ask for something or not.

Dependence and Interdependence

In virtually everything relative to our daily life in the world, we rely on the talents, skills and labors of others—not only on professionals we need in times of illness and emergency, but also on those who provide public services and goods such as food, clothing and utilities. "Your unfailing Providence sustains the world we live in and the life we live," according to a petition included in the Book of Common Prayer. "Watch over those, both night and day, who work while others sleep, and grant that we may never forget that our common life depends upon each other's toil."

A comparable sense of dependence and interdependence is fundamental to faith and prayer. Quite simply, we are not necessary beings; we did not summon ourselves into existence, and we cannot maintain our lives on our own or without reference to others. Dialogue, in word and action, is the condition of all life. Hence if prayer can be considered analogically as a kind of conversation with God, that is only because we sense that God attends, heeds, listens to and provides for us in our particularity: that our existence is somehow significant to Him, and that even our casual steps are known to and guided by Him.

A contemporary spiritual writer, referring to the old adage about no atheists in foxholes, describes the advantage of prayer in emergencies as being that they are almost automatic exercises in faith without our thinking about it. "There's no time for doubt now, something tells us, [as] we cry out to a power greater than ourselves. Inwardly or outwardly, we shout for help. No one has to tell us how to pray."

When we present our needs to God (Who of course knows them before we do), we are rather like students asking questions or raising problems in the presence of a knowledgeable teacher—a comparison that has obvious weaknesses. Although we cannot tell God anything He does not know, this does not mean that prayer is pointless. A more subtle and critical process takes place: our requests reveal us to ourselves, they interpret our desires and show us what is important to us. "To ask" is, therefore, to discover where and who we are before God.

Magic

In regard to petition, doubters are often on the mark when they see magic instead of spirituality. When prayer is the expression of a manipulative, bargaining intention, and when imprecation becomes like casting a spell or relying upon a charm, the request is little more than an appeal to magic, and the supplicant takes on the role of a conjurer.

It is usually easy to recognize when our requests are child-ish, the sort we may once have made for a particular outcome—

for a new bicycle at Christmas; for unmerited success on an imminent school examination; for a touchdown; for a date. These sorts of appeals do often endure into mature years, as people continue to confuse God with a wizard, a matchmaker or a headwaiter scurrying about to satisfy everyone's orders. Not long ago, for example, a Washington society hostess found herself coming down with a bad cold on the morning of an important luncheon. At 10:00 A.M., she put through a frantic telephone call to a Midwest prayer center, and—apparently through divine intervention—by half past noon, she felt well enough to greet her guests.

This sort of account provides comfort to those who regard prayer as mere superstition. In almost all cases, the effectiveness of such magical incantations is linked to a negotiation or bargain (or in this case a donation to the prayer center), to the recital of a specific formula, to the performance of certain gestures or rituals or to the repetition of certain words at hourly or daily intervals. For all the goodwill they may involve, these activities are exploitative deviations from true prayer. They tend, in other words, to direct God toward a specific outcome rather than to place oneself humbly in need before Him.

Praying Where One Is

For all its belief in direct appeals to supernatural beings who had the power to influence everyday life, even ancient prayer was not necessarily synonymous with magic. Babylonian and Assyrian kings, for example, often asked only to be imbued with the spirit of the god Marduk, just as the West African Ewe priests prayed simply to remain near the heart of their great Spirit. The Greeks, too, appreciated the value of asking for spiritual gifts rather than only material benefits: In the *Choephori* of Aeschylus, Electra prays that she "may be a more temperate and more pious wife" than her mother, Clytemnestra. Similarly, a character in a comedy by Aristophanes asks Demeter, the goddess of grain—"who feeds all my thoughts"—to "make me worthy to worship you."

In the Socratic dialogue *Euthyphro* (which comes to us from about 380 B.C.), Plato identified the danger of turning prayer into something like a bargaining transaction in commercial trade:

> *Socrates:* So do you mean that piety is the science of giving to the gods and asking from them?
> *Euthyphro:* Exactly, Socrates.
> *Socrates:* Wouldn't the right way be to ask them what we need from them?
> *Euthyphro:* Certainly.
> *Socrates:* And the right way of giving would be to present them with what they need from us?
> *Euthyphro:* You are right.
> *Socrates:* Then real holiness is the art of doing business with one another—an art of barter between gods and men?
> *Euthyphro:* Yes, barter—if you like to call it that.
> *Socrates:* But I don't like to call it that.

A fragment of a long hymnic prayer to Zeus by Cleanthes, who died in 232 B.C., demonstrates similar evidence of a more refined sensibility:

> From you was our beginning . . .
> For you the whole vast cosmos, wheeling round
> the earth, obeys, and where you lead
> it follows, ruled willingly by you . . .
> To you the unloved still is lovely—
> and so, in one, all things are harmonized.

Praise is then followed by a petition for spiritual enlightenment:

> Scatter the darkness of our souls and grant us
> true understanding.

~

Unlike the Greeks, the ancient Romans tended to pray for material benefits, begging their favorite gods to bestow fortune, protection and victory over rivals; there was virtually no notion of anything more substantive. But to Juvenal, writing in the 2nd century A.D. (and very likely influenced by his predecessor, the philosopher Seneca), this kind of prayer was quintessential folly. Juvenal argues for what one classical scholar has called "an enlightened attitude about prayer: one that is not based on self-prostration before Fortune. . . . We make a deity of [Fortune] because we lack *prudentia*." Because people are mostly enveloped in a cloud of error, Juvenal wrote in his Tenth Satire, they cannot distinguish between true blessings and destructive urges.

The quest for wealth and power is not only vain, he adds: they place everyone in danger, for cupidity often drives even family members to murder. If one must have something to pray for (and he is all but certain the act of prayer is fruitless), it ought to be simply *mens sana in corpore sano*, a sound mind in a healthy body—or, more to the point, a mind liberated from fear of age and death, free from wrath and desire. Juvenal is hardly a Buddhist, but these sentiments echo that tradition's search for enlightenment by detachment from wanting.

~

People close to nature often pray for health and strength in naturally poetic terms drawn from their work in the natural world and their innate sense of being linked to the elements. An old prayer from New Hebrides asks God:

Be the canoe that holds me in the sea of life. Be the steer that keeps me straight. Be the outrigger that supports me in times of great temptation. Let your spirit be my sail, carrying me through each day. Keep my body strong, so that I can paddle steadfastly on, in the long voyage of life.

The metaphor of the voyage at sea is a natural archetype, and water, of course, is ubiquitous in ritual and prayer, whether the speaker is from the desert or the seashore. "Our Father," pray the Sudanese, "everyone is here to ask rain of you. The earth is dry, our families are ruined. You alone are our Father—grant us rain!" The poignant reference to the commonweal and the absence of a bargaining tone distinguish this prayer from the magician's. Closer to water, Ghanaian fishermen sing, "Lord, what a blessing is the sea, with fish for us in plenty." The petition for continued abundance is implied in an exclamation of praise and thanksgiving.

In 10th-century Japan, Shinto prayers known as *norito* were compiled in fifty volumes still consulted today. Like much of traditional Japanese culture, including the simple but grave and graceful tea ceremony, the words used to address deities are carefully formulated in elegant language. Only a heightened form of speech effects good, it is believed; crude or clumsy words, on the other hand, invite only evil. Centuries ago, the sun goddess was asked, in meticulously arranged cadences, to "make the emperor's life a long life, his reign an abundant reign . . . and to cause to flourish in abundance the grains which the common people harvest."

In addition to material concerns, Japanese petitions have not neglected the spiritual, especially after the establishment of a native brand of Buddhism. "Teach us to respect the essence of all religions, and lead us to the One Ultimate Truth. Have us perform our duties out of penitence, and all our work out of gratitude. Enable us to perfect the way of our living by completely submitting to the laws of Nature. . . . Sweep away all evils and save us, O God our Parent! . . . And grant that we may return to the land of [Nirvana] and so walk in the Paradise of Light."

The basic petition of Japanese Buddhism, it should be noted, is frequently misunderstood in the West. Buddhists do not aim only at an ultimate spiritual liberation from the world of sense and matter: they pray (today more than ever) for quite tangible realities related, for example, to issues of political and social justice. Sutra texts and words of patriarchal wisdom are normally included in Buddhist journals addressing people's anxieties, and the Buddha is invoked as a healer.

In Hinduism, the most commonly used Sanskrit word for prayer is *prarthanu,* the root of which may be traced back to the word for "grains"—hence the prayers of pastoral people to various gods for a good harvest. But there is not only concern for "a share in prosperity"—one prays, too, for an enlightened spirit. "You, O great Lord, give brilliance of mind. Illumine me . . . [and] may there be peace on earth as in the firmament. The Supreme Lord is peace. May we all be in peace, peace and only peace, and may peace come unto each of us."

The conjunction of petitions—for material as well as spiritual blessings—has been characteristic of Islam since the time of Muhammad. "O God," he prayed each morning, "I pray for well-being in my existence, in life, health and property—and for my welfare in this world and the next." When a member of his community fell ill, he prayed in terms suggesting familiarity with the Lord's Prayer:

God our Lord, You who are in the heavens, may Your name be sanctified. Yours is the command in the heavens and on earth.

As Your mercy is in the heavens, so let Your mercy be on earth. Forgive us our sins and failures. You are the Lord of those who seek to do good. Upon this person's illness send down mercy from Your mercy and healing from Your healing.

And an acknowledgment of Allah's compassion, with which all Muslim prayers begin, makes of every petition a request for a deeper spiritual life: "Forgive us our shortcomings and failings," a contemporary Muslim woman has written.

Bless all who are suffering, dear Lord, and those in distress of any kind. . . . Bless all those who are outside the fellowship of believers, or who are struggling to cope with personal beliefs that have led them astray. Bless us all, and keep us close to You always. When our eyes are clouded and we do not think clearly, keep us close in Your sight and protected by Your grace. We are bold to ask all these things, confident in Your love for us. Amen.

The Scriptures on Petition

Petitionary prayer embraces every kind of Jewish devotion: lament, praise, thanksgiving, contrition and adoration; every movement of the heart, at every stage of a life, comprises a plea to be heard and heeded. From the time of the patriarchs, petition has articulated the individual's and the people's radical dependence on God as well as a confident request that He may enlighten the darkness of existence and compensate for human perversity. When Solomon succeeded his father, David, to kingship, for example, he prayed: "I do not know how to go out or come in. Give Your servant, therefore, an understanding mind to govern Your people, able to discern between good and evil—for who can govern this, Your great people?"

God's unimaginable wisdom is never forgotten as one prays: to the contrary, faith in God's transcendence inspires every plea. "Before they call, I will answer," says the Lord to His people through the prophet Isaiah. "While they are yet speaking, I will hear." The goodness of God is everywhere proleptic: His providence anticipates human expression and supersedes every other plan.

Nevertheless, the Psalms, from first to last, beg confidently for divine assistance in every department of life. Here, too, an acknowledgment of one's contingency does not imply a spirit of neurotic timidity but rather an attitude of calm certainty that one will be assisted: "O Lord, answer me, for I am poor and needy. . . . You are my God: be gracious to me. . . . Listen to my cry of supplication. . . . In the day of trouble I call upon You, for You will answer me." Here as everywhere in the Hebrew Bible, there is no indication that the person praying can control the action of God or produce magical results. The relationship is always characterized by humble submission and loving trust.

Prayer in the spirit of the Scriptures, as a contemporary Jewish text indicates, "has a double effect: it strengthens faith in God's love and kindness, as well as in His all-wise and all-bountiful prescience. But it also chastens the desires and feelings of man, teaching him to banish from his heart all thoughts of self-seeking and sin, and to raise himself toward the purity and the freedom of the divine will and demand."

In this biblical spirit, Beethoven prayed during times of depression, disillusionment and anxiety over his intermittent (and finally complete) deafness. "O God, God," he cried, noting everything in his journal and adopting the tone of Jeremiah or the psalmist, "look down upon Your unhappy Beethoven. Let not things remain so any longer. Help me, for You see I am

forsaken by everyone. . . . O God, my Refuge and my Rock,
O my All!" But then, just on the edge of complete collapse, he
attained a kind of tranquillity: "Serenely will I submit to all
these changes, and I will place my whole confidence, O God,
only in Your unchangeable goodness." It is prayer that alters us,
not God.

Even a cursory reading of the Old Testament, however, reveals things—preserved for our instruction, if not always for
our edification. The so-called prayer of Jabez, for example (a single verse in 1 Chronicles) is an example of inappropriate prayer:
"Bless me by enlarging my territory," Jabez demands of God.
This description of a man's desire for wealth comes as a crude in-
terruption in what is otherwise a long genealogical list. This
greedy fellow is never mentioned again in the Bible—a silence
surely not irrelevant in assessing him.

Similarly, even the Psalms sometimes contain prayers that
could only be called offensive to God and repellent to us: "When
my enemy is tried, let him be found guilty, and let his prayer be
counted a curse. May his days be few, may his children be or-
phans, and his wife a widow. May his children wander about and
beg. May the creditor seize all that he has. May there be no one
to do him a kindness, nor anyone to pity his orphaned children."
And so it continues. The Psalm is not included as an example of
worthy Davidic prayer; rather it documents a stage of vindic-
tiveness, of anger and bitterness beyond which Hebrew thinking
later developed. (Just so, the great King David's sins are not presented as worthy of imitation.)

The Lord's Prayer

The most sophisticated Jewish prayer from biblical times is the
so-called Lord's Prayer, a compilation of verses that may be

traced to a collection of the sayings of Jesus. We do not have the original Aramaic words he spoke, but only the rendering of them in the Greek New Testament. Once part of an oral tradition, these verses have been preserved most fully in the gospels of Matthew and Luke, and in the late 1st-century document on Christian life and practice called the *Didache*, or teaching of the apostles.

It is critical to recall that in Jesus' time, the texts of prayers devised for use outside formal Jewish liturgies were not firmly fixed but were freely interpreted, with additions and alterations made by those who passed them on. In the case of the gospels, the sayings of Jesus and his Prayer were developed in this manner—not with intent to falsify, but rather to illuminate the sense of the words for people in new circumstances. In other words, to interpret the original words did not mean to be untrue to them, but rather to profess their continuing relevance.

"Even so central a text as this [the Lord's Prayer] is reshaped with relative freedom, adapted to local usage and elaborated," as the biblical expert Eduard Schweizer has pointed out. The early Christian community had no sacred texts other than the Hebrew Bible, of course, for the canon of New Testament writings had not yet been composed. Thus, Schweizer notes, the Lord's Prayer "is not the letter of the law; it is an aid to prayer, a guide to be followed without being bound to this or that precise wording."

In this regard, it is interesting to note that the New Testament writings attributed to John and Paul omit the Lord's Prayer entirely. This certainly does not mean that there is no historical basis for believing that the phrasing, general content and sense of the verses can be traced back to Jesus himself through the collection of sayings that seems to have circulated orally and that were available to Matthew and Luke.

But the absence of this Prayer outside Matthew and Luke,

and the differences evident when we compare their versions, also suggest that there was no legalism or fanaticism involved in the transcription of the Prayer, no attempt to identify and transmit (whether by reportage or research) the actual words of Jesus himself. The translation and adaptation were done quite naturally within the believing communities, who proclaimed that the Risen Christ was alive and present to them, continuing to disclose himself mysteriously in their ongoing faith, and to enlighten those struggling in their common worship, their private prayer and their fidelity.

Jesus knew his disciples wanted to learn to pray as he did, and for that they needed guidelines. Hence we read that, after Jesus returned from a period of solitary prayer, his disciples asked him, "Teach us how to pray, as John [the Baptist] taught his disciples." His reply was consistent with the faith of a devoutly observant 1st-century Jew who knew the Eighteen Benedictions and the Kaddish, Aramaic prayers that concluded several kinds of worship services.

"Whenever you stand praying, forgive if you have anything against anyone—so that your Father in heaven may also forgive you your trespasses." Jesus' brief remark on prayer in general, found in Mark (the earliest of the four gospels), represents a primitive form of what later developed in early communities as the Lord's Prayer; to it, Matthew and Luke added verses from a collection of sayings of Jesus that circulated orally. "When you pray," we read in Luke, "say, Father, hallowed be Your name. May Your kingdom come. Give us each day our daily bread. And forgive us our sins, for we ourselves forgive everyone indebted to us. And do not bring us to the time of trial."

The Matthean version, slightly more elaborated and subsequently preserved in worship services, became the standard form by which the Lord's Prayer is known.

The particular context in which the Lord's Prayer appears in

Matthew is important: it occurs immediately after an injunction "not to heap up empty phrases [and] many words." What Jesus counsels, by contrast, is the serenely brief prayer that follows. The version that has been used for two thousand years of Christian prayer is substantially the same form as what we read in the *Didache*; it is here reproduced in the traditional English style by which it is now most commonly recognized.

> Our Father, Who art in heaven,
>> hallowed be Thy name.
> Thy kingdom come,
>> Thy will be done on earth as it is in heaven.
> Give us this day our daily bread;
>> and forgive us our trespasses,
>> as we forgive those who trespass against us;
> And lead us not into temptation,
>> but deliver us from evil.*

The Lord's Prayer is entirely focused on God and His plan for the world, even when its structure seems to shift from an emphasis on Him (in the first four lines above) to us (in the last five). It is particularly interesting to see how the Matthean version contains three references to God (His name, His kingdom and His will) followed by three petitions (concerning our bread, our sins, our temptations).

Among the remarkable implications of these verses is that petitionary prayer is not about speaking words or performing acts to obtain something from God, nor to achieve a specific

---

*From about the 4th century, some manuscripts of Matthew added a doxology based on 1 Chronicles 29, 11–13: "For Thine is the kingdom and the power and the glory forever. Amen." This conclusion reappeared in 17th-century Church of England services and has recently been included in Roman Catholic worship.

goal. It is rather about harmonizing human life and conduct with the name of God (that is, with His existence, holiness and benevolence toward humanity) and with the presence of His kingdom—the reality outside space and time where all separation from God and all the consequences of sin have been totally eradicated. This "kingdom," or realm of God, begins in this world, where God's presence and activity are welcomed and affirmed in the affairs of humanity.

While the Lord's Prayer may indeed have reached its final form within the context of a Christian ritual celebrated by followers of Jesus, who were a group within Judaism until near the end of the 1st century A.D., it cannot strictly be called a "Christian prayer" except insofar as it was later included solely in Christian usage. Traced back to the teaching of Jesus, a devout Jew, and based on sections of the Hebrew Scriptures and contemporary Aramaic worship services, it could and can be devoutly prayed by any Jew, just as it was composed by one.

"Hardly a clause in the Lord's Prayer either does not or could not stand in Jewish prayers," as one linguistic scholar has observed, "and the effective prayer life of Jesus, as the first disciples record it, clearly has its human roots in the rich prayer life of his people." The English abbot and spiritual director John Chapman went so far as to write that the Lord's Prayer "is natural religion in its highest form." The Lord's Prayer must be considered in our history of personal prayer because of its uninterrupted history in private devotion; it has always provided the standard by which at least all Christian prayer may be assessed.

Our Father, Who art in heaven*

The Lord's Prayer takes a stand against childish prayer by introducing us to the realm of God. In composing the prayer, Jesus released his disciples from the burden of finding their own way to God. He himself very often referred to God, without distinction, as both his Father and the Father of his disciples. This designation for the deity, quite natural in a patriarchal society, occurs 40 times in the Old Testament in reference to God—most notably, in Isaiah ("You are our Father") and Sirach ("I cried out, Lord, You are my Father"); God is Father 260 times in the New Testament.

The contemporary connotation of fatherhood was of loving leadership and strong care, qualities traditionally praised in (but certainly not limited to) men; in any case, Jews certainly did not think of God as having exclusively masculine gender, and there are biblical allusions to the nurturing maternity of God ("As a mother comforts her child, so will I comfort you").

But this approachable God, from Whom we draw existence, also dwells in light inaccessible, in the realm of unimaginable holiness and power. This is implied in the phrase "Who art in heaven," which assures that although addressing God as our Father, we will never be tempted to take Him for granted, and that His very transcendence is the basis for reverence—even as we pray to Him as One Who fills the world.

We should not, however, imagine God as inhabiting some distant, spatially defined "heaven," which is a word that refers to a state of majestic being, not a place. "Wherever God is, there is heaven," wrote Teresa of Ávila. There is no need to die and "go to heaven" in order to speak with Him, she added, "nor is there

*The verses of the Lord's Prayer are discussed here—with the exception of the petition for forgiveness, which properly belongs to chapter 6.

any need to shout. However softly we speak, He is near enough to hear us. All one need do is go into solitude and look at Him within oneself, and not turn away, but with great humility speak to Him." The corollary for prayer is that God is at work every moment, sustaining everything in being—and therefore, He is at the center of every human heart, for every moment is His "now." God's heavenly dwelling, we can say without hesitation, is ourselves.

Hallowed be Thy Name

These words and the following phrase rework a well-known Aramaic prayer, the Kaddish, spoken at the end of the synagogue service and often added as a conclusion to other prayers: "May His name be praised and honored as holy in the world." Ever since Isaiah, "the Holy One" had been the primary name or identification by which God was known and addressed. "The name of the Lord comes from afar"—He has broken through the mists of being the Unknown, has manifested His being in power as the Holy One. The name of God means his innermost Being; if it is to be hallowed, it means that God is to be recognized and praised everywhere as the Holy One. And in praising God, we ratify and deepen His Being, His gifts and His action within us; praise and thanksgiving are ideationally linked.

Origen, in his treatise *On Prayer* in the 3rd century, rightly pointed out that no one can pray that the name—that is, the identity—of God actually be made holy, for it is holy by its nature.

A name is a summary designation descriptive of the peculiar character of the thing named. . . . In the case of men, whose peculiar characteristics are changed, their names also, by a sound usage, are changed according to Scripture. When the character of Abram was transformed, he was called Abraham; when that of Simon, he was named Peter; and when that of Saul, the persecutor of Jesus, he was designated Paul. But in the case of God, inasmuch as He is Himself ever unchangeable and unalterable, the proper name which even He may be said to bear is ever one—that mentioned in Exodus, "He that is."

Thus Origen concludes that we ask, in the Lord's Prayer, to keep a holy idea of Him Who is holiness itself, "in order that we may see His holiness as creator, provider." And we pray for all the world to recognize this.

Thy kingdom come,
Thy will be done on earth as it is in heaven.

The first phrase is also adapted from the Kaddish: "May He establish His kingdom soon." For devout Jews hoping for social and political vindication under Roman occupation, the goal was clearly the establishment of a theocratic state under a political deliverer.

But with the rise of Jewish Christianity, there occurred a shift in focus: the kingdom was no longer considered as a divinely sanctioned political reality. The kingdom is not "of this world," as Jesus said, but rather arrives when God's benevolent will is accomplished "on earth as it is in heaven"—when it is localized and made real, with human cooperation, in the sphere of ordinary human life—not by political sanctions. The kingdom of God—that is, the activity of God at work in the world on our behalf—thus becomes an event in the present, and it is an entirely different focus from an earthly kingdom or a consideration of the kingdom in a future life after death, which is left entirely up to God.

The kingdom here "below," which is a product of our

acceptance of God's saving will for us and our cooperation with it, thus makes visible the kingdom of heaven, the realm of God. It has dawned in the here and now, where it is growing in our midst—not yet fully realized, to be sure, but in process. And this "will of God" requires our collaboration in everything that furthers the humanizing process. It is the fullness of the invitation offered to Adam in the garden—to cooperate in the proper and just ordering of the world, "to name" things, which means to determine their function in the world for the benefit of everyone.

In the years immediately following Jesus' death, his followers expected an imminent end of the world. Although they understood that the kingdom had been inaugurated in Jesus' ministry, they also held that its fulfillment had to await the literal dissolution of creation. At that time, Jesus, as the glorious figure of judgment, the apocalyptic Son of Man announced by the prophet Daniel, would return to earth and establish forever the reign of God. That much was affirmed by the oldest preserved Christian document, Paul's first letter to the Thessalonians (A.D. 50–51). The same expectation was implied a few years later, when Paul concluded his first letter to the Corinthians with a short prayer already well known to them, which he cites in the original Aramaic: *Marana, thà*—Our Lord, come!

Those same words conclude the *Didache*; indeed, some modern scholars claim that the invocation *Marana, thà* may have terminated the primitive celebrations of the Eucharist. Gathering for a meal in Jesus' memory, Christians believed that it prefigured the heavenly banquet for which they longed—the fulfillment of the kingdom in eternal life. Hence their impatience: "Our Lord, come!" Believing Christ Risen to be present mysteriously among them, they prayed to be with him in time and, eventually, in eternity.

This simple, heartfelt prayer (which also became a common private invocation among Christians) typified the tension of early faith. And when it became clear that an early, dramatic, visible return of Jesus was not in the divine plan, the delay itself became one of the concerns guiding the formation of the four gospels.

"Thy will be done . . ." The phrase, as Aldous Huxley said, "is repeated daily by millions, who have not the slightest intention of letting any will be done, except their own."

It is common for many people to think of the will of God as something that is invariably hostile to their own—something terrible and demanding that overtakes and crushes our expectations of happiness or success. In this spurious conflict, God is as dour as the headmaster of a dreary school, where all is mute obligation and there is no free time and no games; or, more subtly, God is regarded as a strict parent requiring our constant subordination, as if his only message to us was a grim threat: "This is for your own good. Some day, you will appreciate what I'm doing." Consider, for example, that the expressions "will of God" or "act of God" have become primarily a reference to something dreadful and unfortunate. The death of a child is "an act of God"; the slaughter of innocents in wartime is a mysterious part of "God's will."

On the other hand, God's will is understood by many today to be synonymous with material success: "God wants you to be rich and happy and successful," we hear so often today from television preachers and even so-called religious writers, who evidently take God for a portfolio adviser, assuming that He has less regard for the countless poor and hungry and disenfranchised (and, therefore, we need not be attentive to them, either). This version of God is nothing more than a counterstatement to the image of Him as a humorless headmaster: this is God as cheerful agent and business manager. The purveyors of this particular vision proclaim that God is on the side of the wealthy and powerful, the one (or the nation) with the most money or the most dangerous weapons.

Referring to the will in this context, using anthropomorphic language, necessarily involves speaking of God, by analogy, in human terms, which is pretty much all we can do. But God does not *have* a will as we do, in the sense of its being a faculty of energy or inclination, of ambition or self-interest, of reaching and grasping, of altruism or self-dedication. God may only be said to *be* His will, which is love, and which works in time and creation only for the good of humanity, for the fulfillment of everything. That conviction underlies faith.

To express this in contemporary terms: everything in the universe is under the mysterious and benevolent control of a providential Power. To pray for the coming of the kingdom, then, means to accept responsibility in the present, to seek and work to become fully human—to actualize the sphere of God's influence by replicating the divine will among us, just as the order of physical creation itself represents and actualizes the divine will ("on earth as it is in heaven").

Sensitivity to the ever-potential clash of the divine wisdom against human decisions is a connective thread throughout the history of Jewish, Christian and Muslim prayer.

"You know what I want," Julian of Norwich said frankly to God in the 14th century. "If it be Your will that I have it, or if it be not Your will—do not be displeased with me, for I want nothing that You do not want." She took her cue, of course, from the prayer of Jesus on the brink of his arrest and execution: "My Father, if it is possible, let this cup [of suffering] pass from me—yet not what I want, but what You want." Jesus did not desire death or seek it out; in fact, he made every effort to avoid it.

The wisdom of hindsight—and the implicit gratitude that his prayers were not answered as he had expressed them—can be read in the words of a gravely wounded Confederate soldier during the Civil War:

> I asked for strength, that I might achieve;
> I was made weak, that I might learn to obey.

I asked for health, that I might do greater things;
I was given infirmity, that I might do better things.
I asked for riches, that I might be happy;
I was given poverty, that I might be wise.
I asked for power, that I might have the praise of men;
I was given weakness, that I might feel the need of God.
I asked for all things, that I might enjoy life;
I was given life, that I might enjoy all things.
I got nothing that I had asked for,
but everything that I had hoped for.
Despite myself, my unspoken prayers were answered;
I am, among all men, most richly blessed.

Give us this day our daily bread

The gospels are clear that Jesus of Nazareth, who fed the hungry and healed the sick, took human need seriously and sought to alleviate want and suffering. The prayer for "our daily bread" includes everything that people require for sustaining life—not just as individuals but as a community, aware of one another's needs.

For some people, the prayer for ordinary food is something of a paradox, in light of what we read a dozen verses after the Lord's Prayer, where Jesus is clear about divine providence and needless anxiety: "Do not worry about your life—what you will eat or what you will drink, or about your body, what you will wear. . . . Do not fret and ask, 'What will we eat?' or 'What will we drink?' or 'What will we wear?' . . . Your heavenly Father knows that you need all these things."

But these verses do not contradict the relevant passage in the Lord's Prayer. Our concern for material necessities is entrusted to God, Who knows our needs and how to provide for them. The choice of the word "bread," while surely representing all that is necessary for maintaining physical life, is magnificently simple, and sublimely instructive for those who pray. One asks not for excess, nor for luxury, nor even for oneself alone: one asks to awaken to each day not with needless abundance, but simply with sufficient provision to prevent despair.

"Do not worry about anything," Paul writes to the Philippians, "but in everything, by prayer and supplication with thanksgiving, let your requests be made known to God." It is well established in both the Judeo-Christian and Muslim traditions that the needs of ordinary earthly life and health are matters for prayer. The Book of Psalms recorded prayers for safety and protection, for food, for long life. "It is permissible to pray for whatever it is permissible to desire," wrote Thomas Aquinas in the 13th century; he, in turn, was citing the Greek theologian John of Damascus (who died about A.D. 750)—"To pray is to ask becoming things of God." What is permissible, what is becoming and appropriate—that is always the gauge of prayer's suitability. Later, Martin Luther, quite in the same spirit, urged that all spiritual and temporal needs be brought to God. Muhammad instructed his followers to "pray God for your welfare in this world and the next," and he prayed each morning and evening "for my well-being in religion, in my existence, in life, health and property." In the prophetic vision, nothing is outside the realm of divine influence, protection and activity.

However, we must understand the meaning of "need" within a proper historical context. The Lord's Prayer comes to us from a culture that did not envision the terrible realities of worldwide famine, which afflicts so many millions in our own time. In the era of Jesus, most people managed, few had excess and wealth was very rare in the life of anyone. Physical needs, in other words, were generally modest, and very few people aspired to or achieved opulence.

This petition, then, becomes not less but in fact more poignant for us today, as we pray not for *my* daily bread, but for *our* daily bread. It is neither possible nor desirable to forget, at precisely the moment of our prayer, the suffering that touched the heart of Jesus himself when he encountered it—and the suffering that has grown to pandemic levels in our own time, when tens of millions are starving worldwide and enduring agonies imposed by man as well as by natural disasters.

Early prayers were expressions of common needs that, it was understood, went beyond the necessity of food. "We beg You, O Lord," prayed Clement, an early Church leader in Rome at a time of Christian persecution, "to help and defend us. Deliver the oppressed, pity the insignificant, raise the fallen, show Yourself to the needy, heal the sick, bring back those of Your people who have gone astray, feed the hungry, lift up the weak, take off the prisoners' chains."

This entreaty of unselfish concern was very likely the inspiration for a later English prayer that has survived in some personal and communal devotional books to the present; it has traditionally been offered at the end of the day: "Keep watch, dear Lord, with those who work or watch or weep this night, and guard all those who sleep. Tend the sick, Lord Christ; give rest to the weary, bless the dying, soothe the suffering, pity the afflicted, shield the joyous—and all for Your love's sake." Prayer for oneself cannot exclude the needs of others.

We lift up to God, then, all those who are today forgotten, and our prayer (as always) reminds us of our obligation—not only to bring before God the needs of the suffering, but to help find ways of alleviating those needs. As the gospel according to Matthew later indicates, the standard of judgment for all of us will be the extent to which we have found some personal means of alleviating human misery when we see it: "I was hungry and you gave me food, thirsty and you gave me something to drink, a stranger and you welcomed me, [for] just as you did to the least, so you did to me."

Amid the social and economic complexities of modern times, this may indeed be a thorny matter, difficult to comprehend, and it may be harder still to see just how an individual can make a difference in light of the enormity of the world's suffering. But the injunction remains: prayer for our own needs must include an active concern for others.

And lead us not into temptation,
    but deliver us from evil.

The Lord's Prayer concludes with a verse that causes some people unnecessary anxiety. "Do not put us to the test" might serve as a good modern translation, "and so save us from evil." We pray not to be kept from all temptation (which would be impossible, in practical terms), but rather to be kept from those critical situations in which we might make decisions that alienate us from God. The second part of the verse is a restatement of the first: we ask God to save us from evil both external and internal. That He can do because He is the Holy One, our Father in heaven.

Hence it is unnecessary to read the final petition as a statement that God leads us into the thicket of temptation to see how we fare. In a way, the concluding verse puts the brakes on all the prayers of petition we utter: "Do not give me what I ask for if You foresee that they would be snares or sorrows." Where, indeed, would I now be if God had granted all the silly, selfish requests I have put before Him?

The Willingness of God

Dante expressed the matter succinctly: *la sua voluntade è nostra pace*—"His will is our peace."

There often lurks, even among devout people, an inclination to suppose that we know better than God what is right and proper for us—that it is our will that really counts when it comes to our happiness and well-being. If only God would get sensible and do our bidding, everything would be so much easier. Well, maybe we can strike a deal!

Without doubt, petition at prayer is a topic often poorly understood—not only because of magical tendencies, and our attempts to manipulate or bribe God, but also because of a false opposition we tend to presume exists between human and divine intent. That divergence is due to the subtle, unspoken notion that submission to God's will means disaster for us, or at least some unpleasantness—that God's ways are at least to be regarded suspiciously, if not avoided altogether. At the root of this misperception is a lack of trust—of faith itself—in God's unimaginable and infinite mercy, and the lingering anxiety that He may not, after all, be Love straight through.

This sort of thinking (never, of course, articulated so crudely) leads by a direct route to a wholly false idea of prayer. The practical result of such spiritual malfunction is "prayers" that are not really prayers at all—not expressions of longing for God and what harmonizes our existence with His, but rather examples of unattractive designs on destiny. Hence we pray to win a lottery, or to be rid of a meddlesome person in our life, or to control someone (by brute power or by romantic ardor, for example) or to be spared the ordinary lot of the human condition. When we are not heeded, the consequence of our disappointment is the complaint, "Why is this happening to me?" To our annoyance, the reply may sometimes be sensed, deep within: "Why not?"

It is always tempting to regard prayer as the solution to a problem—or, worse, to all problems. But prayer is not a means of escape from the ordinary lot of physical and emotional life, which necessarily involves experiences of diminishment, darkness and dying. In fact, prayer is rarely the solution to any problem at all. We do not pray for utilitarian or functional or financial reasons, nor because prayer can produce beneficial results. We pray to know more deeply *Whose* we are; from that awareness derives everything we genuinely need in this life.

And here we come perhaps to the ultimate significance of the term "God's will." We tend to conceive of God as "having" a will much as we do—a faculty of desire, of intent, of motivation. And we think of that will as a blueprint for what God desires. Considered from this perspective, "finding God's will" means locating the part of the blueprint that involves me so that I can measure up and fit into it—no matter what, because that is the way things are to be. The metaphor of a kind of a divine management blueprint, however, not only gives us a vague sense of discomfort; it also may get us into a good bit of trouble, because it can lead to a subtle but strong undercurrent of resentment. The idea of a divine blueprint (which we must locate and into which we must force ourselves) implies strict limitations on human freedom and makes us little more than pawns in God's game of destiny. Surely the notion of "the will of God" means more.

We might instead think of God's *willingness* as the total array of elements He sets before us by which we in fact use *our* will to make choices, even when the choice is to accept what seems inevitable. When Jesus said, "Not my will but Yours," the effect was not a cancellation or annihilation of his own willingness but an offering of it, a joining of it to God. Hence his willingness to suffer was neither masochistic nor a Stoic avoidance of pain; rather, he went through it to God.

The elements of *our* willingness, with which we discover God's willingness to be for us, include but are not limited to our powers of judgment, our discernment of what is right and necessary, our intuition about the proper course of action in a particular situation, the witness of others and reflection on our own experience. All these are also the vehicles of revelation which then become clarified in the deep silence of prayer. As the great Scripture scholar Oscar Cullmann wrote in a classic treatise, "The power to unite oneself with God's will is itself the hearing of a prayer." The divine *voluntas* is the beginning not of our extinction of self but of our recognition, begun here and now, and yet to be fulfilled in eternity.

God answers prayers, then, through the limitless array of experiences, reactions and thoughts that come to us, both despite of and in light of what we may think of as unanswered prayers. There are always responses: realizations about coping mechanisms, about courses of action, where to go for strength, where to find the spiritual and temporal mechanisms for absorbing the fact that our will often must be winnowed and sifted, chastened and elevated. We become more sensitive to what diminishes and enhances us—and so prayer makes us not less but more sensitive to the suffering of others, and more susceptible to their goodness, too.

It is neither irrelevant nor irreverent to say that there is a sense in which we make God's will in collaboration with Him, in specific actions and particular circumstances. There is no preordained blueprint according to which we must live: His only meaning, after all, is to share Himself in love. And because He exists in an eternal Now and creates us at every moment, the meeting of our will with His ought to have an element of astonishment.

The prayer that God's willingness can be accomplished with our active participation is a break with narcissism, anxiety and all the usual preconceptions we bring to a consideration of how He should act on our behalf. And that refined faith may finally bring us to the conviction that (as Julian of Norwich wrote) all will be well; everything will, at last, be well.

This confidence is but the logical term of the conviction that could never be stifled in the long history of the Hebrew people. When they suffered—from the time of the patriarchs through the Exodus and down to the times of their annexation to Assyria in the 8th century B.C. and of the Babylonian captivity in the 6th century B.C.—one prayer returned to their lips time and again: "The Lord hears when I call to Him." Even when the reply was not immediately forthcoming, even when their destiny seemed enveloped in darkness, a faithful courage and a courageous faith sustained them: "I wait for the Lord more than those who watch for the morning."

⌇

It is true that Jesus instructed his followers to ask for any good thing they needed and promised his disciples that anything they asked "in his name" would be granted. But that phrase has a quite specific meaning: "Ask for anything *the way I ask it*"— that is, with full reliance on God's better judgment, and with a complete and serene submission to His will for us, which embraces and finally saves. If prayer is indeed the alignment of our wills with His, then we cannot want what He does not want— and so we shall indeed obtain whatever we ask. All true prayer, according to Julian of Norwich, "ones" us to God by conforming us to Him.

Such prayer needs, she continues, to be "large" in its concern for others. Four centuries later, Samuel Johnson asked God that—if his work and study resulted in an abundance of material rewards—he might be given also "a compassionate heart, that I may be ready to respond to the wants of others." Today when we pray for peace, we pray to be transformed into peaceful people who advance peace in the world; prayer, after all, is always about *us* being changed—not God, not others. The believer never boasts, "I did it my way."

The prophets' passion for being God's instruments, Jesus' undiluted witness to God's fidelity, Muhammad's insistence on the reality of the divine compassion: all the holy ones of history lived and prayed confidently. And when it came to a matter of will, they knew Whom they trusted. They recognized that sometimes they might have to run the risk of losing everything—but that, after all, was only so that they might gain much more than just some thing. They knew that prayer is essentially not about petitions and requests: it is about asking God to give us Himself.

CHAPTER SIX

Prayer as Forgiveness

Grudges, Resentments and Hatred

Perhaps one of the least attractive aspects of the human personality is that it derives strong emotional satisfaction from both short-range aversions and long-term resentments against those it perceives as opponents or enemies. It does not seem to matter much if those perceived foes are familiar personally or whether they are nations, groups, races or individuals who are believed to have trespassed.

By intensifying an antagonism against a presumed adversary, the ego is inflated: one gets a kind of subtle jolt or expressive charge to soothe an apparently disadvantaged self-image. Bitter memories, lovingly recalled and tenderly fondled, sustain the umbrage once taken, often to the point of exaggeration. In any case, slight grudges often grow into profound and permanent sources of rancor, and even legitimate moral outrage against an obvious crime or corruption can lose its balance and turn into a manic thirst for vengeance. The remedy for this tendency to keep wounds fresh (and thus potentially debilitating) can only be a healing of memories. Only by forgiveness can the pain of any injury be treated; only by forgiveness can any wound begin to heal.

We do not, it seems, live in a time that values forgiveness. Broad and various social anxieties; the fear engendered by a world that seems to have gone out of control; a sense of entitlement and of victimization; demands for legal and financial compensation—all these and more have made the very idea of forgiveness seem like weakness. This may be at least partly because the word and its implications are often misunderstood. However, many people quite wrongly presume that forgiveness means to deny the effect of an offense, or to minimize its significance, or to say that something dreadful was not really so bad and can be dismissed without comment or control. But failure to understand the true nature of forgiveness only further stimulates the desire to retaliate.

The verb "forgive," which comes to us from Old High German and Old English, has a quite specific meaning: to remit a debt; to abandon a claim for requital; to discard one's resolve to seek vengeance; to give up a wrathful desire to inflict pain or death on an offender.

And forgive us our trespasses,
    *as we forgive those who trespass against us**

These may be the most challenging (not to say ignored) words of the Lord's Prayer. Said aloud or silently, they implicitly acknowledge that one stands always in need of God's forgiveness—a conviction reiterated for centuries by the Hebrew Scriptures, which proclaim both human sinfulness and God's limitless forgiveness:

Have mercy on me, O God, according to Your steadfast love; according to Your abundant mercy, blot out my transgressions. Wash me thoroughly from my iniquity, and cleanse me from my sin. For I know my transgressions, and my sin is

*Regarding the word "trespasses": the Jewish-Christian Matthew used the Greek word for "debts," which was a Hebrew-Aramaic euphemism for "sins." The gentile Luke, on the other hand, used the Greek for "sins." Both words were represented by the (probable) original Aramaic, *hoba*.

ever before me. . . . Create in me a clean heart, O God, and put
a new and right spirit within me.

An important issue is raised here, and it involves my readiness to be forgiven by God—which I can do only by not yielding
to forces like the inclination toward acquisitiveness, moral superiority and the urge to compete for pride of place. Forgiveness
for myself means also accepting that those who offend me are,
like me, locked in mortal combat with what draws us away from
our full potential as humans.

This is not mere pious rhetoric. In the Jewish faith, God's
mercy is extended to the worst possible sinners. King Manasseh,
for a classic biblical example, is represented as the egregious case
of hardened wickedness: his idolatry and cruelty (even to his
own son, whom he tortured without regret) were considered to
be the cause of the downfall of the kingdom of Judah. "He did
what was evil in the sight of the Lord" is the summary of his
reign; "he shed very much innocent blood and was worse than
all our enemies combined."

But Manasseh was not only the prototypical royal sinner; he
was also an example of an unexpected penitent. When he and his
people were dragged off in chains into what has become known
as the Babylonian Captivity, Manasseh prayed for forgiveness.
"While he was in distress and in fetters, he entreated the favor
of God—he prayed, and God received his entreaty." His prayer
is included in the canon of Scripture, and it is a masterpiece of
penitential devotion, central to Jewish thinking about the unimaginable breadth of divine compassion; at the same time, it is
a proclamation that the long arm of God's forgiveness touches
the worst we can do and the worst of those among us.

You are the Lord Most High, of great compassion, long-
suffering and very merciful. According to Your great goodness,
You have promised repentance and forgiveness to those who

have sinned against You. In the multitude of Your mercies, You have appointed repentance for sinners, that they might be saved. The sins I have committed are more numerous than the sands of the sea. And now I bend the knee of my heart: I have sinned, O Lord, I have sinned. I earnestly implore You: forgive me, O Lord, for You are the God of those who repent, and in me You will manifest Your goodness. Unworthy as I am, You will save me according to Your great mercy . . .

If Manasseh was irredeemable—as many thought—then there would always be doubt about who could repent and be heard, even at a critical last moment; in other words, there could well be limitations on divine mercy. But the Hebrew Scriptures are unambiguous: "God heard him and restored him again to Jerusalem and to his kingdom." To the astonishment of many at that time (and perhaps to more now), the matter was clear: no one was beyond the possibility of repentance and conversion; no one was to be denied the right of repentance.

Precisely the same theme occurs in the first letter of Peter in the New Testament. After his death and in the process of his glorification, wrote the author (citing an early Christian hymn), Jesus visited "spirits in prison"—a reference to the sinners of Noah's flood, whom the Jews regarded as the prototype of unforgivable sinners.

Christ was put to death in the flesh but made alive in the spirit, in which he went and made a proclamation to the spirits in prison, who in former times did not obey, when God waited patiently in the days of Noah, during the building of the ark. . . . The gospel was proclaimed even to the dead, so that, though they had been judged in the flesh as everyone is judged, they might live in the spirit . . .

The sense of the verses is quite clear: God does not judge people definitively until the entire truth of the Gospel has been preached to them. The saving mission of the Risen Jesus, in other words, extends to those whom Jewish tradition had condemned finally and unequivocally.

These excursions into classic Hebrew and early Christian thinking about the nature of repentance, forgiveness and God's mercy are directly relevant to consideration of the extension of human forgiveness. The awareness of my own dependence on divine mercy makes it both possible and necessary for me to forgive others; in fact, forgiveness of others, according to the Lord's Prayer, becomes the condition of my being forgiven by God. "Forgive us our trespasses as we forgive those who trespass against us." In this respect the Lord's Prayer is, we might say, a dangerous formula to recite: I ask God to treat me just the way I treat others.

ॐ

Forgiveness and love of those we perceive to be enemies are absolutely central to the teaching of Jesus of Nazareth, as they were central to his way of dealing with others right up to the time of his death. Unrestricted, other-centered love—which is a matter of will, not of emotions—was at the heart of his proclamation: "Love your enemies and pray for those who persecute you. . . . Be merciful, just as your Father is merciful. . . . Forgive and you will be forgiven. . . . Do good to those who hate you, bless those who curse you, pray for those who abuse you. . . . Do not condemn, and you will not be condemned; forgive, and you will be forgiven." My prayer must be that an offender will repent and turn to God, just as I myself must repent and turn to God. In the late 4th century, Ambrose of Milan—writer, composer, bishop and teacher of Augustine—understood this: "Teach me," he prayed, "to sympathize with sinners from the depths of my heart. May I show compassion when anyone falls and his sin comes to my notice."

The Lord's Prayer takes with absolute gravity the marvelous forgiveness of Manasseh and the words of the Jewish Book of Sirach: "Forgive your neighbor the wrong he has done, and then your sins will be pardoned when you pray. Does anyone harbor anger against another and expect healing from the Lord? If one has no mercy toward another like himself, can he then seek pardon for his own sins?"

"Forgive us as we forgive others. . . ." If we stop to think about it, this is not unrealistic, sententious advice from an idealistic philosopher; to the contrary, it is the height of pragmatism, the only way that concord may be restored among individuals, groups, races and nations. To be sure, it is also an ideal—but one that, if it guides every consideration, affects human nature at the core of its being. As long as we continue to believe that this is impossible—as long as we insist on retribution or revenge—grace is impeded, the process of healing is stymied and God's approach to us is thwarted. And so the world remains mired in impossibility.

※

In his announcement of God's unconditional love for humanity, Jesus also placed forgiveness at the core of his parables. In the famous story of the prodigal son, that poor wretch is forgiven by his loving father even before he has an opportunity to express his contrition for ungratefully squandering his inheritance in a life of hedonism. In another parable, how different is God's unimaginable largesse from the cruelty of the unworthy servant:

A king wished to settle accounts with his slaves. When he began the reckoning, one who owed him 10,000 talents was brought to him; and, as he could not pay, his lord ordered him to be sold, together with his wife and children and all his possessions, and payment to be made. So the slave fell on his knees before him, saying, "Have patience with me, and I will pay you everything."* And out of pity for him, the lord of that slave released him and forgave the debt.

But that same slave, as he went out, came upon one of his fellow slaves who owed him 100 denarii.† Seizing him by the throat, he said, "Pay what you owe." His fellow slave fell down and pleaded with him, "Have patience with me, and I will pay you." But he refused, and he went and threw him into prison until he would pay the debt. When his fellow slaves saw what had happened, they were greatly distressed, and they went and reported to their lord all that had taken place. Then his lord summoned him and said to him, "You wicked slave! I forgave you all that debt because you pleaded with me. Should you not have had mercy on your fellow slave, as I had mercy on you?" And in anger, his lord handed him over to be tortured until he would pay his entire debt.

Jesus concluded the parable: "So my heavenly Father will also do to you, if you do not forgive your brother or sister from your heart."

Forgiveness is the radical corollary of Jesus' condemnation of the old *lex talionis*: "You have heard it said, 'An eye for an eye and a tooth for a tooth,' but I say to you, love your enemies and pray for those who persecute you." This is an entirely pragmatic way of reordering the world, for forgiveness puts an end to retaliation and to final judgment on others. What is here presupposed in a connection of mutuality and responsibility: "Forgiveness," as one Scripture scholar has tersely written, "is a

*A single talent was more than a laborer could earn in fifteen years; 10,000 talents, therefore, was a monumental sum that could never be repaid.

†A laborer could earn 100 denarii in about three months; as a debt, it could easily be repaid.

social necessity if society is not to be paralyzed by an accumulation of grievances of one against another."

Prayer for Enemies

"If you forgive others their trespasses, your heavenly Father
will also forgive you; but if you do not forgive others, neither
will your Father forgive your trespasses."

However uncomfortable we may be with this notion, Jesus
insists that those we regard as enemies are objects of God's love
("Your Father makes His sun to shine on the just and the un-
just . . ."), and sinners are included in His plan—a conviction to
which he was faithful even at the bitterest moment of his life,
when he prayed for those who put him to death: "Father, forgive
them, for they know not what they do." This was evidently so
crucial a model for Christian life that the last words of the deacon Stephen, the first martyr, were "Lord, do not count this sin
[his imminent execution] against them."

The spirit of forgiveness prevailed throughout almost three
hundred subsequent years of violent persecution, as Christian
martyrs routinely prayed for their torturers. An eyewitness
documented the deaths of the martyrs of Abitine, for example,
and recounted how one of the condemned prayed during terrible
agony, "God Most High, do not regard these deeds of theirs as
sins. Have pity on them."

When Christianity was legitimized by Constantine, forgiveness of enemies did not lose its force as a moral imperative—in
fact, it became the standard by which true Christians could be
recognized: "Pray for your enemies from the love of Christ,"
wrote Saint Benedict in his rule for laymen. It is important to
recall that at this time and for centuries after, violence and
brutality were so routine everywhere that even minor social

disputes were very often settled by extreme violence and even murder. The equivalents of courts and police were virtually unknown; hence, fidelity to the command of disinterested love and the prohibition against retaliating violence were both remarkable and necessary.

The belief that concord can be restored and maintained only by forgiveness is certainly not confined to the Jewish and Christian traditions. The complete repudiation of vengeance is also the glory of the Islamic insistence on imitating the merciful and compassionate Allah. Forgiveness, for Muslims, means not taking revenge even when one has the means to retaliate against a guilty party; forgiveness necessitates treating with active goodness those who have hurt us.

The Qur'an, for example, teaches that one must give up resentments as quickly as possible: even in divorce, partners should be quick with mutual pardon. "Those who refuse to forgive and be reconciled with others can hardly expect that God will deal gently with them in the final accounting." A significant saying of Muhammad summarizes his entire program of human relations: "If anyone continually asks pardon, God will show that person a way out of every difficulty and respite from every anxiety, with sustenance from where he least expected it."

In this spirit, an Iranian religious leader famously prayed after the murder of his son:

> O God, we remember not only our son, but also his murderers—not because they killed him in the prime of his youth and made our hearts bleed and our tears flow, not because with this savage act they have brought further disgrace on our country—but because through their crime we now follow Your footsteps more closely. It makes obvious as never before our need to trust in Your love—love that makes us free from hate toward our persecutors; love that brings patience,

forbearance, courage, loyalty, humility, generosity. When my son's murderers stand before You on the day of judgment, remember the fruit of the Spirit by which they have enriched our lives. And forgive.

This extraordinary prayer recalls a moment at the end of World War II, during which thousands of Jewish children were put to death at the Ravensbrück concentration camp. When the place was finally liberated, a piece of paper was found, placed beside the body of a dead child. On it were words written by an unknown prisoner moments before his own death:

O Lord, remember not only the men and women of good will, but also those of ill will. But do not remember all the suffering they have inflicted on us—remember instead the fruits we have bought, thanks to this suffering: our comradeship, our loyalty, our humility, our courage, our generosity, the greatness of heart which has grown out of all this. And when those who have inflicted suffering on us come to judgment, let all the fruits which we have borne be their forgiveness.

Buddhism presumes that the tendency to retaliation must be replaced with a commitment to nonviolent compassion. "Conquer anger by love," according to a Buddhist maxim. "Conquer evil by good. Conquer the stingy by giving. Conquer the liar by truth." The *Tao-te Ching* enjoins, "Do good to him who has done you an injury," just as Paul urges the Romans, "Overcome evil with good." Hindus believe that the universe is held together by forgiveness as the concrete presence of disinterested love. A major Hindu tract claims that "a superior being does not render evil for evil. One should never harm the wicked or the good or even criminals meriting death. A noble soul will always exercise compassion even towards those who enjoy injuring

others or those of cruel deeds—for who is without fault?" The
sentiment is apparently universal in the world's great traditions.

ॐ

No less significant is the issue of forgiveness of self and of another for a personal relationship that has gone wrong or ended,
or that bears a deep wound of pain, remorse and regret. Such relationships cover the broadest spectrum—marital and familial,
romantic and friendly, social and professional. The extension of
forgiveness, it must be emphasized, may not always entail the
resumption of the prior state of relating, or the reconstruction of
a lost relationship with a parent, spouse, friend or lover. In fact,
that kind of reconciliation can be disastrous, for some relationships are better abandoned. A subtle form of sadomasochism
often infects people of goodwill who wrongly think that forgiveness must necessarily be accompanied by an effort to resume what ought to be left behind.

For a variety of reasons, some relationships simply do not
endure. People bear not only the weight and burden of their own
psychic, emotional and genetic baggage; they also grow and
change, and needs alter with time and experience. When it
comes to forgiveness, it is not always possible to renew or to
reconstruct—to return to the cruel or abusive parent, the brutal ex-husband, the neurotic ex-wife or the former friend or
lover who betrayed us, or whom we failed. In mourning these
relationships—perhaps even more than those in which we have
the satisfaction of face-to-face forgiveness—the profoundest
sort of pardon may in fact occur. Free of the need to justify, to
analyze, explain or articulate past events and feelings, we can
move to the level of true benevolence, of wishing wellness and
willing happiness for those whose names still sting us with pain.
All of this can happen in private, in the secrecy and silence that
is prayer: "Forgive me, as I forgive them."

‿

One of the most tragic examples of the failure to understand and offer forgiveness is the existence of capital punishment, abolished in most of the world but still permitted under law in some places (China, some Middle Eastern and African nations, and the United States, for example). "Some people do not deserve to live" is a rallying cry one often hears from supporters of this practice, which is certainly contradictory to the Jewish-Christian tradition and may never be endorsed by anyone claiming fidelity to its branches.

The refusal to kill, the refusal to exact state-sanctioned murder in the form of capital punishment, allows God alone the final judgment on the worth of a human life and on the assessment of its spiritual value. Granting God that judgment breaks the cycle of the criminal's arrogance and refuses to imitate his act of destruction.

Many good people are convinced that extending compassion to a criminal and allowing him the opportunity to repent and to offer restitution represent a tacit approval of his act, as well as a lack of concern for the victim. But like the chroniclers of the Hebrew Scriptures, Jesus evidently thought that the worst people he encountered were deserving of a chance to repent: witness his treatment of the worst of his society—extortionists, prostitutes, embezzlers, thieves, hypocrites. He proclaimed God's embrace of them all.

"I have no pleasure in the death of the wicked," proclaimed the Lord through the prophet Ezekiel. "I desire, rather, that the wicked turn from their ways and live." To that end, God has the patience of God. In saying after saying and parable after parable, Jesus announced that God always provides the sinner an opportunity for repentance. The man from Nazareth was simply following developed Jewish tradition about the unexpected nature of repentance and forgiveness when he set forth forgiving love as the standard of human life and condemned capital punishment—in the rescue of the adulterous woman about to be executed, for example.

From the early days of Christian faith, those who presented themselves as candidates for baptism had to renounce killing and were prohibited from carrying out an execution, however legally permissible it might have been. "A soldier who is in a position of authority is not to be allowed to put anyone to death; if he is ordered to, he is not to do it." So stated the early 3rd-century text *Apostolic Tradition* of Hippolytus. There was nothing revolutionary in this precept: it simply made explicit the teaching of Jesus and his apostles for Christian converts in the Roman Empire.

ॐ

The refusal to exact retribution is not tangential to the truth of our prayer, for it addresses the heart of our relationship with God and one another; it makes real the faith that parallels prayer. Forgiveness, the making right of my relationship with God, is something I need—radically, in the core of my being, so that I may fully become what I am: God's own. Forgiveness is not something elective, not something that I can sometimes offer others and sometimes withhold.

One of the most powerful of modern Christian prayers takes into account all those who have committed grievous offenses against society and who languish in prisons that do not offer them opportunities either to earn repentance or to offer restitution.

Lord Jesus, for our sake you were condemned as a criminal. Visit our jails and prisons with your pity and judgment. Remember all prisoners, bring the guilty to repentance and amendment of life according to your will—and give them hope for their future. When any are held unjustly, bring them release; forgive us, and teach us to improve our system of justice. Remember those who work in these institutions; keep them humane and compassionate, and save them from becoming brutal or callous. And since what we do for those in prison, O Lord, we do for You, constrain us to improve their lot. All this we ask for your mercy's sake. Amen.

Improving the frail systems by which we judge one another, then, means not only seeing that the truly dangerous killer is removed from contact with society by imprisonment (but never by imposition of a death sentence); it also means working to change the conditions that give rise to a violent society—and to see that those imprisoned are not brutalized, dehumanized and further drowned in the poisonous cauldron of hatred. "Forgive me in the measure that I forgive others." If a Jew, a Christian or a Muslim cannot say that prayer with fullness of commitment, then he dishonors the tradition of his religion.

Forgiveness of others is indeed the condition of our own forgiveness and healing. All prayer is encounter with God, and where the bond of forgiveness is withheld—when we deny others the opportunity for repentance, when we cry for vengeance, when we demand specious and impossible "closure" by killing another, then all our petitions for the forgiveness of our own sins become meaningless. And with that, our encounter with God is itself compromised.

CHAPTER SEVEN

Prayer as Suffering

Unanswered Prayers

For those who believe that God hears prayers, one of the most poignant challenges is the experience of a petition that seems to have been unheard, unanswered or flatly denied. The Hebrew Scriptures contain many laments and complaints about this situation: "Have you not rejected us, O God?" runs like an antiphon throughout the Psalms and the prophetic writings. The Muslim asks, "Remove the hardship"— not only of illness, but also of an apparent negative response from Allah.

How do we reconcile this with the fact that the New Testament seems to offer a chain of unambiguous promises that prayers will be favorably answered?

> Whatever you ask for in prayer, believe that you have received it, and it will be yours. . . . Ask and it will be given to you; search and you will find; knock, and the door will be opened for you. . . . If you have faith even [as small] as a mustard seed, you will say to this mountain, "Move from here to there," and it will move—and nothing will be impossible for you. . . . Whatever you ask for in prayer with faith, you will receive.

Of course things are not so simple, as even a child quickly discovers. And the result of disappointment—of feeling that one has been rejected; that prayers have gone unacknowledged; that God is absent—is often additional suffering, whether or not the petition involves any kind of catalyzing prior anguish or affliction.

Part of the problem comes from reading these and similar verses of the gospels without taking into account their mode of expression, or their contexts. "Moving a mountain" is best understood as a Semitic trope meaning that faith can have remarkable, unexpected moments and effects. We are told that we will receive—but not necessarily that we will receive precisely what we request. We are promised that we will find when we seek, and that a door will be opened when we knock—but the finding and the discovery may reveal something other than what we had anticipated. "If you have faith" describes the condition and the atmosphere necessary for all prayer. Faith provides the reins on self-indulgence and narrow self-absorption; indeed, faith determines the very nature of what we ask, for in faith one seeks nothing so much as God's wisdom, protection and embrace. Faith, which is unconditional trust, means being aware that God knows what is better for me than I could ever ask. In other words, "if you have faith" and "if you believe" forestall any dejection caused by an apparent refusal.

Consider, by analogy, ordinary personal relationships. A request I make of a friend is always subordinate to and a sign of the plea I make for the friend's support and devotion. But if a request for a particular favor is denied, I do not terminate the friendship: I trust that the friendship goes deeper and has greater value than the specific request.

This is even more true of my relationship with God. I collaborate toward my ultimate fulfillment, based on a deeper relationship that I can imagine, and my prayer is not simply a reflection of the frail certitudes of my own desires, plans and provisions. "Sometimes it seems that we have been praying a long time," wrote Julian of Norwich, "and still it seems to us that we do not have what we ask for. But we should not be too depressed on this account, for I am sure that either we are waiting for a better occasion, or more grace, or a better gift."

Any consideration of unanswered prayers has to confront with consummate earnestness the situation of Jesus of Nazareth, whose entire life and ministry was based on trust in his Father and submission to His will. Facing the terrible outcome of an arrest and execution that seemed inevitable, he prayed on the last night of his life, "My Father, if it is possible, let this cup [of suffering] pass from me—but let not my will but Your will be done." The prayer was offered (according to the established tradition of the New Testament) "with loud cries and tears."

Jesus' absolute trust and submission did not vanquish his terror, which was very real. The hard truth is that he was not spared the cup of suffering: his petition to avoid a cruel death was denied. While Christian faith proclaims that he was indeed heard—that God's final answer was the Resurrection—there is no avoidance of the fact that his prayer to be spared suffering was not granted. There is perhaps no greater evidence that not all prayer is answered in precisely the way one anticipates, and this represents part of the profound struggle that is an ineluctable aspect of authentic prayer. As a wise man said many centuries ago, "Prayer is warfare to the last breath." The enemy in these skirmishes is not God; it is rather the accumulation of selfish patterns in our own lives, and the darkness and dimness we too often prefer to liberating light. The clue to victory in the battle is the absolute trust that goes by the name of faith—the path to eternal light, as believers have always claimed.

From biblical times to the present, it is not surprising that light and darkness are among the most common metaphors—archetypal symbols, as academics prefer to say, that were especially eloquent in a preelectric world where nighttime meant literal darkness. Nocturnal hours were full of danger, for a moonless or stormy sky provided ample cover for highwaymen, invading armies or hostile neighbors, wandering lunatics, rapists, the inebriated and all sorts of scoundrels. Oil and paraffin were always scarce, and everyone but the hardened criminal welcomed dawn's first light. Poets and psalmists accordingly referred often to interior light, to God as light and to darkness as confusion, ignorance, terror, sin and death.

Physical Suffering, Death and the Problem of Evil

Into the collective memory of Israel was burned the anguish of centuries of persecution and of exile, each epoch compared to the people's formative experience—the long desert wandering of the Exodus. Doubtless because there was enormous bodily suffering and deprivation associated with these national traumas, Hebrew prayer sustained the metaphor of pain even when describing inner turmoil, individual depression and the temptation to despair that came from a feeling of desolation.

> There is no soundness in my flesh, no health in my bones. My wounds grow foul and fester, I am utterly bowed down. . . . The terrors of death have fallen upon me, fear and trembling come upon me, and horror overwhelms me. . . . But I call upon God, and the Lord will hear me.

Aware of their frailty, insufficiency and helplessness, their infidelity to God and their confusion over His plans for them, the psalmists and prophets complained often about their suffering and prayed for relief.

The Christian complaint about evil is even more full of

paradox, for it derives from the reality of Jesus crucified. This is, it must be acknowledged, an event that has become, after two thousand years, perhaps too familiar through paintings and sculptures, crosses and crucifixes, movies and tableaux. The horror is almost impossible to reclaim, especially given the ubiquity of images that desensitize it, and the documentation, even in so-called entertainment forms, of all kinds of real and fictionalized violence in our own time.

In addition, it is difficult for many people to take seriously the reality behind an event that has so often been distorted through mawkish piety, cheapened by movies, sentimentalized by music and even falsified by bad preaching. The cross itself is often little more than a chic fashion accessory, studded with emeralds and encrusted with diamonds, its wearers unaware of the glittering contradiction.

The images, however distorted, require reclamation. The torture and death of Jesus of Nazareth are calmly described in the four gospels, with utmost dignified brevity, in remarkably understated diction, without focus on the physical aspects of the suffering itself; the text contains neither embellishment nor dramatization. Jesus is not portrayed as a brave martyr whose death arouses admiration, nor is he set forth as an intrepid warrior, enduring his destiny with solemn detachment. Faithful to the end, he has believed in and surrendered himself to the unassailable, unimaginable love of God.

This does not mean, however, that he did not experience psychological, emotional or spiritual suffering; compared with the bodily pain, the inner agony of Jesus must have been unspeakable. Too often a wrongheaded interpretation of the Passion has been proclaimed or at least implied: the notion, for example, that Jesus never lost sight of his transcendent identity and so only *appeared* to suffer. Never must orthodoxy more fervently cling to the truth of the full humanity of Jesus than for the period at the end of his life. His brokenness, his spiritual desolation, his sense of futility, his failure—all these contributed to the depth of his agony. And he was utterly alone, without the slightest shred of consolation from anyone, friend or relative.

On the cross, Jesus cried out, "My God, my God, why have you forsaken me?" His lament was a citation from Psalm 22, well known to all Jews. The words as he uttered them must be heard with all their implication of the abandonment Jesus felt: they expressed neither a hymn of trust that God would vindicate him (as is implied by later verses of that Psalm), nor a shout of abject despair. They were what they were: an appeal, a supplication—"Why have you forsaken me?"

Jesus did not accept death patiently. He endured it in all its agony, screaming out to God Who remained his sustenance at the end. But Jesus felt none of that support: he experienced nothing but a complete emptying of self. He was, by any standard of his world, a complete failure—cut down in his prime, his work suppressed, his honor destroyed, his loved ones alienated and, at last, subjected to a hideous death reserved for the worst criminals. He who had abandoned everything to God seemed abandoned by God. Everything seemed drenched in futility.

Could it be that the mockers had been right all along? Ought this man—of good intentions, perhaps, but finally a hopeless, even quixotic character—to have been compassionately dismissed into the pages of history? Have not too many people already been deluded far too long?

So much in the background and life of Jesus, after all, seemed to have predicted the collapse of any grand hope or noble intent on the part of his people. The race from which he came was of bygone grandeur, its magnificence diminished by its enemies. There were no real achievements to which he could lay claim, either—no secure body of work to leave as a monument, no school of teachers to take up his preaching. His friends were unremarkable people without any greatness to recommend them, and they had no very clear idea of just what he had been about. Jesus had been upsetting expectations and overturning polite religious standards since the beginning of his ministry; in fact, he was a frighteningly simple man who went about doing good, being accessible to others, reaching out to their needs.

But in the end his enemies seem to have been vindicated, for his teaching took root nowhere, and it had apparently been stamped out forever. Jesus ended his career not with a great triumph but a prisoner put on trial and then punished on a windswept patch of desert.

As for his death, it was far from a heroic, trailblazing martyrdom. He was not a great philosopher dying for his ideas, nor a military hero struck down in the glory of battle. He was not a great statesman who, coming within sight of the pinnacle of success, fell under the knife of assassins. He was not a wise old man, surrounded by comforting companions. The only people reacting to his death spoke for everyone, and they mocked and challenged him. Every consolation was denied; everything in creation was against him.

~

That must have seemed equally true to the early Christian martyrs, too, as they were herded to torture and execution for refusing to worship the emperor as their god. There are numerous reliable texts witnessing the final hours of those who died rather than deny faith, and the record is of a quite human struggle, of fear as well as of confidence.

"Lord, Lord, Lord—come to my help! I turn to You for refuge!" cried Agathonike, a young Christian wife and mother, as she was dragged off to be burned at the stake in Asia Minor, at the end of the first century. Her fidelity did not help her overcome her terror.

Euplus, a Sicilian deacon, approached the block to be beheaded: "Take care of me, Lord Christ," he prayed, "because it is for you that I am suffering." He was both faithful and fearful.

Genesius, a Roman actor, would not worship the emperor in place of God even after being stretched on the rack, torn with iron claws and burned with torches. Given one last chance, he replied to his torturers, "There is no king but him whom I confess. He it is whom I worship and adore. Were I to be killed a thousand times for my allegiance to him, I would still go on as I have begun. I would still be his man. Christ is on my lips and in my heart, and no one can take him from me. I am sorry only that I came so late in my life to worship him."

George Bernard Shaw dramatized just such a heroic death in his play *Androcles and the Lion*. A Roman captain asks a young Christian named Lavinia why she is willing to endure a martyr's death:

Captain: Are you, then, going to die for nothing?
Lavinia: Yes—that is the wonderful thing. It is since all the stories and dreams have gone that I have now no doubt at all that I must die for something greater than dreams or stories.
Captain: But for what?
Lavinia: I don't know. If it were for anything small enough to know, it would be too small to die for. I think I'm going to die for God. Nothing else is real enough to die for.

We cannot avoid the inevitable question such accounts raise: What sort of God treats people this way? What sort of God puts his Chosen through so many centuries of woe and wandering? What sort of God abandons Jesus, who has been unfailingly faithful, and then seems to forget those who have taken him as a model? What sort of God stands by idly while evil triumphs in each new emergence of genocide?

But is not the more pertinent question, "Where was *mankind*

at the time of the Shoah?" As for asking what kind of God allows
suffering, the only reply can be: A God Who takes human suffering with absolute gravity indeed—a God Who has entered fully
into that suffering and does not allow it the final victory; the sort
of God Who completely alters the meaning of suffering and death
and provides the mysterious means with which we can cope with
it and thus collaborate with Him in transforming it.

Not least of the corollaries is the fact that the reigns of Assyria, Babylon and the Third Reich are no more, but the Jewish
people have survived and done more for the world than any of
their persecutors. The Roman Empire collapsed, but Christian
faith endured. The people of Islam, too—subjected to cruel colo-
nizing and commercial exploitation by Western dominions from
medieval to modern times—have not been obliterated from the
world. "I believe in the sun even when it is not shining," a Jewish prisoner wrote on the wall of a concentration camp. "I believe in love even when I cannot feel it. I believe in God, even
when He is silent."

The Talmud was recited in the camps, and Jewish rituals were
secretly observed. There were also virtually constant prayers even
in the face of death. At the request of fourteen hundred young
Jewish men sentenced to death, Rabbi Zvi Hirsch Meisel blew the
ram's horn on Rosh Hashanah. When he had done so, one of the
youngest victims cried to his fellows: "The Rebbe has strength-
ened our spirits by telling us that even if a sharp sword rests on a
man's throat, he should not despair of God's mercy. I say to you
all, we can hope that things will get better, but we must be prepared for them to get worse. For God's sake, let us not forget to cry
out *Shema Yisrael* with devotion at the last moment!"*

---

*The *Shema* is the great Jewish proclamation of faith and also a summons to prayer, from Deuteronomy 6, 4: "Hear, O Israel: the Lord is our
God, the Lord alone!"

In another camp, a Christian compatriot—Dietrich Bonhoeffer, a pastor who had joined the German resistance against Hitler—was languishing in prison and awaiting imminent execution. "Help me to pray," he wrote on a scrap of paper,

> and to concentrate my thoughts on You: I cannot do this alone. I am lonely, but You do not leave me; I am feeble in heart, but with You there is help; I am restless, but with You there is peace. In me there is bitterness, but with You there is patience. I do not understand Your ways, but You know the way for me.

For the Jewish, Christian and Muslim traditions, there is no final explanation for the existence of evil and suffering in the world, and no solution to the apparent contradiction between suffering and the existence of a merciful God. "If I were to know Him, I would be Him," runs the old Jewish saying.

It is important that we take seriously and never lose sight of the reality of sin. The struggle to free people from selfishness, hatred, cruelty and prejudice retains a grip on human motivation, and we can identify examples everywhere.

But perhaps it is not the existence of the negative realities for which we should attempt to account (they are the result of humanity's failures, after all) so much as the surprising endurance of goodness, self-sacrifice, philanthropy and gentleness in the world. Are they not attributes of Ultimate Reality? The violent clash between man-made evil and the benevolence of God continues, but once we realize that it is indeed a battle, then —even though we cannot understand it— we can accept the paradox that the world's Creator is the source of the love that will finally triumph. And the evidence for that living, driving, reasonable expectation is the existence and the force of effective goodness in the world. It does not give up; it does make a difference.

This does not, of course, take into account the existence of evil other than moral evil—physical suffering, for example, whether the death of a child, or the starvation of millions, or the devastations caused by floods and tornadoes. No satisfactory explanation may be possible for these, either. But we might ask if we could have a world without them—or, for that matter, without the suffering caused by wickedness and perversity? All we can say is that we would not have *this* world without the components of suffering.

From prayer comes at least a partial answer to these questions: God does not merely regard evil and suffering with remote concern. Somehow He is present alongside them and brings us to Himself through and despite the suffering. How this happens we cannot always discern, but we can (and perhaps must) pray especially when we confront pain and suffering in this world. "Often prayer consists more in groans than in words, more in tears than in speech," as Augustine wrote sixteen centuries ago to someone enduring troubles. "But God collects our tears; our groaning is not hidden from Him Who created all things."

Such is the spirit of prayer found in several African tribes today—the Aro of Sierra Leone, for example, who have a litany for a sick child addressed to the sacred ancestors. "The little one I hold in my hands is my child—she is also your child; therefore, be gracious to her. She has come into a world of trouble, sickness, cold and pain—the pain you knew and the sickness with which you were familiar. Let her sleep in peace, let her grow and become strong."

᠅

Prayer itself contributes to the evolution of our collective consciousness concerning the power of good in this world, and the necessity to take a stand against evil. And finally, of course, there is the faith of the ages: that life finally triumphs over death.

"Could the immortal God have given us life with no other horizon but death?" asked Hilary of Poitiers in the 4th century. "Could the Giver of good inspire us with a sense of life only to have it overshadowed by the fear of death?"

In his own way Francis de Sales, in 1605, addressed the issue. When writing to a woman troubled not only by evil in the world but also her own inability to counter it effectively, Francis asked: "Why does anyone who is doing the best he can let himself be disturbed? Why is he troubled? What has he to fear? No, no, God is not so frightening. He is content with little from us because He knows very well that we don't have much to offer."

Pierre Teilhard de Chardin, a Jesuit priest who died in 1955, was an internationally renowned scientist, paleontologist, philosopher, theologian and mystic (and one of the discoverers of the so-called Peking man, which revolutionized the history of anthropology). Reflecting on the inevitability of his diminishment and death, he prayed:

> Grant, when my hour comes, that I may recognize You under the species of each alien or hostile force that seems bent upon destroying or uprooting me. When the signs of age begin to mark my body (and still more, when they touch my mind); when the illness that is to diminish me or carry me off strikes from without or is born within me; when the painful moment comes in which I suddenly awaken to the fact that I am losing hold of myself and am absolutely passive within the hands of the great unknown forces that have formed me—in all those dark moments, O God, grant that I may understand that it is You Who are painfully parting the fibers of my being in order to penetrate to the very marrow of my substance and bear me away within Yourself.

Finally, one must ask if embracing atheism is a more comforting response to the world's suffering, its agony and its beauty, than clinging to a hope in God. Does denial bring us any

consolation in our anguish? The contrary position was explored
in the Hebrew Book of Job, which insists that God remains unknowable to us—yet, at the same time, we can place undiluted
trust in Him. God does not, then, preserve us *from* all suffering,
but He does preserve us *in* all suffering. Some find in a phenomenon like Auschwitz the strongest argument against the
reality of God. But we can place a boundless and completely reasonable trust in God, despite everything. This may be the ultimate meaning of the great Muslim injunction to "hold fast to
the rope of God."

～

That the world contains both goodness and evil is taken for
granted in Eastern thinking. Chinese wisdom, for example,
emphasizes the two great cosmic forces, yang and yin. Included in this duality are all the oppositions basic to our experience: spring/fall, night/day, movement/immobility, truth/error,
beauty/ugliness, creativity/destruction, life/death—one could
set down a long list. The fundamental dialect of yin/yang has
deeply spiritual implications for the way in which the world is
perceived and accepted. What is beneficial to the universe as a
whole, for example—what is necessary for its sustenance and
growth—may involve the diminishment and even destruction
of an individual being. That principle is perhaps most immediately evident in the food chain and, indeed, in the great chain of
being itself. It becomes more immediate, and more complex,
when we become aware of the conflict and strain within our own
being. Desires clash with duties, and various internal dishar-
monies mark every stage and condition of our reactions to outer
events and circumstances.

Suffering is, then, built into the human condition. When our
interests are threatened, we become hostile, and our hostility is
expressed by either aggression or retreat; either way, we become

more anxious. Today, the Judeo-Christian tradition is often presented by its partisans as a system that offers tidy answers to life's problems and long-term effective results, an attitude that can come dangerously close to a kind of spiritual capitalism. In this regard, the West has something critical to learn from Buddhism.

Often accused by Westerners of being characterized by a fundamentally fatal pessimism, Buddhism is in fact a way toward profound enlightenment that approaches suffering earnestly, and liberation from it even more so. The core of Buddhist wisdom is synthesized in the belief that none of our great joys or sorrows is permanent—that life in this world is radically frustrating, a constant cycle of painful and fleeting experiences. This realization leads not to a nihilistic despair, however, but to a confident expectation (through quite specific disciplines developed in the Zen Buddhist tradition) of ultimate liberation from pain and suffering.

The state is achieved through the Eightfold Path of right view and thought, right speech and action, right livelihood and effort, right mindfulness and concentration. And while Buddhism does not share with the West a tradition of prayer as we consider it, the development of meditative techniques offers a discipline and a process toward the achievement of liberation from the tyranny of suffering often caused by blind craving. In Buddhism, the goal is enlightened compassion—the gate through which one passes from judgment and immobility to the kind of freedom that allows every being to be itself.

Pain and Suffering in Prayer

As disorienting and potentially overwhelming as physical agony can be, there are also forms of spiritual menace that threaten the

life of prayer. In 16th-century Spain, John of the Cross—one of
that country's great poets and mystical theologians—identified
several types of them.

Born Juan de Yepes, John worked as a nurse and acquitted
himself brilliantly at the university in Salamanca. Ordained a
priest, he met Teresa of Ávila when he was in his twenties, she in
her fifties; together, they set about to reform the Carmelite Order, which had become ignobly lax. His dedication led him into
disputes with religious authorities, and he was even imprisoned.
But he never stopped writing. Worn out from work and jail, he
continued to compose some of the finest poetry to come from
Spain.

In the matter of our relationship with God in prayer, John
was remarkably modern. "Many people feel sad about the spiritual good of others," he wrote in his classic *The Dark Night of
the Soul*.

> They dislike hearing others praised. Hearing of the virtues of
> others depresses them; they cannot bear to listen while an-
> other person is praised without contradicting what is being
> said or interjecting some criticism intent on unraveling the
> compliments being paid. They are angry, you see, because
> they are not receiving the praise themselves and because they
> long to be the center of attention.

Laziness is likewise a hazard. Often we become weary with
the challenge that discipline requires, and believing that times of
prayer ought to bring concomitant emotional pleasure, people
sometimes abandon it if instant satisfaction is not forthcoming.
"When we begin our spiritual journey, we often want God to desire what we want. . . . We measure God by ourselves and not
ourselves by God."

On the other hand, people of good will and effort often become prey to a prolonged period of aridity, of spiritual dryness.

Medieval spiritual writers spoke often of *acedia* or *accidie*, when God seems absent and prayer is a matter of weary persistence and apparent emptiness. "Pray wholeheartedly, though it seems to you that this has no savor for you," wrote Julian of Norwich. "Pray wholeheartedly, though you may feel nothing, though you may see nothing, for in dryness and barrenness, in sickness and in weakness, your prayer is most pleasing to [God], though you think it almost tasteless to you. . . . God accepts the good will and the labor of His servants, however we may feel, and therefore it pleases Him that we work in prayer."

This time of joyless perseverance was called "the night of the senses" by John of the Cross, who further described it as a period of challenging distress and obscurity when one seems to have lost everything that had been gained or had made sense. Only a fierce clinging to God through faith enables one to survive so poignant a time of trial.

A sensitive reader of souls, John recognized that a state of spiritual dryness might be due to deliberate distraction and laziness; or that it might be the result of "bad humor or bodily indisposition." And so he offered what he called "signs" by which the situation could be gauged as an important phase in spiritual growth.

First, John taught that a person who finds comfort neither in the things of God nor of the world may well be enduring a dark night sent by God "to purge [one's] sensory appetite—that is, to distance someone from everything that is less than God and prepare for even richer spiritual blessings." Second, he insists that when a person remembers God with painful anxiety, then surely the spirit is becoming stronger, for indifferent people do not care much for the things of God. Third, when, despite all efforts, a person cannot meditate or pray, "God certainly is now beginning to communicate Himself, no longer through the channels of sense, as formerly, but in pure spirit."

John of the Cross set forth a remedy for the kind of depression

that can often afflict people who, because they do not experience pleasant feelings at prayer, think either that they have
given up on God and so are at a distance from Him, or that
they have been abandoned by Him. Practical as well as mystical,
he insisted that at such times God is, as it were, transferring
His blessings from our senses to our spirit. "The spirit grows
stronger and more alert, and becomes more intent on not fail-
ing God."

This absolute trust should become our focus at such times of
aridity and melancholy. "Be patient and persevere," John counseled, adding that we "must not be anxious about meditation,
[but] be content simply with directing attention lovingly towards God—and all this without anxiety or effort, or any desire
to feel and taste His presence."

Hence the deprivation of spiritual consolation has a quite
beneficial effect on our prayer, for it prevents us from "a harmful
attraction toward sweetness"—that is, from becoming attached
to a psychological or emotional state of pleasant reverie (for
which John uses the word *embelesamiento:* a pleasurable sensa-
tion somewhere between a dream and a swoon). Few masters of
the art of prayer have so sensitively articulated the ways in
which we can discern the spirit of our prayer and turn ourselves
wholly to God, leaving behind any anxious self-assessment.

John of the Cross, who died in 1591 at the age of forty-nine,
guided many (his friend Teresa of Ávila among them) through
the thickets of spiritual confusion. He emphasized that we must
always distinguish between desolation and despair when it
comes to our moods and humors in prayer, a caution that has
been taken up by wise counselors down to our own time. "You
have been in desolation," wrote John Chapman to a devout
woman in 1928. "When you are quite convinced that you have
nothing, not even a gift [for] prayer . . . then you will have gone
a long way. . . . I think it likely that God *wants you to learn to ac-*

cept the state of dissatisfaction with yourself in which He has put you [italics his]." The point of this suffering within the condition of prayer, Chapman continues, is that we ought to wish in prayer

> only what God provides *at any given moment* . . . If you do your best, at that moment, the result of your prayer—however dry, weak and unsatisfactory—is just exactly what God wants you to have here and now. Worry is useless and harmful. Try to be absolutely at peace, because you are satisfied with God as He is with you at this moment.

This kind of counsel has its roots in the ancient confidence expressed in the Hebrew Scriptures: "The Lord will fight for you," Moses reiterated to the people at critical moments, "and you have only to keep still."

ॐ

Another benefit spiritual suffering can offer, even though it may be unclear to the one who endures it, is a kind of death to selfishness, which is the root of so much pain.

Buddhists point to *shunyata*, to emptiness and nothingness, as the principle that purifies and holds everything in the universe together. This nothing, paradoxically, is not nothing: it is an essential quality of our existence, which is mired in suffering and in the transitory. Everything we hope for, desire and fear encourages us to place useful values on things and people, and so they become means to ends. *Shunyata* means emptying ourselves of such self-centered, materialistic approaches to what is outside ourselves, and instead attempting to see everything in itself. Hence the concept of emptiness or nothingness "is really a way to see things as full in a new way," as one scholar has suggested.

This refusal to cling to any external thing as merely useful leads us very far beyond the limitations of self. As the mystics of every tradition have discovered in their deepest meditations, nothing comes into existence or survives on its own, and everything is impermanent. Ignoring this truth encourages us to look for a core of permanence where it cannot exist. *Shunyata* reminds us that beholding everything in its own being, without reference to its usefulness to us, frees us from unrealistic dependence on things even as we try to trick ourselves into controlling them. Similarly, John of the Cross wrote often about the richness of *nada*, a difficult concept that seems to imply an embrace of desolate darkness. In the darkness and the nothingness, however, we can detect the first stirrings of true peace.

From ancient Buddhism through Renaissance Spanish mysticism all the way to the 20th-century Anglo-American monk Thomas Merton runs a common theme that was perhaps first articulated in the East. In the emptiness, life may seem like a dead and dark cave where we can neither pray nor think, where prayer is without light or pleasure. But this is the fertile emptiness of the enlightened Buddha, and here begins the forgetfulness of the false ego, as Merton has written:

Prayer and love are really learned in the hour when prayer becomes impossible and your heart turns to stone. . . . [Then] peace lies in the heart of darkness. Something prompts [us] to keep still, to trust in God, to be quiet and listen for His voice; to be patient and not to get excited. . . . When [we] stay quiet, attentive to the darkness, a subtle and indefinable peace begins to seep into [our] souls. It cannot be grasped or identified. It slips out of focus and gets away. Yet it is there. What is it? It is hard to say: but one feels that it is somehow summed up in "the will of God," or simply, "God."

꙳

For much of her life as a nun, Teresa of Ávila found prayer a tedious, depressing duty that left her feeling frustrated, a failure;
it is said that during these years, she regularly shook the hour-
glass, as if to hurry time along. "I spent nearly twenty years on
that stormy sea," she wrote in her autobiography. "I had no joy
in God and no pleasure in the world." In addition, she endured a
series of grave illnesses: hers was not, in other words, a comfortable and soothing life of easy piety.

On the brink of despair, she thought of Christ alone and
afflicted, praying to God in agony the night before his death—
"simple thoughts of this kind." Then someone gave her a copy
of the *Confessions* of Augustine, "and I seemed to see myself
in them." And so she persevered in prayer despite the emptiness, the spiritual blankness and humiliations. "I only asked for
grace and pardon for sins . . . and indeed, He showed me great
mercy in allowing me to be with Him and bringing me into His
presence."

From about the age of forty-two until her death at sixty-
seven, she became one of the most profoundly prayerful and active reformers in European history. Her awareness of God's
presence transformed her life, and the transformation took place
in silence. Now undeterred by confusion, Teresa entrusted herself entirely to God even in darkness and aridity, and so she discovered the true meaning of prayer. From this point, she knew
it would be "an intimate sharing between friends; it means taking time frequently to be alone with Him Who we know loves
us." Another reformer—her contemporary, Martin Luther—
expressed a similar conviction: "I am sometimes so cold and
cheerless that I cannot pray. Then I close my ears and say, 'I
know God is not far from me, therefore I must cry to Him and
invoke Him.' "

Teresa of Ávila warned gently but repeatedly about the perils for beginners in the art of prayer—primarily, the danger of placing a high value on emotions and feelings. "Set little store by consolations and tenderness in devotion, and do not be elated when the Lord gives them nor disconsolate when He withholds them. . . . When I hear men of learning and intelligence making such a fuss because God is not giving them feelings of devotion, it revolts me to listen to them: they should master themselves and go on their way."

Teresa's remedies against the tendency to assess oneself by analyzing emotions were often refreshingly commonsensical: "Have good conversations with people and take a country walk"—activities that will help keep us from being "depressed or afflicted because of aridities or unrest or distraction of the mind, [nor] troubled if we have no conscious devotion." What matters is clinging to God.

Teresa's spiritual descendant, Thérèse Martin (known as Thérèse of Lisieux, who was also a Carmelite nun), did not live as long as the woman of Ávila. "The little flower," as she is popularly known, died at twenty-four after enduring the ravages of tuberculosis and of a terrifying spiritual darkness and sense of abandonment: "One must have passed through the tunnel to understand how black its darkness it."

When she was advised to take up a volume of prayers, she confided in her notebook: "I do not have the courage to search through books for beautiful prayers," she wrote. "They are so numerous that it would make my head ache. Unable either to say them or to choose between them, I do as a child would who cannot read—I just say what I want to say to God, quite simply, and He never fails to understand."

After years of illness and disappointment, Julian of Norwich could still write: "God did not say, 'You will not be tempted, you will not be belabored, you will not be disquieted'—but He did say, 'You shall not be overcome.' "

The reassurance to which she held fast is still relevant for very many people amid every variety of suffering—even the sort that renders one powerless and inactive. Amid the unimaginable suffering of a Nazi death camp, Corrie ten Boom could still claim, "No matter how deep our darkness, God is deeper still."

CHAPTER EIGHT

Prayer as Abandonment

In some spiritual traditions, suffering is represented by darkness. But for John of the Cross and others, the image of darkness does not, in the final analysis, convey either doubt, despair, anxiety or tribulation. It is, on the contrary, an extraordinary metaphor that illustrates—like the symbol of the cloud of unknowing— that our relationship with God neither depends on nor has its origin in our senses or our rational thought. Our link to God (and consequently our prayer) is not a matter of reason, but of a growing bond of love. Nowhere is that bond clearer than in our willingness to abandon ourselves.

The Senses of Abandonment

Perhaps the most poignant kind of suffering involves one sense of the word "abandonment"—the feeling that one has been left behind by God, or that a relationship with Him we had thought to be firmly in place has faded like a half-forgotten dream. Those with a heightened spiritual sensitivity and an acute awareness of their own insufficiency may even feel that their own past indifference to God has finally brought about a complete collapse of their spiritual moorings—that they are tossed on waves of chaos and confusion, not only abandoned by God but also reduced to a feeble dependence on their own incompetent mechanisms for spiritual equilibrium.

It is at precisely such critical moments that one of the great paradoxes of prayer emerges. The way to cope with desolation and a sense of being abandoned is in fact a deliberate and willing surrender to God. To abandon myself is the challenge and condition of escaping a sense of my own futility; and the act of abandonment—to continue the paradox—leads to a deepening conviction that my life in its particularity and my entire existence itself have meaning, even if that meaning is not always, or even rarely, clear.

In abandoning myself to eternal mercy, I no longer have to rely on the pathetic illusions of "my strength" or "my resources." In abandoning myself to God—in giving myself up completely to the dark mystery of His presence—I can enter into a new, open and freer territory than I have ever known. Thus liberated from the delusion of existential self-reliance and the concomitant fear of annihilation, I can, with the psalmist, cast all my care upon the Lord. As one wise modern contemplative has written: "Prayer is, at bottom, the surrender of the whole self to God. It is genuine in the measure that the surrender is genuine and that must be our objective, not self-gratification." That means "abandoning our own little ship of which we have the control . . . and crossing over into the boat of God, which we cannot control."

To many people, a total surrender of the self seems like the most pathetic sort of escapist self-delusion, probably because we have been trained to think that we are in complete charge of our lives. We decide what politics we espouse, what philosophy of life we follow, whom we love, what we will do tonight, tomorrow, next year. We plan, we control, we arrange, we account for our lives down to the last cent and second. But then we learn that a healthy friend is afflicted with a grave illness or that a shy young man has taken up a shotgun and opened fire on a crowd of pedestrians. Closer to home, one fine morning we suddenly

notice that, contrary to every expectation, we are indeed growing older!

There are daily examples of loss of control, too. We may
miss a travel connection and have to cancel an appointment. A
headache makes work impossible for a day, or a virus forces us to
postpone a celebration. We cannot alter the weather, and even
subtle conditions in body chemistry affect our moods and our
ability to respond to others. For all our ability to use technology
in the service of planning, things can still go horribly wrong.
But what finally determines the effect a negative event has on us
is not the event itself, but our inner attitude to the event. In any
case, we find that we often have no choice but to abandon ourselves to circumstances.

Whether or not one employs overtly religious language to
describe it, an act of abandonment—of turning everything over
to God in absolute trust—lies at the heart of every world religion; it certainly is implicit in every true prayer. Beginning with
a sense of contingency and proceeding through cycles of struggle and suffering, Zen practitioners, for examples, are comparable to their Jewish and Christian counterparts. All accept that
abandonment is not an act of weakness, or of stony stoicism, but
a deliberate self-donation toward a fundamentally reliable and
benevolent condition of being.

As the best-known form of Buddhism in the West, Zen has
become particularly popular since World War II. At the root of
"Zen" are Japanese and Chinese words for a meditative state of
awareness; as such, Zen is not a religion, but a disciplined way to
understanding, insight and eventual enlightenment. Periods of
silent sitting and concentration under the mentorship of a master or *roshi* aim at transforming one's vision, of liberation from
mundane existence. Zen tries to comprehend that life has a sacred core that cannot be learned from any conventional method
of education or reading.

It is crucial to stress that abandoning ourselves in calm confidence to eternal benevolence and to limitless compassion (personalized in an affirmation of God in the Judeo-Christian tradition, but not in Buddhism) does not mean submitting blindly to fate, nor yielding to an indifferent or even hostile force in the universe, nor simply doing nothing, and waiting to see what happens. But it does mean freely giving up the illusion of power and ultimate control, and cultivating the kind of assurance and trust that springs from faith.

ॐ

A father tosses his child high into the air, and the child giggles, certain that loving arms are waiting to catch him. A mother in a swimming pool invites her baby to leap in from poolside, and the baby laughs and jumps into her embrace. However we attempt to analyze such behaviors, they are acts of abandonment at their fundamental level—a faithful trust that one's known, experienced source of love and protection will not fail in this breathtaking moment. Doubts arise only later in life, when we begin to trust no one but ourselves. Abandonment does not mean the annihilation of our willingness, nor does it mean the denial of what makes us ourselves; the child floating in midair does not have to make any such psychospiritual effort, for he acts with full confidence he will be safe.

Abandonment means cultivating an interior passivity, like that of a child, a state of being receptive. The passivity that enables us to trust in One greater than ourselves, and to hear, to be addressed, to fall into those arms: all of this requires calmness, not a numbing in fear. Abandonment to God, which is the reasonable consequence of all true prayer, does not imply an emotionless acceptance of whatever tragedy or fortune comes along, as if abandonment narcotized us equally to pain and joy. It is, on the contrary, a conviction that there is a limitless Ground of

Being, and that all our experiences can deepen our capacity for
reaching that Ground. Abandonment is a daily giving of self to
what is greater than self; in so doing, we come to know the truth
that no great pain lasts forever, and no great pleasure, either.
This is better news than is immediately apparent.

༄

The connective threads of meaning that I can discern in the pattern of my life demonstrate this principle: the choice of one
school or profession or job or new residence over others, which
in turn led to the emergence of unsuspected talents, or to a lifelong relationship, for example. Reflection on such felicitous ac-
cidents enables me to move forward in trust toward the future,
to give up a futile dependence on myself alone, and hence to find
in abandonment the surest means of preserving my true identity. I reflect, I consider (in other words, I pray), and then I abandon myself to what emerges. Indeed, perhaps on no other point
is the life of prayer more profoundly paradoxical. "Those who
want to make their life secure will lose it," said Jesus of Nazareth,
"but those who lose their life will keep it."

How odd these emphases seem to us, for an integral part
of the social fabric of our time is that everyone ought to be
constantly active. Part of this attitude may derive from Anglo-
Puritanism and the stress on independence that place a high
value on *doing something*. Everyone is supposed to be in control
of life, of relationships, of roles in social and professional situations. To choose not to assert this control often engenders a kind
of panic, which explains why we so often encounter people who
are busy making a living but who seem to take very little real
pleasure in life itself. This confusion often engenders a great
deal of neurotic aggression.

But to those who, however vaguely, have sensed a Beyond in
their midst, and to those who have felt even the first vague stir-

rings of being finally comprehended—indeed, embraced by—unimaginable mercy, abandonment provides the single sure route to God. Hence abandonment means much more than an acknowledgment that I am not in all respects the master of my destiny: it means accepting the much happier situation that I am at the mercy of Another. As one wise contemporary writer has observed, "The goal, in prayer, is to give ourselves away." To do so, or at least to attempt to do so, is to enter into the inherent transcendence of our own being—in which we are receptive to the mystery of God. This sort of surrender-in-trust is a fundamentally human inclination that guided our behavior even before we were tossed into the air and giggled rather than gasped.

Abandonment as a Consequence of Judeo-Christian Faith

Abandonment to God, which occurs every time we sit in silence for prayer, is at the core of religious experience. For the Jewish people, history as presented in the Scriptures may be represented schematically as a series of cycles of suffering, survival and confident trust that God is faithful: that He continues to act as He always has, on humanity's behalf. This may not always be clear, and we may make a muddle of our participation in the human-divine economy, but the affirmation of God's fidelity is central to Jewish faith.

The same is also true of Christianity, which asserts the ineffable reality of the Incarnation—the affirmation that in the person of Jesus, God has indeed entered into time, space and matter; that in Jesus, God has united Himself once and for all to a portion of this world and its physical reality. But Christian faith goes even further, for by virtue of the Resurrection of Jesus—his complete transformation into the realm of the divine in his humanity—everything in existence is drawn into the process of reaching toward that final state in which God triumphs. The successful outcome of the material universe, all sin and evil notwithstanding, is in principle guaranteed by the Resurrection.

Abandonment in faith to this mystery is abandonment to life exultant. The God of the beginning is also the God of the end, the One Who creates and completes. The daring of the logic is literally awesome: the Creator God reveals Himself; the revealing God embraces and summons; the summoning God finally acts in love to save what He has made. Christian faith and prayer, in this matter, constitute what one 19th-century writer called "a mighty interference" in the world.

Hence God has an existential empathy with the world He makes—not the world He made once upon a time and then deserted, but a world He continues to hold in existence. The divine compassion is not a matter of celestial paternalism—it is a matter of a profound affiliation between God and us. And that relationship is at the heart of prayer.

Islam and the Eastern Traditions

The very word "Islam" means abandonment—a conscious, deliberate submission and surrender to God that springs from a longing for Him. Muslim faith is grounded in this single reality of the God Whom the Qur'an proclaims "The Compassionate and Merciful," the two most common among the ninety-nine Most Beautiful Names of God. In light of this, all Muslim prayer is directed to this gracious and present God Who is kind and caring for all.

Some Jews and Christians see a discontinuity when certain Muslim groups endorse violence, which seems contradictory to the authentic faith of Islam and its ongoing prayer life. So it may be, but those same Jews and Christians have to confront the facts of their own continuing attempts to justify systematic war as a means of peacemaking—greater aggression as a response to aggression, violence compounding violence, and a high-toned militaristic rhetoric that calls on a God of righteous vengeance and conveniently ignores the God of universal love. As the bilateral brutality continues, one can see Islam staking a position on one side and Judeo-Christianity on the other, but it is often difficult to locate anything like authentic belief in the One God so blithely claimed as firmly situated in the camp of each. "God is on our side," according to the adage printed on every American dollar bill—*annuit coeptis* (literally, "He has approved of what we have begun"). This kind of thinking can lead to perilous undertakings, just as the medieval Christian crusader's claim "God wills it" has an echo in the questionable Islamic claim "Allah fights for us."

These observations are not tangential to a consideration of prayer in the great traditions. In fact, the authenticity of our faith and the reality of prayer may be assessed by the way in which individuals perceive, confront and behave toward those considered to be enemies—an aggregate of individuals, after all, comprises a government. It is at least a tenable hypothesis, and one worth deliberation, that a commitment to the power of violence and the stratagems of war are inconsistent with faith in God and jeopardize the possibility of prayer.

The 16th-century mystic Nanak, founder of the Islamic-Hindu sect of the Sikhs, expressed his confidence in God through abandonment: "You are my Father, Mother, Brother and everywhere my Protector. What fear or care can come near me, O Lord? Through Your mercy I have felt You. You are my support, my trust. Everything created is Yours—and nothing is ours."

A century later, Tukaram, the Hindu peasant mystic, urged abandonment to God as the remedy for national tribal conflicts and a loss of purpose. "Of what avail are this restless, hurrying activity, this weight of earthly duties?" he asked rhetorically. "God's purposes stand firm, and you, His little ones, need one thing alone: trust in His power to meet your needs. Your burdens rest safe on Him, and you may play securely at His side. This is the sum and substance of it all: God is, God loves you, God bears all your care."

Such prayers found their way into regular usage by devout sectarians, who usually adopted the accompanying practice of the profound bow—the *pranam*, a custom still often employed today. Kneeling on the floor, one joins hands at chest level and then bends at the waist until the forehead touches the floor. Placing oneself in the posture of surrender, one finds that "the posture becomes a means of instruction," as one Western practitioner has written. "The body teaches the mind what it feels and looks like to let go." Thus abandonment has a bodily expression for the Hindu tradition, as it does for the Muslim (the profound bow to the floor), for the Buddhist (the traditional lotus position, cross-legged), for the Jew (standing in silence or for communal prayer) and for the Christian (for whom standing, bowing, kneeling and sitting are all appropriate attitudes for prayer and contemplation).

Hebrew and Christian Scriptures: Abandonment as Trust

The fully developed faith of Israel, reflected in the Psalms and the prophetic literature, presumes that a provident God in Whom one can fully place one's trust is therefore also the Lord to Whom one can completely abandon oneself.

> With You I lack nothing, for You hold my destiny secure. In God alone I trust, and I will not be afraid. And so I listen for my God, Who will answer me.

Your love for me is so great that You have rescued me from the depths of death and annihilation. You are a God of tenderness and mercy. You, my Lord, my loving and faithful God, will never abandon me, and You are coming to meet me and to take me to Yourself forever.

And for Jesus, the cry of abandonment on the cross ("My God, my God, why have You forsaken me?") was not the final testimony. "Into Your hands I commend my spirit" are his poignant last words: silent and apparently absent, God is still clung to in complete abandonment.

Beneath this dark and mysterious faith lie not pious thoughts about God, but God Himself. The God of Israel and the God of Jesus are the One who is ever present to us in His creative power: our existence is rooted and grounded in His—we exist more really in God than in our own being. "What is needed, if we are to be at peace," as one modern spiritual master has written, "is that we should be consciously aware of this fact. Such an awareness would constitute 'enlightenment' [and] would enable us, at last, to understand ourselves." That profound self-understanding is the paradoxical result of the abandonment enjoined by Jesus of Nazareth: losing ourselves, we find ourselves forever. Complete self-donation to God in faith defines abandonment; in a way, it makes of one's life a kind of sacrifice.

The Prayer of Abandonment

Precisely where we might least expect it—in the midst of cultures in social and political upheaval, and just as Church authorities were stressing strict obedience to traditional doctrines—the motif of abandonment in freedom to God became a major theme in the development of personal prayer. The most eminent names in the history of Spanish and French spirituality led the way.

For all his emphasis on the proper use of intellect and will, Ignatius of Loyola clearly recognized that human faculties must finally be quiet in the presence of God. His own prayer was one of profound renunciation, even of the gifts he most prized: "Take, Lord, as your right, and receive from me, all my freedom, my memory, my mind and my will. Whatever I am and whatever I possess, You have given to me. I give it all back to You. Dispose of me, and the powers You gave me, according to Your will. Give me only a love for You, and the gift of Your grace—then I am rich enough, and I ask for nothing more." In Germany, Ignatius's contemporary Martin Luther prayed similarly: "I put myself in Your care, body and soul and all that I have."

At the same time, Teresa of Ávila wrote in some detail about the prayer of abandonment. She admitted that in the early stages of our explicit communion with God, certain verbal prayers and methods of prayer were helpful and perhaps even necessary—they are both the fruit of and the response to our particular personalities. But words and methods take us only so far, and then there is a deep and nonverbal point of abandonment, a level where we let go of every agenda, every expectation, every direction of our own will in prayer; that is the point, to use Teresa's phrase, where we "abandon ourselves into the arms of God's love."

This message is at the heart of the teaching of Teresa's great friend, John of the Cross; indeed, it may well be the key to understanding the deepest level of his idea of the dark night of the soul. Ordinarily such darkness is perceived as a purifying period, a negation of knowledge. But something greater emerges to fill the prayer that was once fired by intellect and will. The mind is darkened only so that a clearer light may shine from the prayer of abandonment—abandonment very much like that of a spouse or lover who drifts confidently to sleep in the presence of the beloved, without fear. This stage of prayer is characterized by the kind of trust in the presence of another who does not require our words to maintain the bond between us; presence alone achieves that.

For John, the prayer of abandonment marks the point at which we move from active meditation (thinking about the things of God) to passive contemplation (a simpler, intuitive awareness of God's proximity, by which we are held attentive without any particular motions of our mental apparatus). This passivity then bestows a greater light, "even as the light of the sun overwhelms all other lights, so that when it shines and disables our power of vision, there appear to be no lights at all."

This may be a difficult stage in the process of our prayer, but for Teresa and John it is both inevitable and necessary. In addition, the abandonment has psychological corollaries that John expresses, as so often, in the language of paradox:

> In order to have pleasure in everything,
>> desire to have pleasure in nothing.
> In order to arrive at possessing everything,
>> desire to possess nothing.
> In order to arrive at being everything,
>> desire to be nothing.
> In order to arrive at knowing everything,
>> desire to know nothing.

The meaning is not quite so obscure as it may at first seem: in order to gain more than just some thing, we find it possible to risk losing every bit of achievement we think we have made. "I abandoned and forgot myself," John wrote. "All things ceased. I went out from myself, leaving my cares. On the road to union with God, this night of faith guides me."

A generation later, another Carmelite—Lawrence of the Resurrection (Nicholas Herman)—urged more directly: "Once and for all, we must trust God and abandon ourselves to Him alone, for He would not deceive us." And at the end of the 19th century, Thérèse of Lisieux, dying of tuberculosis at twenty-four, struggled in her final illness and spiritual darkness to abandon herself to God.

In abandonment, she sensed, was her true liberation from suffering. Comparing herself to a toddler who throws herself into the arms of a loving parent, she relied on the unimaginable love of God to be her ultimate security and freedom from the fear of death. "I expect nothing of myself but everything from God," she wrote. At the end, despite hideous suffering, she at last felt a serenity that had eluded her after years of spiritual struggle.

This attitude of expecting everything from God is faithful confidence of a very high order, but it is not the special prerogative of saints. Thérèse's abandonment involved a simple but difficult interior motion: letting go of everything that had spelled security. Everyone within the process of faith must experience this sort of prayerful endurance: our attachments to our systems of thinking and of doing things, our plans, our forms of prayer, our ideas about what constitutes a proper spiritual path, our preconceived ideas about God and His ways for us, must all be given up; even our virtues must be burned away.

Every tradition in the world has stressed the necessity of abandonment—most obviously, abandoning an inordinate desire for security, for endlessly youthful looks and uninterrupted good health, for material possessions, for a good name. These are not, it must be emphasized, bad things in themselves. But to covet them as if they could bring us absolute serenity and bestow upon us an earthly paradise is to entertain the ultimate self-deception. After all, security is an elusive reality, and is never experienced if considered as something this world can guarantee. Just so, health must sometimes (and of course finally) fail; possessions do not protect us from boredom, much less from spiritual crisis; and a good name often derives from a well-designed social mask.

Jean-Pierre de Caussade and John Wesley

Perhaps the warmest appeal on behalf of abandonment was set forth by a French Jesuit teacher and spiritual director who died in 1751. Some of Jean-Pierre de Caussade's letters, notes and miscellanea were compiled a century later under the title *L'Abandon à la Providence Divine (Abandonment to Divine Providence)*, a short book that has never gone out of print and has been translated into many languages.

His debt to Francis de Sales and Jeanne de Chantal (both of whom died earlier in the century of his birth) is clear almost on every page. Jeanne—Francis's spiritual daughter—encouraged her community of nuns to a simple faith without undue self-concern and with "total dependence on God," so that they might recall His goodness "in everything that happens to them from moment to moment."

Francis and Jeanne had developed a straightforward spirituality that stressed the process of prayer and the slow, anxiety-free awareness of God's work in us—unseen, unfelt but real for all that. As wife, mother, widow and (with Francis's assistance) founder of a community of religious women, Jeanne remarked wisely that "the great method of prayer is to have no method at all. Prayer happens by grace, not by artfulness." In the spirit of de Sales, she counseled "a very simple practice of the presence of God effected by a total abandonment of oneself" to God's providence.

This method of the simple practice of the presence of God was of course not new at the time and was the sole concern of

Jeanne's contemporary, Brother Lawrence of the Resurrection. As a method of prayer, it may be traced back to the so-called Desert Fathers of the early Church.

John Cassian, for example, had been a monk in Egypt before he founded monasteries in what is now southern France in the early 5th century. A contemporary of Saint Augustine, Cassian urged the practice of the presence of God through the silent repetition of an expanded verse of Psalm 69 ("Come to my help, O God; Lord, hurry to my rescue"). The anonymous author of the 14th-century treatise *The Cloud of Unknowing* simplified this form of prayer even further: by repeating in silence "a little word of one syllable," the attention could be firmly fixed on the presence of God.

After centuries of more complex and complicated "schools" of prayer, this purer form has been widely taken up again and has found exponents in modern times: the American Trappist monks Basil Pennington and Thomas Keating developed the method of Centering Prayer with laypeople in mind, while in England, the Benedictine John Main taught a similar contemplative method.

꒰

Unlike his predecessors—Cassian, de Sales and de Chantal—Jean-Pierre de Caussade's external life had little drama; he lived virtually unknown outside a small circle, first as a professor and then as a counselor to a convent of cloistered nuns. Contrary to some extremists of his time who misunderstood abandonment as a sort of total spiritual passivity requiring no concomitant effort, discipline or care, Caussade emphasized attentiveness to God through the actual circumstances of each day.

Abandonment is therefore not a psychological self-deadening but an active response to an ever-present, ever-revealing God of love. "To wait with folded arms for everything to drop from heaven would be an absurd and culpable quietism—and so while leaning on God, you must never leave off working yourself." When we look on ourselves as collaborators with God (which is, after all, the point of virtually every page of Scripture), "we shall then act quietly, without anxiety, without hurry, without uneasiness about the future, without troubling about the past, giving ourselves up to God and relying more on Him than on all possible human means. In this way, we shall always be at peace, and God will infallibly turn everything to our good."

Abandonment is itself, then, a component of and type of authentic prayer. Caussade admits that often our lives seem to be composed of insignificant details, routine tasks and humdrum chores. But it is just this ordinary life that is the forum for God's self-disclosure to us: "We are often bored with the small happenings around us, yet it is these trivialities that would do marvels for us if only we did not despise them, for God speaks to every individual through what happens moment by moment. The events of each moment are stamped with the will of God. If we have abandoned ourselves to Him, there is really only one rule for us: the duty of the present moment."

This is an intensely pragmatic spiritual path, along which abandonment can virtually be identified as a hallmark of every prayer life, for prayer derives from faith, and faith moves us to deliver ourselves into the arms of God. On every page of his writings, Caussade's psychological balance combines with his unthreatening and gentle injunction of simple attentiveness to a living God: the duties and demands of ordinary life thus provide the forum through which we encounter God. To discover Him in the small details as well as in the great events is to sustain a relationship—and that, after all, is the meaning of true prayer. "God's action penetrates every atom of your body," he wrote in a letter to one nun, "indeed, into the very marrow of your bones. Have perfect confidence in all the activities of God, for He cannot do anything but good."

Caussade shares none of the bleak severity so common to

18th-century religious rhetoric, and none of its stark, cautionary suspicions about human nature. "This fortunate habit protects me from danger," he said in another letter, acknowledging the influence of Francis de Sales. "God will keep us in peace in the midst of the greatest disasters of this world, which pass away like shadows. Nothing surprises me in this life—by now you ought to know my way of always looking at the best side of things and setting everything in a favorable light, as St. Francis de Sales advises. This somehow makes it impossible for me to think badly, to judge harshly or to speak unkindly of anyone, whoever he may be. I strongly advise you to have confidence in God, Who alone can fill the place of everything else."

Caussade's spirituality has a remarkable resemblance to what we have learned of Hindu thinking since the early 20th century: "The existence we have received from God," he wrote, "remains, as it were, in the bosom of the Divinity and remains plunged and engulfed therein. God, then, is the author of all being; nothing is, nor lives, nor subsists, nor moves but by Him. He is Who is, by Whom and in Whom all exists, and Who is in all things. Things, compared with nothingness, seem to have an existence—but compared with God, they seem nothing—they only possess being and substance by the gift of God." Caussade likewise shares the confidence of Buddhism: "We shall finish by arriving at the complete annihilation of our entire being before God. Thus alone shall we be true, and shall be before God in our proper state—that of nothingness." His words could have been written by a modern Zen master.

Few spiritual directors are so perennially relevant as Jean-Pierre de Caussade; few expressed with such lively simplicity the conjunction between ordinary life and prayer; few so clearly demystified the notion of abandonment. His influence on spirituality has never diminished over the course of the last 250 years; it can be discerned in the teachings of many traditions about prayer, and even in the meditations of great academics, occasionally in spite of themselves. The 20th-century French Jewish philosopher Simone Weil, for example, asked rhetorically: "Why should I have any anxiety? It is not my business to think about myself. My business is to think about God. It is for God to think about me."

We are living in touch with God at every moment, Caussade insisted; we are living in God's action as a fish lives in water. Our life and our prayer, then, are not a matter of trying to *feel* that God is here; rather, they are a simple acknowledgment that we are at all times enveloped and embraced in His providential presence.

The notion of abandonment is found not only in various Roman Catholic traditions of prayer in Europe. Among Caussade's devout contemporaries was the Protestant John Wesley, founder of English Methodism, whose private prayer was remarkably similar in spirit to that of Spanish and French spirituality. "I am no longer my own but Yours," he prayed in private. "Put me to what You will. Put me to doing. Put me to suffering. Let me be employed for You or laid aside for You, exalted for You or brought low for You. Let me be full, let me be empty. Let me have all things, let me have nothing. You are mine and I am Yours." His words became the basis for a Covenant Service that Wesley conducted on the first day of each year, when he urged people to commit themselves unreservedly to God's benevolence.

The Simplicity of Abandonment as Prayer

For those who consign themselves in faith to God's mercy, things can be right even when they feel hopelessly wrong. Hence the great paradoxes continue, for a true prayer can be merely the weary complaint to God, "I cannot pray—I cannot even keep still and attentive in Your presence." After all, so much in our prayer depends on circumstances—our physical disposition, our concerns, our exhaustion or wakefulness. But for those who abandon themselves to God, these distractions and apprehensions dissolve. "The only thing is to take life as it comes," John Chapman wrote in 1926 to one who was enveloped by spiritual discontent. "Providence arranges everything, so all is right in the end. Meanwhile, if we worry, we must try also to take that fact with simplicity, however paradoxical it sounds. . . . Confidence in God is what we want."

Although he was over fifty, Chapman volunteered as a chaplain in World War I, and he endured all the horrors of trench life in France from 1915 to 1919. While the experience permanently broke his health, it also deepened his dependence on God. In 1927, he wrote to an old acquaintance in words that could have been an excerpt from Jean-Pierre de Caussade: "Our whole environment and everything that happens is God's hand upon us, and we are in touch with Him at every moment. . . . Every detail of life is a means arranged by Him to lead us to Himself."

Life with God, which is just another way of describing the life of prayer, is not a problem to be solved but a mystery to be experienced. By "mystery" we do not mean something esoteric and incomprehensible, but rather the depth of all reality. "Mysteries are not truths that lie beyond us," as the philosopher Gabriel Marcel memorably wrote. "Mysteries are truths that comprehend us." Through the habit of abandonment, that mystery and that truth embrace us in the unimaginable but ineluctable reality of the divine compassion.

CHAPTER NINE

Prayer as Serenity

The astonishing paradox of the prayer of abandonment is that, far from putting us at risk of losing our way in a cloud of helpless anxiety, it eventually effects a profound and hitherto unexpected serenity. Surrender to the Lord of infinite, compassionate benevolence, by a simple, habitual act of inner dedication, establishes in us an attitude about reality that we may not have known earlier. Because surrender is itself an act of prayer, the concomitant serenity is not a matter of a wistful, narcotized detachment from the world. It is rather a conviction that things are better off where they in fact are: in the hands of God.

Surrender, Serenity and Silence

As with every part of the journey to the God Who is near, this stage, too, is approached in the most secret and silent part of our being. Teresa of Ávila is a trustworthy guide in the matter, precisely because she had to balance exhausting activity in the world with a consuming desire for silence and prayer—a dilemma endemic to our own time, five centuries later. But she succeeded in experiencing an inner serenity through surrender to the demands placed on her. While engaged in business, the funding of convents, the reformation of religious life and the nearly continuous composition and dictation of books, she found that the habit of abandonment to God established her more deeply than ever in silence, even amid the crush and press of constant work.

The metaphor Teresa chooses to describe this kind of prayer-amid-the-din is the ancient tradition that the great temple at Jerusalem, erected during the reign of David's son Solomon, was constructed in silence. The place "was made of stone finished at the quarry," according to 1 Kings 6, "so that neither hammer nor ax nor any tool of iron was heard in the temple while it was being built." This is the kind of Semitic hyperbole that enriches the religious language of the Scriptures, and it conforms to the profound silence that prevailed during prayer in the completed temple. "The Lord is in His holy temple: let all the earth keep silence before Him," as the prophet Habakkuk enjoined; similar statements may be read in the Book of Psalms, and in the writings attributed to the prophets Zephaniah and Zechariah.

Just so, Teresa observes, prayer builds an interior temple where God dwells within us:

> Having committed oneself wholly to God, so tranquilly and noiselessly does the Lord teach the soul in this state that I am reminded of the building of Solomon's temple, during which no noise could be heard. In this temple of God, He and [the individual] rejoice in the deepest silence. There is no reason now for the understanding to stir, or to seek out anything.

Teresa is too wise to believe that there can be any depth in prayer if it is attempted only in the midst of ceaseless activity: one must also seek out solitude and stillness, or the serenity will soon be revealed as illusory and sterile. Whenever she met people dedicated to a life of constant motion and the pursuit of achievement, Teresa was quick to warn them that the whirl of such goings-on could be a short route to exterior and interior chaos; with less and less of the interior strength that derives from periods of quiet recollection, people can fall apart—or at least come perilously close to losing a sense of real meaning in their lives. Mere busyness can cause a harrowing disconnection of the self; an attitude that appropriately keeps business in the realm of work can improve both the world and the worker. This Teresa knew from firsthand experience—hence her insistence on periods of withdrawal, however brief.

Addressed by God and committed to the truth of His unfailing goodwill toward us, we can experience a profound sense that (as Julian of Norwich put it) all shall be well precisely because God is faithful. This conviction can become a kind of spiritual life-support system, through which we feel the gradual evanescence of every kind of fear and anxiety. But such a liberation means we must take with absolute gravity the fact of our contingency, of our creaturehood; we must give up the misconceived notion that we are the source of our own being and the sustenance of our existence.

The East

Outside of the Judeo-Christian tradition, the matter of spiritual serenity is linked not to one's relationship with a personal and loving God but is rather the achievement of inner harmony derived from right thinking and the discipline of meditation. For devout Buddhists, profound inner serenity is ultimately the fruit of universal compassion. The tradition of the so-called Ten Perfections, for example, involves attitudes of giving, duty, renunciation (abandonment), insight, courage, patience, truth, resolution, lovingkindness and finally serenity. "As indeed the earth looks with serenity on all the pure and impure that are cast upon it, even so shall you approach with serenity both joy and sorrow—if you are to attain wisdom." This nontheistic form of human development, Buddhists insist, is available to all who will submit to its disciplines of conduct and focused meditation.

A venerable tradition in Buddhism contradicts the erroneous assumption that the wisdom of the East is a grim business fixated on endless cycles of birth, death and rebirth—an attitude about reality that would seem to undermine anything like serenity. A monk, it is said, consoled a grieving king on the death of his wife by reminding him that all human life is impermanent—a truth not to be taken as bad news, however, but good. It means that old age itself will age, sickness will fall ill, death will die, impermanence will pass away. In this regard, "the final goal of Buddhism remains liberation [and] escape from the wheel of rebirth."

Equivalent misperceptions abound in Western presumptions about Islam and Muslim believers. The Arabic root of both words (S-L-M) connotes a sense of wholeness, serenity and balance that are the result of having in order one's relationship to God and to others—a state called *salam*, which is linked to the Hebrew word for peace, *shalom*. "When a person pursues that state [of right relationships], it means attributing to God and to none else what belongs to God," as a contemporary Islamic scholar has rightly insisted. "That is the root meaning of *iSLaM*. One who achieves that state of propriety in relation to God is a *muSLiM*." One knows serenity, in other words, by an active awareness that God Alone is to be held at the center of life.

Blessings

The same sense is at the heart of the Hebrew Book of Psalms, which sets before those who pray the blessing of serenity that comes from abandonment in faith. "I lie down and sleep; I wake again, for the Lord sustains me. I am not afraid of those who have set themselves against me." At the end of temple prayer services, priests spoke the biblical blessing attributed to Aaron: "The Lord bless you and keep you. The Lord make His face to shine upon you and be gracious to you. The Lord lift up His countenance upon you and give you peace."

The notion of blessings is often difficult to comprehend. What does it mean to bless God and to invoke blessings on others?

To bless God is not only to express gratitude: fundamentally it acknowledges that He is the Author of all that is good. Blessing God is an act of dedication to Him—an acknowledgment of His sovereignty even as one understands that human effort is not the final guarantor of a right relationship with God; that is achieved only by the free act of God's dedication of Himself to *us*—what the theologian calls grace. If an awareness of this mutuality of dedication does not bring a measure of serenity, it is certainly a proper step in that direction.

As for invoking blessings on others, we may regard them as prayers for the entire human family, of which the one who prays is an exponent and representative. "May the peace of God, which passes all understanding, keep your hearts and minds in the knowledge and love of God and of His Son Jesus Christ our Lord," is the 16th-century blessing found in the Book of Common Prayer, "and may the blessing of God Almighty, the Father, Son and Holy Spirit, be among you and remain with you always." The one who utters the prayer is not excluded from the prayer for solidarity with God; nor, of course, is the speaker bestowing the blessing. God alone, as Maker and Sustainer, is the One who saves forever and brings the dead to life with Himself.

This spirit is at the heart of a prayer composed by the American theologian Reinhold Niebuhr. Widely known as the Serenity Prayer, it was taken up by Alcoholics Anonymous, a group that understands the illusion of human control and its power to lead to addiction and grief. "God, give us the grace to accept with serenity the things that cannot be changed, the courage to change the things that should be changed, and the wisdom to distinguish the one from the other."

Theophan the Recluse

"God is closer to us than our own soul," wrote Julian of Norwich, "for He is the foundation on which our existence stands. If we want to know ourselves, we should seek in the Lord God, in Whom we are enfolded." Her contemporary in the Rhineland, the anonymous 14th-century author of *The Book of the Poor in Spirit*, emphasized that serenity derives from the fact that "God is nearer to me than I am to my own self," and that this awareness was itself the first response in prayer.

The link between the experience of God's presence in silence, and stillness as itself a prayer that bestows serenity, has not often been described, but it is surely the essential element in mature prayer. "Madame, you are seeking outside yourself for what is inside," said a wise guide in 18th-century France, to one who was spiritually unbalanced and psychologically self-absorbed. "Seek God in your own heart and you will find Him." The listener had a tiresome taste for excessive rituals and pious observances, the discharge of which is often mistaken for a deep prayer life.

An unfailing route to spiritual serenity, on the contrary, was movingly set down by the great 19th-century Russian Orthodox priest, professor and bishop, George Govorov, who died in 1894. Better known, in the Russian tradition, as Theophan the Recluse, he remains one of the undisputed masters of the interior life.

At the age of fifty, after having served as a highly respected educator, rector of the Saint Petersburg Academy and then as a bishop, he resigned his positions and withdrew to two small rooms in a modest provincial monastery, where he lived in great simplicity until his death twenty-eight years later. His life as a recluse encompassed three related activities: prayer, literary work on prayer and a continuing correspondence of spiritual direction with women and men from all over Russia; for relaxation, he painted icons and did minor carpentry.

At his death, Theophan's legacy included vast commentaries on religious history and biblical literature, as well as ten volumes of correspondence (in an engaging and unpretentious style). It is entirely possible that the Orthodox Church's spiritual tradition cannot be understood without at least a familiarity with the content and spirit of this remarkable man; his personal austerity and scholarly disposition never alienated him from a profound sympathy with the lives of ordinary people and their struggles to find God in the world.

In prerevolutionary Russia, Theophan greatly appreciated, for example, the desire for serenity. What have we to do in order to enjoy true peace of soul? he asked.

Secure for yourself inner solitude—which is not a mere vacuum, nor can it be gained simply by creating complete emptiness in oneself. When you retreat into yourself, you should stand before the Lord and remain in His presence, not letting the eyes of your mind turn away. . . . It is an excellent thing to go to church, but if you can accustom yourself to pray at home as if in church, such prayer at home is equally valuable.

To be with the Lord is the aim of our existence, and when we are with Him, we cannot fail to experience a feeling of well-being. . . . Just as one person sees another face to face, try to stand before the Lord so that your soul is face to face with Him. This is so natural that there really should be no need to mention it, for the Lord is always near. There is no need to arrange an introduction between you and Him, for you are old acquaintances.

For all his erudition, Theophan took a radically simple view of prayer: "The principal thing is to stand before God, and to go on standing before Him unceasingly, day and night, until the end of life." This is primarily a matter of silence and solitude, of an inner direction of our attention (and by extension of our entire being) to the transcendent depth within us. Without slavish dependence on fashionable or exaggerated theories, Theophan gently and directly set forth what he considered three degrees or stages of prayer. The first degree is bodily prayer, consisting of formal prayers accompanied by various traditional postures. The second degree is attentive prayer, in which readings from books or formulas of prayers are silently uttered as if they were one's own. The third degree Theophan called the prayer of feeling, without words: a phrase of penance becomes a habit of contrition; a word of petition become a conviction of one's dependence on God. As Jeanne de Chantal likewise wrote, "There is no danger if our prayer is without words—it is the simple raising of our hearts to God, and the more simple and stripped of feeling it is, the surer it is."

This approach toward attaining serenity has nothing to do with achieving a sense of personal satisfaction nor developing a surefire "method" on which we can congratulate ourselves. Like Teresa and John, Caussade and Chapman—indeed, like everyone who has written meaningfully about prayer—Theophan urged us to pray daily, to make it a habit. "The less one prays, the worse it goes," as Chapman wrote memorably, thirty-five years after Theophan's death; and the worse it goes, the less there is of real serenity.

As we experience this depth and this unique kind of inner calm, there occurs what the gifted contemporary writer Emilie Griffin calls "transparency," a gradually greater clarity and insight not only into the true self but also into the matters of our daily lives. We come to comprehend that people and things and events do not belong to us, but it is we who become more open and available to them, and therefore to the constant astonishment that communion with God effects.

꒰꒱

In contrast to the tranquil but never presumptuous or self-righteous spirituality of thinkers like Theophan, there is a long list of misleading and sometimes even dangerous books on prayer and the inner life—those that encourage us to measure and judge our progress. This is little more than spiritual capitalism, a system that attempts to place precise evaluations on matters of the spirit.

Since the medieval age first expressed this tendency to codify and intellectualize, a "science" of the spiritual life has developed, with even some saints being led into tortuous speculations about the "stages" of our development in prayer. But human beings are not good judges of our own spiritual state, and the desire to assess ourselves (or to have another assess us) stands opposed to true prayer, which is not about discovering how good we are, but how good God is.

We do not pray in order to find answers: we pray to turn ourselves over to God and to allow Him a greater field of operation within us. We do not pray for personal fulfillment, which is mere modern egotism: we pray so that our truest fulfillment may be God's greater presence to us. We do not pray to bring about a desired outcome, nor to gain some kind of mystical insight into reality, nor to gain any kind of possession: we pray in order to give ourselves away. We do not pray to achieve some altered state of consciousness or behold extraordinary things: we pray to belong to God.

Our task is therefore to be more aware of the journey ahead than of the way already traveled. But if we find that prayer has brought us a fresh serenity, a gradual diminishment of fear and a deepening of trust, then it is likely that we are indeed on the right path, even though we are constantly aware of the disparity between our ideals and our lives as we live them. In the privacy of our solitude, in the secrecy of our serenity, we find our deepest links to others, too—hence we move back into the world with a keener sensitivity to the needs of others. We find that we more patiently sustain situations and persons we would otherwise dismiss with resentment. We find, most of all, that our serenity enables us to endure our own failure and insufficiency.

ॐ

A prayerful life is fundamentally a joyful life—an existence grounded in trust that God cannot fail us. Hence, prayer establishes deep roots of serenity, even amid spiritual and physical crises. As the consequence of faithful abandonment and the result of prayer as a life of love and constant transformation, serenity provides not a comfortable cushion for life's challenges. It is, to the contrary, an experience of the truth that God can be trusted—a God Who is always available to us, always ready to provide what we really need. It is no facile kind of reductionism to say that serenity is in some sense inevitable if we persevere in prayer.

If you do not have the hopeful conviction that there is a living, loving God as the ground of your existence, it is unlikely that you have read thus far. And if there is indeed a living, loving God Who is both near and within, you have every imaginable right to expect a serenity unlike any in the world.

CHAPTER TEN

Prayer as Loving

"We succeed in prayer and in love," wrote the great 20th-century theologian Karl Rahner, "when we lose ourselves in both, and are no longer aware of how we are praying or in what manner we are loving." For Rahner, both prayer and love had to be as devoid as possible of self-consciousness, self-assessment and self-aggrandizement. Prayer itself (as a responsive relationship) is an act of love, and love itself (as a commitment to the well-being of others) is an act of prayer.

✢

Throughout the course of history, wherever we find people praying, we find the single consistent motif of a response to a Reality that may not be ignored—a turning of attention toward and a reply to a personal invitation. That response goes much deeper than emotions, however; indeed, as we have seen, the emotions may be clouded and untrustworthy, submerged (now and then or mostly) in dark waters of confusion.

For countless centuries, people have claimed to have been comprehended and addressed by the transcendent yet immanent God—a Reality they did not seek but rather were sought by. They have spoken and written about these encounters in terms of a frankly personal attachment, a dedication, a bond that, for all its magisterial mystery and its being subject to the constant peril of cliché, is typically described as loving. This is certainly true of the saints; it is also true for those who come to understand that prayer is nothing if it is not the dialogue of an intimate relationship.

But how can we speak of the love of God, in both senses: His for us, and ours for Him? What does it mean to say that God loves me? What does it mean to speak of my own love for Him? Are we not doomed, given the imprecision of our language, to uttering clichés of romantic illusion, fastening our feelings to a comforting, dreamy escapism?

Jonathan Edwards, who died in 1758, was a philosopher, theologian and president of Princeton University; he was also one of the great intellects in American colonial history. Often superficially branded as a bombastic preacher driven by an intolerably severe and even cruel religious extremism, Edwards in fact placed as much emphasis on faith and love as he did on sin and guilt: for Edwards, it is love for what God does in us that draws us to prayer, and the discipline of prayer in turn inculcates love. Preaching on prayer, he told his congregation, "It is the nature of love to be averse to absence, and to love a near access to those whom we love. We love to be with them; we delight to come often to them, and to have much conversation with them." From this common experience of human friendship, Edwards rose to a consideration of the duty and the richness of prayer, which is nothing so much as an expression of relationship—and relationship presumes the bond of love.

The Scriptures on God's Love

In the Bible, God's love for Israel is described in terms of human love and fidelity, and the command to love God wholly and entirely is seen in concomitant faithfulness to God's covenant. God first acted salvifically on behalf of a beleaguered people, drawing them to Himself and remaining faithful when they were disloyal. "I have loved you with an everlasting love" were words addressed to the people through the prophet Jeremiah. This love becomes emotionally specific in the words of Hosea, who spoke of God's activity on Israel's behalf as a sign of both paternal love ("When Israel was a child I loved him, and out of Egypt I called my son"—a reference to the Exodus) and marital love ("... love a woman just as the Lord loves the people of Israel").

Israel was, then, a kind of corporate personality—the people named for the patriarch. The Israelites were well aware of being loved by God *as* a people, for in the entire Old Testament, only David's son Solomon is singled out as the object of God's love; everyone else experiences that love through affiliation with Israel and through the forgiveness of sin. As a member of God's blessed people, one knows love precisely because one is among those who have been saved for meaning and purpose despite their failings.

For the Jewish faith, a consequence of this calling is the necessity of prayer. As a modern rabbi has said, prayer "in its highest form and its most sincere levels, is called a 'service of the heart,' and constitutes one of the many ways by which *love of God* [sic] is expressed."

That spirit infuses the Jewish foundations of the New Testament. A noteworthy aspect of the first three gospels is that they say nothing explicitly about God's love for humanity at all. Jesus never addresses the subject, except to indicate in parables how gracious, accepting and forgiving God is of all who fail or are disenfranchised. The matter of God's love for us, in other words, is presented strictly in terms of how God acts toward us: there is no attempt to offer Jesus' example as an alternative to, say, the various Greek cultural and philosophical concepts of love.

The gospels do, however, enlarge upon the traditional Hebrew notion of God's love—the person, ministry and final glorification of Jesus are a tangible sign of God's love not only for the people of Israel but also for the whole world. The fourth gospel

and the letters attributed to John are crucial in this regard, setting forth the ethical blueprint by which human response to divine love may be understood. The famous verse "God is love"
does not proclaim that God is merely a poetic metaphor for the
sentiment of human love; it is not a statement of philosophical
essence but rather of ethics. The reverse is *not* true, as the author
of 1 John makes clear. "In this is love: not that we loved God,
but that He loved us." The love of God for us is clear from our
existence and from God's climactic self-disclosure in Jesus of
Nazareth.

Hence the New Testament preserves, first, the mystery and
incomprehensibility of God, Who embraces human history but
is not identical with it, and, second, the standard by which we
may understand what it means for us to love God. The first
letter of John brings us to the core of both how we are assured
that God loves us and how we can determine whether or not
we respond to that love: "No one has ever seen God; if we love
one another, God lives in us, and His love is perfected in us." If
we love one another, we know that "those who abide in love
abide in God, and God abides in them. . . . We love because He
first loved us."

And then comes the unavoidable result, and the single statement that answers the question regarding how love for God is
recognized: "Those who say, 'I love God' and hate their brothers
or sisters [i.e., any other persons], are liars; for those who do not
love a brother or sister whom they have seen, cannot love God
Whom they have not seen." There is no ambiguity: "Those who
love God must love their brothers and sisters also."

At the core of the biblical and postbiblical notion of love is a
simple principle: loving God means counting on Him and responding by love for others. "Faith means believing in God in
spite of appearances," said Jacques Rivière. "Charity means loving our neighbors in spite of what they may do to us. Hope

means to look forward to spiritual goods even when they seem to be impossible."

Love as Adoration

To speak of "God" and to use the word "love" in the same frame of reference is to invite any number of difficulties, for nowhere else is the language of analogy both so necessary and so weak. God does not "love" us in the way people love us, nor can we say we "love" God when we have in mind anything like the sentiments we feel toward other human beings.

We can, however, know that there is a Ground of meaning to existence; we can know that we are, in the core of our being, recipients of so much that is good and beautiful. From the love offered to us by those we know, admire and love in return, we understand how essential love is in our lives: we can survive without romance, but we cannot live without love. And that realization alone tells us something, it reminds us of the benevolence at the root of all that is.

For some people, there is further evidence of a grounding love in the enormity of the world's beauty; in the breadth and depth and sheer uninterrupted volume of creativity and imagination that have given understanding and purpose to lives; in the richness and mystery of the physical universe; in the sublimity of human communication; in the greatness of spirit, the heroism and magnanimity that surface all the time and everywhere. No matter the darkness, there is somehow always light: for it we yearn, to it we respond. Our capacity for that response is, indeed, infinite. We never have enough goodness, enough beauty, enough mercy, acceptance and love. It matters that we matter.

Strange though it may at first seem, we can perhaps come

closest to an understanding of the nature of the dual dynamic—
of God's love for us and ours for Him—if we consider how necessary it is for us to adore something or someone. The word
"adoration" is an intensive form of the words "to pray" (ad +
orare: not to pray to, but to move in prayer toward Someone);
adoration is at the heart of every religion in history.

Behind my need to adore is the absolute claim of God on me
as one created and sustained by Him; at the foundation of my
need to adore is the recognition that I am but a fragment—
dependent on people and things outside myself. Yes, I can adore
if I am responsive to the breathtaking, complex mystery of the
universe, and to the unexpected flowering of humanity's finest
instincts. And I can say that God is indeed present when one person is kind to another. Surely that is not too small a thing among
all the great issues; saints and mystics tell us that God is manifest most of all in human caring and gentleness.

That may have been among the reasons why Augustine of
Hippo, Anselm of Canterbury, Julian of Norwich, Catherine of
Siena and others referred to "God our Mother." It is that kind of
nurturing, tender love of which they were (however dimly) always aware, perhaps even before they prayed.

Adoration does not leave us detached, intimidated and distant from this Ground of benevolence, and this assurance, too,
comes by way of paradox. The God of the universe comes down
to my level; different from everything created and finite, He
is infinitely close, keeping every fiber of my being. "Paying
honor" or "offering homage" to God is not, perhaps, appropriate
language for a fitting response to this God—it has too much of
impersonal human service about it.

I do not adore God because of His limitless power, but because of my limitless capacity to be touched and transformed by
what is beautiful and sublime. It may be that reference to aesthetic experience is a more apt analogy to the nature of adora-

tion than the idea of homage, as the contemporary theologian John Macquarrie has observed. What is sublime is not far from Rudolf Otto's *mysterium tremendum,* from the holy.

That may be why there has always been a link between religion and art, and why even people who say they have no religious sensibility seek the sublime in artistic experience. There is within us a need to adore, to bend the knee of the heart, to relate to that which is absolute. And when I know that I am touched and somehow deepened by this connection to the creative source of all life, I can say that I am at my most human.

Whatever else it is concerned with, religion is essentially adoration before the Fact of God. And more than a distinct or independent action, prayer in this context becomes a condition of our spirit, a habit of being, an attitude toward reality that claims the priority of God.

Prayer and Life: Love Active

To care about the plight of the poor, the sick, the victims of war, poverty, epidemics and injustice; to cry out against those who would exploit the disenfranchised and abuse the powerless; to love our friends and those who have a claim on our compassion; to attend wholeheartedly, generously and passionately, insofar as we can, to the needs of others—this is what it means to love God. The great prophets of Israel, the Buddha, Jesus of Nazareth and Muhammad—they did not go about the countryside proclaiming abstractions about the meaning of love: they reached out to human need and addressed it.

To love God, then, means to want what is good—to seek the benefit of others in this world. This is the profoundest ethic of Judaism, the deepest meaning of Buddhist compassion, the basis for Islamic submission and the simplest elucidation of Christian charity. To love God also means to love everything that is right and beautiful in the world, and to work for what furthers the humanizing process and what decreases strife, hatred and suffering in the world. Love in faith is, after all, a mystery. We cannot give to God anything but what He has first given us, and to the issue of how I love God, there can perhaps but be one reply: by adoring, confirming and contributing to all that is good in the world. In this spirit, we may say that prayer-in-action is a two-way route by which I accept and respond to God's love for me. "And if we are to love God," said Austin Farrer, the 20th-century Oxford professor and priest, "we must feel Him in the whole substance of our life. We cannot love disembodied ghosts."

$$\sim$$

For four millennia, the great religions of the world have stressed awe and reverence before the reality of the divine. Whether one kneels or stands, sits or bows, external gestures at prayer both in public and in private are signs of our acknowledgment of the sovereignty of God. Postures and positions are secondary to the expression of humility that is the prayer of adoration itself. We do not grovel as if before an exacting master: we rejoice in intimacy with the Lord of the universe.

That the world is completely infused with the presence of the living God is an act of faith that is, for mystical poets like Rabindranath Tagore (Nobel laureate for literature in 1913), a completely reasonable view of reality:

> Have you not heard his silent steps?
>> He comes, comes, ever comes.
> Every moment and every age, every day and every night,
>> He comes, comes, ever comes . . .
> In the fragrant days of sunny April through the forest path,
>> He comes, comes, ever comes.

In the rainy gloom of July nights on the thundering chariot
>   of cloud,
> He comes, comes, ever comes.
> In sorrow after sorrow, it is his steps that press upon
>   my heart,
>   and it is the golden touch of his feet that make my joy
>   to shine.

This is a fair expression of the contemplation of God manifest in the universe; in this spirit, prayer as a habitual act of loving adoration is less about words, or even thinking about God all the time. The prayer of adoration, then, means acting consciously as responsible adult human beings, while ever on the alert for the moment that pulls us forward, advances our cohesion with others, augments our compassion, drives us to a fresh awareness of hitherto unexpected depths. Lawrence of the Resurrection was right when he observed that very often he "was more united to God in his ordinary activities than when he devoted himself to those religious activities that left him with a profound spiritual dryness." In the same spirit, Francis de Sales urged the kind of adoration that is "spontaneous prayer, whenever you can and in whatever setting, always seeing God in your heart and your heart in God."

Adoration, then, is an underlying stance toward God-in-the-world that is consistent with ordinary life; its consequence is a life-in-the-world that is consistent with God. "Let us all belong to God in the midst of so much busyness brought on by the diversity of worldly things," de Sales wrote—adding, perhaps with a sly and knowing smile: "Where could we give better witness to our fidelity than in the midst of things going wrong? Solitude has its assaults and the world its busyness; in both places, we must be courageous."

Hinduism and Buddhism

The Bhagavad-Gita, which presents a highly sophisticated and deeply mystical sense of God, has been called the crowning glory of Hindu theism. In its theology, God is not an impersonal Absolute but the pursuing and merciful Lover of the human soul: "Turn to me as your refuge. I will deliver you from all evil—have no care." The Hindu notion of devotion, of the love of God—*bhakti*—is an active and affective participation of each person in the divine nature; it implies a loving abandonment to the Lord's greatness.

This principle motivated one of the great individuals of modern times. Dedicated to the correction of injustice, racism and violence, Mohandas Karamchand Gandhi—called by his countrymen Mahatma, "the great-souled"—progressively deepened a vision that was wholly loving, prayerful and involved in the world's suffering. He was, one might say, the personification of *bhakti*.

Mediator, reconciler and peaceful revolutionary against colonialism, racism and violence, Gandhi also found time to write more than eighty volumes. Albert Einstein, for one, saw in him a living counterstatement to the horrific brutality unleashed in the nuclear age.

Asked to describe the goal of his life's work, Gandhi once replied: "What I have been striving and pining to achieve is to see God face to face. All that I do by way of speaking and writing [is] directed to this same end." He did not come upon this philosophy from the solitude of meditation in a mountain cave, for like Gautama Buddha and Jesus of Nazareth, he spent himself amid the crush of his people's need and reached out to it. Gandhi saw the danger of ignoring what we do not understand; he emphasized that we tend to minimize and regard as commonplace what is radiant with significance.

Gandhi's own conviction was an unshakable intuition of a loving God—and of our capacity for response—that went further than intellectual analysis:

> I do dimly perceive that whilst everything around me is ever changing, ever dying, there is underlying all that change a living power that is changeless, that holds all together, that creates, dissolves and recreates. That informing power or spirit is God. And is this power benevolent or malevolent? I see it as purely benevolent. For I can see that in the midst of death, life persists; in the midst of untruth, truth persists; in the midst of darkness, light persists. Hence I gather that God is Life, Truth, Light. He is Love. He is the Supreme Good.

Gandhi understood that something of the unknowable God could in fact be known through His absence. Sharing the enormity of his people's misery and understanding that it required both profound loving compassion and political reaction, he enlivened his prayer in and through his work. Just so, his work was his prayer only (he insisted) insofar as it was a process of freeing himself from chains both material and sensual.

The foundation of Gandhi's own faith was Vaishnavism, a path centered round the Hindu god Vishnu; his family had also exposed him to the influence of Jainism, a morally severe Indian denomination. From these traditions, he came to the Bhagavad-Gita, where he was struck by two concepts: *aparigraha*, or the necessity of being free from possessions; and *samabhava*, or the goal of remaining undisturbed by pain or pleasure, success or failure. His belief in the omnipresence of the Eternal amid the world's agony was further enriched by his astonishing openness to all religions and their exponents (especially their mystics). He seems clearly to have embraced monotheism during his mature years, and he was also very much in the tradition of the 16th-century Hindu mystic Caitanya, who spoke of humble love in all

social relationships—peaceful love, love as service, love as intimacy with God, love as submission to God and love of God as
one's true lover.

Russian Christianity fascinated Gandhi when he read Tol-
stoy; Islamic fear of God, implicit or explicit on virtually every
page of the Qur'an, reinforced his sense of reverence for all
life, religious and secular (which, in any case, he saw as aspects
of one world); and his strong connections to the Quakers during his time in South Africa nourished his pacifism. As for
religions, he taught (without smugness or rancor) that they all
refracted something of the truth, but were "interpreted with
poor intellects, sometimes with poor hearts—and more often
misinterpreted."

The significance of Gandhi's character and work cannot be
overstated. His presence in the world was as full a representa-
tion of *bhakti* mysticism as one could seek, and his longing for a
personal God was expressed in terms of a bond of love-in-action
and tireless courage—right up to the moment of his assassination, at the age of seventy-nine, in 1948.

᠅

Although the literature and practice of Buddhism only addresses in passing the notion of love, its meditation practices
direct the spirit away from concern only with one's desires,
emotions and the kind of gratification that often characterizes
human love. "Rather than personal fulfillment, selflessness emphasizes relationships through recognition of the interdepen-
dency of all things," as one contemporary Zen master has said.
Love as a condition and habit, therefore, is expressed through a
spirit of mindful attention and universal compassion. When the
mind is expanded in its view of love, compassion informs, parallels and deepens ordinary human passion. This attention to others, the willingness to give and to help others, would certainly be
called a prayerful attitude by the theist traditions of the West.

The Muslim mystic Junayd, who died in the early 10th century, expressed a direct sense of the love of God: "Even if Your sublime grandeur has kept You inaccessible to my eye's glance, loving ecstasy has caused me to feel Your touch within me." Junayd's contemporary Zahra prayed to Allah (with some boldness for her time) as "my ultimate desire, my Friend." And Rabi'a al-'Adawiyya, a century earlier, boldly addressed God in a loving prayer:

> I love You with two loves—a selfish love and a love that You are worthy of. As for the selfish love, it is that I think of You to the exclusion of everything else. As for the love that you are worthy of, ah!—that I no longer see any creature, but I see only You!

The Language of Love

"The madness of lust, licensed by human shamelessness, took me completely under its scepter, and I clutched it with both hands," wrote Saint Augustine of his wild youth, when he had lovers and mistresses and (at seventeen) sired an illegitimate son. "You were always present to aid me," he said to God in his *Confessions*, "so that I might seek after pleasure that was free from disgust. But I was left a desert, uncultivated for You, O God, Who are the one true and good Lord of that field which is my heart."

For obvious reasons, the metaphor of human love had always been a complicated matter in the language of prayer—until Augustine made it the major theme of the *Confessions*. Passionate hedonist that he had been, he retained his fiery style after his conversion, but his energies found a new focus in his faith. From the time of his baptism at thirty-two until his death at seventy-six, he wrote and dictated a vast library of scholarly works, memoirs, poems and letters; bishop and guardian of orthodoxy, he employed the method of Platonic philosophy to defend Christian faith. *Confessions* and *The City of God* are among the great standard works of late classical literature, and Augustine's brilliance as an apologist influenced almost every medieval thinker of consequence. (So, less fortunately, did Augustine's lingering Manichaeism, a deviant Christian sectarianism that was deeply suspicious of the world of matter and the flesh.)

His *Confessions*, completed about the year 400, were composed in the form of a long prayer to God: the text is nothing short of a love letter and virtually establishes a new form of prayer as an explicit act of love.

> Too late have I loved You, O Beauty so ancient and so new—too late have I loved you! Behold, You were within me, while I was outside: it was there that I sought You and, a deformed creature, I rushed headlong upon these things of beauty which You made. You were with me, but I was not with You. You called to me, You cried out and You shattered my deafness. You blazed forth with light and have shone upon me. . . . When I cling to You with my whole being, my life will be life indeed, filled wholly with You.

Good Platonist that he was, Augustine saw everything in creation as if it were a prism refracting the attributes of God, Whom he then describes in terms of His divine effect on the soul, and by means of metaphors that are remarkably sensual:

> Not with doubtful but with sure knowledge do I love You, O Lord. By Your word you have transfixed my heart, and I have loved you. Heaven and earth and all things in them say to me that I should love You.
>
> What is it, then, that I love when I love You? Not bodily beauty, and not temporal glory, not the clear shining light,

lovely as it is to our eyes, not the sweet melodies of songs, not the soft smell of flowers and perfumes, not limbs for the body's embrace—not these do I love when I love my God.

And yet I do love a kind of light, a kind of voice, a kind of odor, a kind of food, a kind of embrace when I love my God: a light, voice, odor, food, embrace for the man within me, where I am bathed in a light no place can contain, where a voice is heard that no passage of time can ever take away, where a fragrance abounds that no gust of wind can disperse, where there is a food that no eating can lessen—and where there is an embrace that no fulfillment can bring to an end. This is what I love when I love my God.

Augustine's contemporary, John Chrysostom, was unwillingly drafted to be patriarch of Constantinople in 398, in which post he exposed corruption among both clergy and empire and fell afoul of just about everyone—such was his moral outrage at the laxity of his time and its blithe dismissal of the needs of the poor. Attention to their needs and those of the sick, he insisted, was proof that one's prayer was indeed a "loving conversation with God—something that comes from the heart, not limited to set hours or minutes, but night and day, it is a continuous activity." Homilies like this, which linked prayer to action, won Chrysostom few friends: he was twice sent away from Constantinople on orders of the empress Eudoxia. Finally, after being forced into exile on foot during severe weather, he succumbed to exposure, exhaustion and starvation at the age of sixty.

ॐ

So began the tradition of the metaphor of love to describe the deepest affect of prayer. The biblical injunction to the Hebrews to love God with all one's heart, mind, soul and strength had to do with covenant fidelity; the psalmist sang of love as gratitude; the evangelists and letter writers of the early Christian communities regarded love as a divinely established bond of grace, and they hesitated to use categories of love that had been intellectualized by Greek philosophers. Augustine, whose soul had perhaps more Hellenistic than Hebrew spirit, was attempting something quite different: centuries before the language of courtly love and long before the rhapsodies of the medieval and Reformation mystics, he spoke and wrote frankly that God fell in love with him, and he with God. In subsequent ages the idea of "falling in love with God" would at times lead to a hyperemotionalism that often derived from psychosexual factors, even in the writings of saints and mystics. But the occasional excesses of self-indulgence need not force us to abandon the conviction that love is made clear in generosity and selfless service—God's generosity and service, and ours.

᠅

Six centuries after Augustine, another restless youth experienced a conversion to seriousness of purpose; this led him to priestly duties in his native Burgundy and, in 1093, to the archbishopric of Canterbury, where he was much admired by William the Conqueror. Saint Anselm, as he is known, continued the Augustinian tradition of prayer as a response of love, but his style is his own. Author of some of the profoundest theological treatises of the High Middle Ages, he also wrote intensely intimate meditations and prayers in rhymed prose—all of them inspired by his own awareness of God in silence.

"I have written," he said of his *Monologion* or soliloquy before the divine presence, "from the point of view of someone trying to raise his mind to the contemplation of God." He advised those who would pray to "enter the inner chamber of your soul, shut out everything except God, and seek him." And then they might pray:

O Lord my God, teach my heart where and how to seek You, where and how to find You. You are everywhere, so You must be here. You have created and re-created me, and all the good I have comes from You, and still I do not know You. . . . Let me seek You by desiring You, and desire You by seeking You. Let me find You by loving You, and love You in finding You.

꙾

"By love, God may be caught and held—but by thinking, never," according to *The Cloud of Unknowing*, whose anonymous author urged prayer as the means to authentic love of God: abandoning ourselves to His mercy is itself an act of loving trust. Two centuries later, Teresa of Ávila was quite succinct: "The important thing is not to think much, but to love much. Perhaps we do not know what love is, but love consists not in the extent of our own happiness, but in the firmness of our determination to please God in everything. Do not imagine that the important thing is never to be thinking of anything else and that if your mind becomes slightly distracted, all is lost."*

John Wesley, founder of Methodism in the 18th century, was clear and direct about prayer: "Whether we think of or speak to God, whether we act or suffer for Him, all is prayer—provided that we have no other object than His love and the desire of pleasing Him. Prayer continues always in the desires of our hearts, even though our understanding be employed on outward things. If you are really full of love, your desire to please God and to do good is a continual prayer."

---

*Teresa's friend John of the Cross, in his *Spiritual Canticle* and *Living Flame of Love*, was far more poetic: his language of love is frankly baroque, and it often falls harshly on modern ears. Translations require more than mere language equivalence—a cultural commentary and a cool assessment of John's background are essential to avoid dismissing his rhapsodies as slightly feverish. But of their value in describing stages of spiritual development there can be no doubt.

Etty Hillesum

Prayer presupposes one's readiness to assume responsibilities, especially for those who suffer. The forms and means of this are many, and a few individuals in the modern world have conjoined a profound life of prayer to a heroic alliance with the disconsolate and oppressed in wholly remarkable ways.

A notable example of this fusion amid the horror of Nazi atrocities is the life, prayer and sacrifice of Etty Hillesum. Her story has only recently been told, partly through the discovery of eight handwritten notebooks she wrote in 1941 and 1942, and partly through eyewitnesses to her deeds, whose testimonies are still being documented. Esther (known as Etty) Hillesum was a Dutch Jew, born in January 1914, the daughter of a classical scholar and a Russian refugee. She received degrees in law and Slavonic languages and then undertook studies in psychology. Around the time of her twenty-seventh birthday, she met Julius Spier, who was fifty-three, a former student of C. G. Jung, and a charismatic psychologist. He became her mentor and her lover, a concurrence of roles that brought them at first a fiery passion and eventually (not least because he was married) a profoundly unsettling guilt.

That year, she began to keep diaries that chronicle her intellectual and spiritual development. Her first entry was made in January ("I am accomplished in bed"), which summarizes the most important element of her life that season—the aim of satisfying Spier with her sexual technique and youthful abandon.

But by May 1940 Holland had fallen to the Nazis. At first, Jews had only to register or be forcibly enrolled as hostile to the Reich. Denial of all civil rights soon followed, and then it was not long before more and more Dutch Jews were transported to Westbork, the last stop before Auschwitz. "Mortal fear in every fiber," Etty wrote on November 10, 1941. "Complete collapse. Lack of self-confidence. Aversion. Panic."

In July 1942 (just as twelve-year-old Anne Frank was beginning to keep her famous diary), Dutch Jews were being dragged off in ever greater numbers. "What they are after," Etty wrote of the persecutors, "is our total destruction. I work and continue to live with the same conviction, and I find life meaningful—yes, meaningful." The means for this shift in sensibility seems to have astonished even her: by this time, she has begun to think and write about God in intensely intimate terms. She had her own religious sensibility that (like Simone Weil's) cannot be accurately characterized as traditionally Jewish or Christian but is certainly firmly God-centered. She also broke off her affair with Spier and began to give herself completely to the care of her fellow Jews.

At the age of twenty-eight, Etty Hillesum had social and professional contacts that could have effected her escape from Holland. But she chose not to abandon those suffering the most appalling fear and facing almost certain death, and so she voluntarily went to Westbork. There, from August 1942 to September 1943, she worked in a hospital, tending the sick and bringing spiritual consolation to all she encountered.

Permitted to travel back and forth to Amsterdam, Etty obtained medicines and delivered messages to and from prisoners' families; each time she was offered escape, she refused. She also would neither despise nor kill Germans, insisting that she could not add to the cauldron of the world's hatred: "I see no alternative. Each of us must turn inward and destroy in ourselves all that we think we ought to destroy in others—and we ought to remember that every action of hate we add to this world makes it still more inhospitable." Her refusal to take vengeance, she added, "in no way implies the absence of moral indignation."

In September 1943, she, her parents and her brother were

shipped off to Auschwitz, where her death was reported on November 30. She was twenty-nine. A letter from a survivor describes Etty as she joined her fellow Jews in the crowded, dark train: "She walked lightly, bearing the burden of these her people, yet conveying an inner calm. She had not been deserted by her God." Another who was present observed that "she had a kind word for everyone—and then the shrill train whistle, and a thousand victims moved out."

Etty Hillesum's last diary entry indicates the distance and depth of her inner journey, from scholar to ardent mistress to one whose love of God impelled her to share the lot of the least fortunate: "We should be willing," she wrote, "to act as a balm for all wounds. This much I know: you have to forget your own worries for the sake of those you love. All the strength and love and faith in God one has must be there for everyone who chances to cross my path and who needs it. For that, I draw prayer around me like a dark protective wall, and I withdraw inside it as one might withdraw into a convent cell—and then I step outside again, calmer and stronger."

The aim of her prayer was simple: "so that something of God can enter, and something of love, too. . . . There is a deep well inside me, and in it God dwells. . . . There are those who pray with their eyes turned to heaven: they seek God outside themselves. And there are those like me, who bow their heads and bury their faces in their hands. I think perhaps we seek God inside." At the end, she was certain of her calling to be with the frightened and the imperiled: "All that is left to me is to yield myself up to God. Truly, my life is a long listening to myself, to others and to God. And if I say that I listen, it is really God Who listens inside me."

Shortly before her death, she hastily wrote a prayer in her notebook: "I feel a growing need to speak to You alone, God. I love people so terribly, because in every human being I love something of You. And I seek You everywhere in them and often do find something of You."

Intercession: Praying for Others

As Etty Hillesum and others in many different traditions discovered, the encounter with God in prayer opens a door to a new, unwalled world in which our association with humanity grows. Etty did not seek refuge from the common lot of suffering, nor did she believe that prayer meant pleasant thoughts and poetic feelings. She conquered dread with compassionate concern for others, and she was able to radiate God to them because something in her conveyed the sure sense that God would not finally abandon them.

This was possible because first of all she had prayed. A truly spiritual life must of course have specific times for silence and withdrawal, for solitary prayer, for spending time with the source and Ground of Being, with the living God. But if it is indeed a spiritual life that encounters God, the inner life can never be pursued in isolation from others: even cloistered contemplatives, and those confined by illness or age or imprisonment, are mysteriously present to one another and to God by virtue of the material unity of the universe. We live and die in solidarity and communion with one another, and so the whole tangle of this world is the concern of all who have known something of God in prayer.

Etty Hillesum's ancestor in faith, the great 12th-century Jewish philosopher Moses Maimonides, was appointed chief physician for his community in Egypt. He composed an oath for doctors that for centuries has borne his name; it is a highly refined example of the conjunction between work and the prayer of intercession:

May the love for my art actuate me at all times; may neither avarice nor miserliness, nor the thirst for glory or for a great reputation engage my mind, for the enemies of truth and philanthropy could easily deceive me and make me forgetful of my lofty aim of doing good to Your children. May I never see in a patient anything but a fellow creature in pain. . . . O God, You have appointed me to watch over the life and death of Your creatures. Here I am, ready for my vocation.

⌇

God enlivens each being; God is the principle uniting everything that is. When John Donne wrote that no man is an island, he was simply putting into poetic terms a datum of every religion in history. We cannot, therefore, think of ourselves in isolation, nor can we ignore others to pursue a rarefied inner life that takes no account of others, for such a narrowing of perspective leads ineluctably to suspicion, fear, a quest for power, distrust, greed and war.

Contrariwise, successful societies since primitive times have been characterized by a strong sense of solidarity: the family, the clan and the tribe are interrelated in every regard. The head of a family prays for the entire family; the family prays for the wider clan; the clan works and prays for the tribe and its chief (who is charged with praying for the recovery of the sick).

Ancient Hindu prayer is remarkable for imploring Agni, the god of fire, to protect every living being. Babylonians and Assyrians dedicated an entire rank of priesthood to entreat the gods on behalf of all people. In Euripides's play *Alcestis* (first performed in 438 B.C.), the title character, before dying, prays for her children to Hestia, goddess of the hearth and protector of domestic life.

The Hebrew people understood that their patriarchs stood as intercessors with God. Abraham and Moses prayed for deliverance from enemies ("O Lord, do not bring disaster on Your people"), and Solomon prayed for the holiness of the people when the temple was dedicated ("Forgive the sin of Your people Israel, and bring them again to the land You have given to their ancestors").

Just so, early Christians remembered beleaguered apostles in prayer ("While Peter was kept in prison, the church prayed fervently to God for him"), and prayed for those who were ill ("Call for the elders and have them pray over the sick"). The quintessential Christian prayer of intercession takes its cue from Jesus on the cross, praying to God for his own executioners. That entreaty was repeated by the first martyr, Stephen, who prayed for those taking up stones to kill him. At the root and ground of intercession is faith in the Risen Christ, the one, true and final high priest who is "ever living, to intercede for all those who approach God."

༈

As Jesus prayed for the entire world on the eve of his execution and taught his followers to pray even for those who are considered enemies, so the most notable characteristic of early Christianity was a sense of communion, of interdependence. Praying for others became the natural and even the logical corollary of praying with others. To be near God, with God, is to know that we live in God with everything that lives—in God we *all* live and move and have our being. Hence we are linked, in our spiritual poverty, our darkness and our pain (of whatever category), to the even greater enormity of the world's total burden and open wound of suffering.

There was nothing like a single bishopric of primacy (much less a papacy) in the early Christian Church, and hence no monarchical leader in any community. But the writings of two significant early "fathers"—the bishops Clement of Rome and Ignatius of Antioch—were received with enormous respect.

About the year 96, Clement (in a position of honor and service to the Church at Rome) wrote a letter to the community at Corinth. In it, he included a prayer of intercession the faithful might recite, asking God to

> deliver the afflicted, pity the lowly, raise the fallen, reveal Yourself to the needy, heal the sick and bring home Your wandering people. Feed the hungry, ransom the captive, support the weak, comfort the faint-hearted. Let all the nations of the earth know that You alone are God, that Jesus Christ is Your child, and that we are Your people and the sheep of Your pasture.

In the same spirit, Ignatius of Antioch urged Christians: "Regarding the rest of mankind, you should pray for them unceasingly . . . that repentance may enable them to find their way to God."

But the early Christians knew that intercession was not mere benevolence or noble intentions for the common good: intercession was a way of life, of working with and for others, and as such it was a direct consequence of faith in the Incarnation. God discloses Himself in Jesus of Nazareth (the man who lived for others) and through our active cooperation remains at work in the world. Hence, those who pray intercede—they work, intervene and join in prayer with everyone in the world.

Throughout history, intercessory prayer has been based on the universal intuition that (as Tennyson put it poetically)

> More things are wrought by prayer
> Than this world dreams of. Wherefore, let thy voice
> Rise like a fountain for me night and day.
> For what are men better than sheep or goats
> That nourish a blind life within the brain,

If, knowing God, they lift not hands of prayer
Both for themselves and those who call them friend?
For so the whole round earth is every way
Bound by gold chains about the feet of God.

To pray for others is a matter of presence, of intention and of collaboration. Perhaps it is worth adding, at this point, that when others recommend themselves to our prayers, we take them deeply to heart at that moment, and when we are present to God in prayer, they are with us, too.

Prayer for and to the Dead

Praying for those no longer living is among the most ancient forms of prayer, as is evident from the Egyptian *Book of the Dead* and the witness of the ancient Near East. It is linked not only to social and familial continuity, but also to belief in a life beyond this world and to the notion that the dead are somehow in process of reaching a final state of being. African tribal rituals, for example, often included prayers to the dead:

O good and innocent dead, hear us: attend to us, you guiding ancestors, for you are neither blind nor deaf to this life we live. You did yourselves once share it. Help us, then, for the sake of our devotion, and for our good.

As for intercessory prayer on behalf of the dead: perhaps we do not pray so much *for* the dead as we pray that we may maintain a relationship with those who have preceded us. We find them in God, we meet them in prayer, for those we knew and loved are not apart or remote but rather alive in God—and hence not separated from us. That may be the deepest meaning of the tradition of prayer to the saints of old. Our honor toward them, our communion with them in the reality of the Spirit, our meditation on their example and our friendship with them can only deepen the life of faith and affirm our relationship to everything that is in God.

This sort of veneration is very different from the unfortunate deviation that occurred in the Middle Ages, when emphasis on Christ as eternal judge brought the saints (and especially Jesus' mother, Mary) to the foreground of faith and invoked them as intercessors, more accessible to us poor mortals than God is, and "more human" than Jesus. Against this, biblical faith has always claimed that there is "one mediator between God and humankind—Christ Jesus, himself human." But there is perhaps a valuable balance to maintain—the saints, like all those we loved in this life, are part of our religious inheritance. It is not, therefore, inappropriate to honor them, for they live in God.

In this spirit, it is important to understand that the cult of the mother of Jesus was not only a result of the era of courtly love: it was also very much a healthy counterstatement to the cruelty toward and exploitation of women. The gentleness and maternal qualities of God took form in and remain reflected in the person of Mary and in the iconography that honors her and, through her, the motherhood of God. Perhaps it was at least partly in this belief that medieval English bishops enjoined the *Ave Maria* on all Christians.*

*The first part of the venerable prayer known as the "Hail, Mary" is drawn from the gospel of Luke 1, verses 28 and 42; the second part is a simple invocation for the help of Mary, mother of Jesus, during one's own life and at the time of death. But this prayer must not be considered as distinct from a plea to God Himself. Friendship and advocacy with those who have preceded us, and with those once particularly close to the event of Jesus Christ, are part of the legacy of faith, but God alone is the source and giver of meaning, and He alone bestows eternal life.

Our connection with those who have died can be as real as with those who are alive—sometimes even more real, in fact. This relationship is not a poetic metaphor or a reverie about our ancestors and their benevolent influence on us. It is, rather, a profound sharing in the life of God, which is always of the present. Encountering God means meeting who and what are always present in Him. And the bond of love conjoining all who are created by God includes not only the formally canonized saints or the heroes of old, but all of our ancestors and old friends; all are gathered in the eternal love of God. It is always God Who hears our prayers—for the dead, to the saints, for the living.

৵

"Love is a direction—and not a state of the soul," wrote Simone Weil. Our need to love and be loved, to be accepted, our capacity to reach out to others—all of these derive from our fundamental orientation to God, the source from Whom all love becomes possible. Our prayer of adoration, then, is our response to Him; our reliance on intercession brings us into communion.

CHAPTER ELEVEN

Prayer as Transformation

If anything at all can be said about true prayer, it is this:

Prayer is a dangerous business. Pursued seriously (can it be otherwise?), it will modify the way we think, act, feel, deal with others, work in the world, behold the universe. It will change us in ways we can never have imagined; it will alter our perspective and transfigure our lives. More than an aesthetic vision and deeper than a moral stance, prayer—by virtue of opening ourselves to God—produces a transformation that will somehow be perceived by others. When we really pray, our interior life takes precedence over the exterior. We are no less active, perhaps, but our activities are more seriously assessed, and our real home, we come to recognize, is within. And prayer requires refreshment and renewal, and a loving attention to the gravity of what we are doing.

Contrary to those who market religion as the pursuit of spiritual consolation, or a pleasant way to live—which is what Karl Marx meant by religion as an opiate—the encounter with God is not a comforting addition to our lifestyle, like a new and easier diet or a five-minute regimen of aerobic exercise. Nor is it a neat little mental trick by which we can block out the difficulties of life in the world, or a convenient way to justify withdrawing from the challenges and disorder and suffering around and within us.

Our habit of openness to God is not a poetic attitude or a heartening program of good thinking that provides emotional satisfaction, improves our self-esteem and makes us feel particularly good about ourselves. If we expect that of prayer, we will give it up in short order. One of the means by which we can in fact know that we are on the right path when we pray is a sense of growing dissatisfaction with what humanity has done in and to the world. This is a meaning of the "night of the senses" described by John of the Cross: when the invisible light of God shines on the mind, a paradoxical darkness overtakes one's normal, easy enjoyment of material pleasures. We do not perceive them as bad—they simply no longer satisfy.

The life of the spirit, the direction of ourselves toward God, is something like taking a deep breath and leaping into waters whose depths we cannot plumb, where we risk exposure to an unknown temperature. We entrust ourselves to the power of change, to transformation at the core of our being. This usually occurs in a long, slow process—by small steps, of which we are mostly unaware. But the change does occur, the transformation happens. Truthfulness becomes something we do as well as speak; courtesy, kindness and gentleness are more evident; courage and honor characterize our response to the events of life.

❧

"Iron sharpens iron," runs the ancient biblical proverb, "and friend shapes friend." In other words, my friendship with another person changes me, just as a piece of iron changes the shape of another piece of iron if I strike them, one against another. And if God is the ultimate friend, then we cannot help but take on a new shape under His influence over the course of time. A gradual, increasingly clarifying light will shine on the tangled fabric of our lives, and eventually we will see a hitherto unexpected pattern. The Changeless One reveals meaning, and we are changed.

This transformation is often most evident at key moments in life. If we cast the net of memory back over our histories, we can identify certain events or occurrences whose significance cannot be discounted. An unexpected meeting with someone who became important in my life, a path suddenly disclosed to me, a way blocked, the job I took, the place to or from which I moved, a relationship formed or broken, an illness contracted, an awareness of aging: does it not make sense to perceive a hidden, providential Power at work in circumstances out of my control or even my desire, moving me toward a certain direction in life and (more gently than iron) shaping me and leading me toward a certain meaning I could not anticipate?

It is of course possible to assert that everything that happens to us is the product of mere chance or coincidence or luck, but this reduces the significance of history and of people in our lives. After all, the slow process of humanization has been responsible for so much goodness, art, heroism, sacrifice and sheer beauty in the world. If we cannot see those and perceive them developing, and if we consider everything as a jumble of chaos without pattern or meaning, then we are perhaps doomed to regard the world and everything in it as quite negligible, and there is no reason to encourage precisely those human qualities that make the world a better place. How long can we survive with such a negating, even cynical turn of mind?

No, prayer—from the primitives through the progressive Judeo-Christian revelation to those who practice *zazen* today—is about a transformation of the self because of a relationship that may fairly be described in human terms. As we have seen, prayer is not about achieving functional results, about having wishes granted by a remote Being. It is about becoming more and more alert to the One Who sustains us in love and awakens us each day to the reality of His presence, if only we give Him a chance; how awake we are depends on us. As one contemporary spiritual writer has asked, "What is the point of complaining that God is absent if it is we who are absent from God, and from ourselves, by our lack of awareness?" In light of this cogent question, we come to understand that prayer must always grow and find new expression.

And just how are we changed? Others will notice a certain patience and calm clarity in us, a shift in our values, a closer attention span, a lightening of anxieties, an awareness of people's needs and a greater compassion for them, an ability to live in the present and to respond intuitively to what cannot be predicted. Most of all, perhaps, we come to know the depths of ourselves better—as works in progress, not as fixed and formed once and for all. In effect, we gradually become what we love, what we value, what occupies our minds.

We should not, however, be tempted to rate or grade ourselves on our performance. "Don't waste time during prayer trying to understand exactly what you are doing or how you are praying," Francis de Sales wrote to the devout Madame de Granieu, daughter of a royal counselor. "The best prayer is that which keeps us so occupied with God that we don't think about ourselves or about what we are doing. In short, we must go to prayer simply, in good faith, and artlessly, wanting to be close to God. True love has scarcely any method."

Living Buddhism and Silent Transformation

Gyomay Kubose, a Buddhist monk residing and teaching in the United States, distinguishes between living and dead Buddhism: the latter describes mere academic knowledge, the former is a spirit comprehended by both heart and body. While acknowledging that there is no prayer as such in classical Buddhism, Kubose has stressed that the techniques of Eastern meditation may effect a stillness that may indeed be helpful for Western, theo-centric meditation and prayer. (The equivalent richness that Western experience has to offer the East is another matter and should not be ignored.)

Those Eastern techniques, much taught worldwide by the Ti-betan Buddhist Sogyal Rinpoche, involve not methods them-selves but attitudes. Rinpoche has emphasized, for example, the necessity of the stillness of the body in sitting meditation, of allowing thoughts to come and go without giving them much regard. This effort at inner focus is at once a discipline and a clearing, so that the mind may be transformed to stillness and be the repository of a universal compassion. "Just remain quietly until you are a little open and able to connect with your heart essence."

The gradual effect of this practice is a calm mind and a clari-fied perception. "Then, whatever you do, you are present, right there—as in the famous Zen master's saying, 'When I eat, I eat; when I sleep, I sleep.' Whatever you do, you are fully present in the act. Even washing the dishes, if it is done well, can be very energizing, freeing, cleansing. You are more peaceful, so you are more you."

This instruction may seem simple to the point of simple-mindedness, but it is a very real path to spiritual transformation. Zen Buddhist practice insists that if one perseveres, without be-coming perturbed by emotions, one will achieve an inner stabil-ity, and the real depth of meditation will take effect. "Your attitude begins to change, and you are transformed. You do not hold on to things as solidly as before, or grasp at them so strongly."

Hence, according to Sogyal Rinpoche, crises can be handled better, and one can even laugh at difficulties a bit, since there is more space between them and oneself. "Things become less solid, slightly ridiculous, and you become more lighthearted."

At this point, we can observe a link to the methods formulated by Ignatius of Loyola five centuries ago—a connection that may at first seem contradictory, since his *Spiritual Exercises* are modeled on highly structured forms encouraging the visual imagination of events in the life of Christ, the construction of conscious thoughts and the focus on verbal inner dialogue about specific "things."

"But what nourishes the soul," as one noted interpreter of Ignatius has found, "is not the multiplication of words but the inner experience of things" as they are in themselves—whether pious reflections or simply being in the presence of God.

Focus, Discipline and a Change of Heart

"Do not let me be scattered about in pieces, my God," prayed Teresa of Ávila, "with each part of me seeming to go off on its own!" Work brought its distractions, and the discipline of focus did not come easily to her.

No matter how many years we have been at it, prayer is not an easy enterprise. It is laced with distractions, darkness and dryness, and very often we come to it as to an irksome duty; the fact that we sometimes consider it a task only reveals how much more progress we have to make. If the few minutes I spend in deliberate converse with God is thought of as a burden or annoying exercise, what then?

We are immersed in the things of this world, usually to the neglect of inner discipline; as Wordsworth wrote:

> The world is too much with us . . .
> Getting and spending, we lay waste our powers . . .
> We have given our hearts away . . .
> For this, for everything, we are out of tune.

How do we prevent too much of the world from determining our every moment? How do we get our hearts back and retune ourselves? In other words, how can the pursuit of inner discipline begin and sustain the daily process of transformation by which (we are assured) real serenity and real joy may be known? And just what is meant by discipline?

The traditions of both East and West stress the centrality of discipline in the spiritual journey, but too often discipline is regarded as synonymous with certain exercises of asceticism, of denials, of physical discomforts, fastings and rigorous penances. This can be dangerous thinking, for such practices can put the attention where it ought not to be: on the self, and on achieving some sort of laudatory standard, as if we were committed to a kind of spiritual Olympics.

For those in the Christian tradition, for example, this unfortunate equation of discipline with penitential, ascetical exercises has been based on an inaccurate reading of an important verse in the New Testament: "Repent, for the kingdom of heaven is at hand." The original Greek of the first word in the verse is μετανοίετε (metanoiete), which means literally a change of mind and heart: not physical mortification, but something deeper. The call to become Jesus' disciple—a word that means a learner—was not a summons to abandon an easy life, for those who responded had nothing like that. The summons was, rather, to a change of perspective, to conversion as a turning away from prejudices and preconceptions. One begins to change one's life, to learn anew, precisely because the action of God in the world is here.

The practice of discipline, then, means becoming a disciple— a learner, one who attends, and answering this summons calls for alertness, docility and a certain pliant, malleable manner before God. To those who carry heavy burdens of whatever sort, Jesus of Nazareth extends an invitation by sustaining and extending the metaphor of one who is burdened: "Take my yoke upon you, and learn from me—for I am gentle and humble of heart, and you will find rest for your souls. For my yoke is easy, and my burden is light."

The paradox—how can a yoke be easy?—disappears when we understand that the yoke is not only the device that enables animals to pull a plow: the word "yoke" (in Scripture, ζυγός— zugos) also means a bond of partnership. (In *The Merchant of Venice*, Shakespeare wrote of "companions . . . whose souls do bear an equal yoke of love.") It is interesting to consider that a single Indo-European stem gave us both the Old English root of "yoke" and the Sanskrit root of "yoga"—a word that, in Hinduism, refers not primarily to an exercise but to union with God. My acceptance of the need for discipline, then, involves withdrawal from excessive absorption in the things of the world, to be sure; but it is most of all about learning the pattern of a new life, of a daily turning (conversion) unto God.

Obviously a primary element in this discipline is simply making time to come deliberately and consciously into God's presence, which is where we live. Times and places simply have to be reserved for the effort of prayer. Sometimes, we have to be quite creative in carving out a hospitable environment, but the universal witness is that the time we give to God bestows precisely the freedom to be transformed.

This element of discipline is, at its heart, about attention (heeding and regarding) and attentiveness (listening). Peter Forsyth, the outstanding figure of early 20th-century English Congregationalism, believed the paradox that we pray freely only when we force ourselves to pray: "The great liberty begins in necessity." We ought not to say, "I cannot pray, I am not in the mood." Instead, we ought to pray until we *are* in the mood, for I not only learn to pray by praying—I learn to *want* to pray by praying. And that demands discipline.

༂

While Forsyth was preaching in central London, Austin Farrer was teaching at Oxford. He set forth, in a memorable sermon at the university, the necessity of a clarifying discipline en route to the transforming effect of prayer. To deepen the quality of our prayer, it must become more and more a habit, which may be encouraged by forming the simple resolution to pray. "Not like the absurd resolutions of New Year's Day," he added, "not like resolutions for the next twelve months, but resolutions for the next twelve hours. Make them few enough to be practicable . . . and if you break them, repeat and renew them. 'What does God ask of me?' is a part of every sincere prayer."

Farrer died in 1968, just as the catchwords of self-fulfillment were emerging into popularity. But prayer, he advised, was not about attending to self-improvement, or rating ourselves on the level of our decent conduct or of enjoying emotional forms of worship. It is rather about fidelity—the habitual effort to see things as God sees them, for what they are, and without stopping at merely weighing their usefulness to us. That principle, of course, is at the heart of authentic contemplation, and with this aim of seeing things "for what they are," every Buddhist would concur.

Austin Farrer's notions about the attention necessary for the disciplines of prayer were very like those of John Henry Newman, the brilliant Anglican scholar who became Roman Catholic and a cardinal and whose many important writings were so influential on (among other groups and events) the debates of the first Vatican Council in 1870. "Is it an easy thing to pray?" Newman asked. "It *is* easy to wait for a rush of feelings . . . but it is not easy at all to be in the habit day after day and hour after hour, in all frames of mind, and under all outward circumstances."

ॐ

No habit is formed at once, after all, a fact to which English divines of the 19th and early 20th centuries seem to have been particularly sensitive—perhaps because life in Victorian and Edwardian times was characterized by a clash between polite religion and true faith; and because traditional preachers, emphasizing moral fitness, cried out so often about immoral habits. But in the case of the best English preachers, for perhaps the first time since Aquinas in the 13th century, habit was now discussed as a manner of being, not merely a repeated routine.

As we form the habit of prayer, Newman wrote, our entire lives are enveloped in its spirit: "we shall see God in all things and can be said almost literally to pray without ceasing." Newman added that if prayer is to transform us, it must have form, structure, order and rhythm—not a slavish adherence to forms or structures others have established, but to those that emerge from the motions of the Spirit within. This calls for a constant state of alertness.

Forsyth, Farrer, Newman and their company were much in the spirit of that extraordinary French advocate of the poor, Vincent de Paul, whose prayer derived from his complete dedication to the sick and the disenfranchised. "What do you do when you pray?" de Paul once asked a young woman

"Father," she replied, "I listen to God."

"You could not do better—only would it not be more correct to say that you listen *for* God? You put yourself in His presence, and you take up an attitude of devout attention. That is all you can do."

ॐ

That life is transformed by prayer is a theme sounded throughout Judeo-Christian history. The Northumbrian monk Bede—

the foremost scholar from Anglo-Saxon England, an exegete, historian and polymath—remarked that "prayer as a whole consists not only in the words by which we invoke the divine mercy, but also in all the things which we do by the devotion of faith. For how could anyone invoke the Lord with words in every hour and moment without a break? No, we pray without ceasing when we perform those works which commend us to our Maker." This spirit was later formulated in the Anglican Book of Common Prayer, in a plea first written for private recitation: "Grant that by Your holy inspiration I may think those things that are good, and then by Your merciful guidance may perform them."

By the time of the late Middle Ages, the connection between prayer and the transformation of one's life had become all but diluted: the monastic type of prayer was so much the standard that those working in the world were considered to be hanging on to spirituality by sheer force of dogged will. Later, Caussade's simplicity countered this unfortunate development, as did the author of *The Practice of the Presence of God*, who was aware of God "in the bustle of my kitchen, where sometimes several people are asking me for different things at the same time."

In the Baha'i branch of Shi'ite Islam, which took its present form in 19th-century Iran, one finds considerable emphasis on prayer as the essential ingredient in a transformed life: "Prayer and meditation are very important factors in deepening the spiritual life of the individual," wrote Shoghi Effendi, a teacher and missionary, in 1944. "But with them must go also action and example, as there are the tangible results of the former." This is consistent with the foundation of Baha'i: "Words without love mean nothing."

Life as Process: Prayer as Transfiguration

To assert that a life of prayer (like faith) is always in process may be to state the obvious, but it is helpful to outline three stages of this development and their attendant experiences. These are not stages through which we pass and to which we never return: to the contrary, they may occur now and again and in no specific order in the lives of all who take steps to find a deeper life.

Primary prayer, with which we are here concerned, is based on our personal, immediate experience of God in silence—an experience to which we long to return. At this point in the process, there is an element of wonder and awe, of a mystery that enlarges one's capacities and transforms one's outlook. In primary prayer, one begins to see the world through a different lens. This prayer is dynamic—it invests life with a fresh meaning and alters our behavior toward others.

Another corollary of primary prayer is that it has a social outreach: one's sense of interdependence increases, along with the conviction that a truly good life must, in some way, involve a concern for the welfare of others. The development of primary prayer does not begin with moral injunctions as a path to prayer, but the reverse: one begins with the reality of God and one's connection to Him, and laws and moral standards follow quite naturally. Living a prayerful life, we do not have to be warned not to hurt or harm a loved one; love creates the atmosphere in which those diminishments are avoided at all cost.

One of the subtler results of primary prayer will be a clearer knowledge of the true self, also a work in progress. "Our greatest protection in this life is self-knowledge, so that we do not become enslaved to delusion and end up trying to defend a person who does not exist. This is what happens to those who do not scrutinize themselves."

So wrote Gregory of Nyssa in the 4th century, long before there was transpersonal psychology or any glorification of self-esteem. This sympathetic man was born in what is now Turkey, was married, ordained and appointed a bishop. His writings fill many dozens of volumes, and he was much prized as a preacher. Within the space of a year, his beloved brother (Basil the Great) and his sister (Macrina) died, pitching Gregory into a profound darkness; from this, there emerged one of the richest spiritualities in the first centuries of Christianity.

For Gregory, we meet God not as an object to be understood, but as a mystery to love and in Whom we are enfolded. Those who do not pray, he continued, "look at themselves, and what they see is strength, beauty, reputation, political power, an abundance of material possessions, status, self-importance, bodily stature, a graceful appearance and so forth—and they think this is the sum of who they are!" Such people ignore the inner life and leave it, as Gregory put it, "unguarded—and how can a person protect what he does not know? The most secure protection is to know ourselves: each of us must do so—know ourselves as we are, and learn to distinguish ourselves from what we are not."

A secondary kind of prayer is a mere remnant, vaguely recalled, of what was once primary—like the memory of a lost love. And a third degree or stage is prayer as only a theoretical conviction or an aesthetic occupation, taken up simply in imitation of someone else (even our former selves) for reasons that have little to do with God and thus produce shallow results.

Thus prayer shows us more and more who we are; it enables the process of self-knowledge to continue, for we come to see ourselves, step by little step, in God's perspective. At this point, we may be able to understand, with greater clarity and psychological health than ever, precisely what is meant by sin. Quite apart from deliberate acts that alienate us from God and humanity, sin is really a condition of need, of our failure in the one necessary relationship. Our sinfulness, in other words, is not so much a matter of what we have done as it is of what we leave undone, what we have missed. "He passes by me, but I do not see Him," laments poor Job, all too aware of his own spiritual myopia. "He moves on, but I do not perceive Him." The biblical sense of sin in large measure concerns this profound awareness of human insufficiency.

Primitive people knew something of this. The Ewe tribe, for example, threw a bundle of twigs, representing sins and offenses, into the air, while saying words they hoped to hear back from the deity addressed: "All your faults are forgiven." Hinduism shares this sense ("Varuna is merciful even to him who sins"); Zen presumes the fragile and undisciplined vision of every human; Buddhism requires monks to confess sins publicly twice monthly; and awareness and acknowledgment of one's sin—of how one has failed and of how far one has to go—is fundamental to Judaism and Christianity. One has only to think of Yom Kippur, the annual solemn day of atonement for sin; to the motif of humility and pardon in the Psalms and in the gospels; and to the vast literature of confession by saints and mystics (most notably, of course, the autobiography of Saint Augustine).

A transformed and transfigured life begins with the forthright acknowledgment of one's imperfection and dependence—a recognition that virtually necessitates prayer, as Martin Luther knew. "Behold, Lord, an empty vessel that needs to be filled," he prayed.

My Lord, I am cold in love; warm me and make me fervent, that my love may go out to my neighbor. I do not have a strong and firm faith; at times, I doubt and am unable to trust You completely. With me there is an abundance of sin; in You is the fullness of righteousness. Therefore, I shall remain

with You, from Whom I may receive but to Whom I can give
nothing.

In the same spirit, the English writer William Law, who published *A Serious Call to a Devout and Holy Life* in 1728, saw a
logical development from growth in faith to awareness of sin to
an inclination to prayer. Those who lead an earnest spiritual life,
according to Law, always keep certain questions in mind: "What
is the best thing for me to intend and drive at in all my actions?
What shall I do to make the most of human life? And what ways
shall I wish that I had taken, when I am leaving the world?"

In the English tradition, perhaps the healthiest model of balance between a sense of sin and serene confidence that God will
bring everything to a good end is found in the writing of Julian
of Norwich. Her spirit was well summarized in a 19th-century
prayer that asks God to "let the whole world feel and see that
things which were cast down are being raised up, that those
which had grown old are being made new, and that all things are
returning to perfection."

The final, saving transfiguration of all things, promised
throughout the New Testament and the major theme of its last
chapters, begins in time with the transformation effected by
prayer. To enter this process, as John Chapman wrote, "the natural thing to do is obviously to acquire the habit of looking up to
God, praying to Him, at *any* moment [his emphasis]." We wait
for the moment that compels us to pray—the moment when we
know we are being touched and greeted.

Waiting for God

"I wait for the Lord," sang the psalmist; "my soul waits, and in
His word I hope. My soul waits for the Lord more than those
who watch for the morning." What we wait for, we do not see, as

Saint Paul remarks when he takes up the theme in his letter to the Romans: "Who hopes for what is seen? But if we hope for what we do not see, we wait for it with patience."

As Paul Tillich observed in a memorable address, Scripture describes our lives in relation to God in terms of waiting—anxious waiting, for the psalmist; for Saint Paul, patient waiting: "Waiting means *not* having and having at the same time." We do not see, we do not know, we do not grasp, and as Tillich reminds us, "a religion in which that is forgotten replaces God by its own creation of an image of God."

Spiritually minded people (as they are often considered in our time) often do not wait for God, and are not on the alert for His coming—simply because they believe they already possess Him in doctrines, dogmas and traditional teachings. Scripture scholars often do not wait for God to manifest Himself in the everydayness of their lives—because they are confident that they possess Him, enclosed and defined within the pages of a sacred book. Devout churchgoers and churchmen often do not wait for God to come to them via the needs of others and the small things of their lives—because they think they possess Him in an institution. And even the most sensitive and humble believers may not wait for God to whisper—because they are certain that they possess God, neatly comprehended within the contours of their own private, prior experience and nothing else.

But the fact is that we do not possess God, we do not "have" God at all. "Much of the rebellion against Christianity," according to Tillich, "is due to the overt or veiled claim of the Christians to possess God." How, indeed, can God be possessed? God is not a thing that can be comprehended among other things—God is not, in other words, less than a human person, and we always have to wait for a human person. Even in the deepest relationships we know, "there is an element of *not* having and *not* knowing, and of waiting."

But that is not the whole story. Although waiting means not

having, it is nonetheless also a *kind* of having. We can only wait for something or someone if in some deep sense we already possess some part of it: the power of what we wait for is already effective within us. Hence those who wait in an ultimate sense are not very far from that for which they wait. Those who wait in absolute seriousness are already grasped by the reality for which they wait. Those who wait in patience have already received the power of that for which they wait, and those who wait passionately know the power of transformation.

When we say we possess God and know everything about Him we need to know for certain, we cannot be transformed, for we have reduced God to a small thing, an idol. "There is much of this idolatry among Christians," Tillich added. But if we know that we do not know God, and if we wait for Him to reveal Himself to us, then *we* are grasped and *we* are possessed by Him.

And in that patient waiting, in being known to and claimed by God, our final transformation proceeds even now as we live. We find that, more and more, we are able to live in the capacious light of God's presence. We find that, more and more, we turn to and yearn for God. With this come both a deeper compassion and a greater sense that all the world, and all who are in it, are bound together in a love we cannot define or describe. But we know that somehow nothing is more real than this.

CHAPTER TWELVE

Prayer as Silence

The Fractures of Noise

Although it is impossible to state so definitively, we may be living in the most clamorous era in world history. A cacophony of noise assaults us almost everywhere. The traffic in our cities becomes louder and more congested each year. Theaters and cinemas are overamplified, and loud recordings seem to fill every store and restaurant. Telephones, pagers and portable entertainment devices ring, hum and beep, filling the spaces of our lives. The roars, shrieks and rumbles of airplanes, sirens, motorcycles and massive trucks assail us, and people seem not to speak if they can shout.

On radio and television, there is the ceaseless blare of advertising, and even program content seems secondary to the volume, as the production of distracting noise very often seems to be the main concern—as are artificial effects to raise the noise level higher, presumably to attract attention. The media provide constant commentary on everything from politics to gossip, and there is endless chatter on the talk shows. But despite all the babble, there is hardly any authentic communication—much less, some feel, is there intelligent public discourse.

We have very little silence in our lives. Most of the time, only brief intervals separate the bursts of noise, whose effects on our nervous systems (and those of animals) are only beginning to be assessed. Noise pollution—the sheer ubiquity and volume

of sound—produces a verifiable somatic tension, with a conse-
quent dislocation of ourselves from ourselves. The result is that
contemporary society seems to have developed a collective case
of spiritual hypertension.

As if to keep pace with the beat, we move and are being
moved more swiftly every day. It is now taken for granted that
we ought to be doing something all the time, and doing it everywhere. Continually busy and harried people are presumed to be
successful, important people. And since travel by automobile
and airplane is no longer limited to the wealthy and privileged,
journeys that were once exceptional have now become routine,
with the result that many excursions seem pointless. Local geo-
graphic stability, often a nurturing factor in establishing and
deepening enduring relationships among families and friends, is
certainly no longer the norm; the mobile telephone, after all, can
keep us in constant contact (if not always in communication)
wherever we might relocate.

The Nature and Necessity of Silence

In the 19th century, the Danish philosopher and theologian
Søren Kierkegaard lamented that "the present state of the
world, the whole of life, is diseased. If I were a doctor and were
asked for my advice, I would reply: Create silence! Bring men to
silence. The Word of God cannot be heard in the noisy world of
today. Create silence."

But to create it is perhaps even more poignantly difficult today. Wayne Oates, the American author, psychiatrist and pastoral counselor, has written that silence "is not native to my
world, [and] more than likely, is a stranger to your world, too. If
you and I ever have silence in our noisy hearts, we are going to
have to grow to it. . . . We will do so on silence's terms for
growth—terms which are not yet our own."

Silence is not simply the absence of sound or noise or speech. It is creative and formative; from silence, we come to understand how effete and emaciated language can become if it loses its connection to its opposite. Conception occurs in hidden silence; time passes in silence. The moon and planets move in silence; the sun, stars and constellations shine silently, and night and dawn come the same way. The growth and blossom of trees and flowers cannot be heard. Playwrights and composers know the indispensable value of silent intervals; directors and actors rely on the dramatic value of pause. And in the depths of all categories of love, there is more silence than speech.

Silence is not the absence of anything; it is not nothingness, nor is it denial or deficiency. Silence is the fundamental and essential condition of everything that lives, grows and changes.

Our spiritual ancestors cherished silence, for it (as much as great events) was the carrier of extraordinary experience. In silence, the prophets and patriarchs knew something of the divine presence among them: "Be still, and know that I am God," the psalmist reiterates: "For God alone, my soul waits in silence." Just so, the prophet Zephaniah urges, "Be silent before the Lord God." And Habakkuk summarized the profound awe in which the Hebrew people approached worship: "The Lord is in His holy temple—let all the earth keep silence before Him." The words themselves almost demand a reverential stillness . . .

Recalling the primal, formative event of the original Passover, when God acted to liberate their forebears from bondage in Egypt, the framers of the Hebrew wisdom literature asserted how God revealed Himself: "While gentle silence enveloped all things, and night in its swift course was half gone, Your all-powerful Word leaped from heaven." And in one of the Bible's most powerful and dramatic scenes, Elijah goes to Mount Horeb to seek God:

Now there was a great wind—but the Lord was not in the wind. And after the wind, an earthquake—but the Lord was not in the earthquake. And after the earthquake, a fire—but the Lord was not in the fire. And after the fire, a sound of sheer silence.

The language of paradox was no accident: "a sound of sheer silence." And at that moment, Elijah wrapped his mantle about his face, aware that he was—in a sound of sheer silence—in the presence of God.

The basic language of God, as John of the Cross said, is silence. "And it is only in silence that we hear it."

At the end of the 1st century A.D., Ignatius of Antioch referred to "mysteries for shouting about, wrought in silence but manifest to us"—the word "mysteries" denoting not puzzles, but rather realities and events through which God discloses Himself. Good old Ignatius knew that the silence of God speaks more loudly and effectively than any human speech. The same notion is taken for granted by practitioners of Zen today, and by Hindu yogis. In silent solitude, the Buddha began his path of enlightenment; in stillness, Muhammad was summoned to be Allah's messenger. "I hold firmly to stillness," said Lao-tzu. "And so I do my utmost to attain emptiness. Returning to my roots is known as stillness."

The connection between silence and prayer is perhaps the great legacy of the Eastern tradition of Hesychasm—from the Greek word for quietude. In the broadest sense, Hesychast prayer is silent, imageless, even without concepts. The experience of Philoxenus, an Iraqi mystic and master of prayer, taught him that silence led to the simplest and deepest kind of prayer: "One should be secretly swallowed up in the spirit of God," he wrote around A.D. 500. A century later, Abraham of Nathpar added that "prayer does not reach fullness as a result of words—for it is not, after all, to a man you are praying, before whom you can repeat a well-composed speech. . . . No, God is silence."

A hundred years after Abraham of Nathpar, the Syrian monk Isaac of Nineveh taught that "the conversation of prayer comes about through stillness.... Every man who delights in uttering a multitude of words, even though he says admirable things, is empty within. If you love truth, be a lover of silence. In the beginning, we have to force ourselves to be quiet. But then there is born something that draws us to it." What is born, Isaac concludes, is "the silence of insight."

This is the goal of authentic private prayer in Judaism, wrote Maimonides: to attain *kavvanah*, the appropriate frame of mind for true devotion, the devout must situate themselves in the presence of God and put aside all worldly concerns. Without *kavvanah*, Maimonides insisted, prayer is like a body without a soul. "Occupy yourself with true prayer," runs an old Islamic text. "Do not be among the heedless—serve the Lord generously."

From these great antecedents, there is a straight line to the development of the so-called Jesus Prayer, the meditation encouraged by the medieval author of *The Cloud of Unknowing*, the contemporary American expositors of Centering Prayer, and the teaching of John Main, who died in 1982 and made the tradition of silence comprehensible for those living amid the commotion of modern life. Inner stillness and receptivity, according to Main, are not achieved in a day, but may be experienced within the quiet focus on a single word, taken as a mantra.

"To pray is to be attentive to the supreme reality of God's presence within our own hearts," Main wrote. "So we must learn to stop thinking about ourselves. We must learn simply to be in the presence of the One who is, and Who is the ground of our being and of all being." To that end, he recommended the slow, silent repetition of an ancient Christian prayer— *Marana thà* (Come, O Lord).

His colleague, Bede Griffiths, moved from London to India in

1955, thereafter devoting himself to uniting the silent contemplative experiences of Asian religion with those of the West. "In the silence," he wrote,

> I become aware of the presence of God, and I try to keep that awareness during the day. In a bus or a train or traveling by air, in work or study or talking and relating to others, I try to be aware of this presence in everyone and in everything—in the midst of noise and distractions of all sorts, as in times of peace and quiet, of joy and friendship, or prayer and silence. The presence is always there.

The aim is a spiritual state that permeates all of life—what theologians call an extensive kind of prayer. We cannot, of course, place God at the center of our attention at every moment, but God can be there, always at the margin and edge of our awareness, like the atmosphere in which we live; He is then the One to Whom our full attention regularly and spontaneously returns, and not always (or even primarily) in formulaic prayers. "We have learned a great lesson when we have learned that saying prayers is not praying," said the Victorian prelate John Charles Ryle, first Anglican bishop of Liverpool.

⁘

As loving and familiar as prayer should be, it is primarily a matter of absolute gravity, for it is the God of the universe and the Lord of all reality Whom we acknowledge and address: what else can we do but fall silent before Him? Our solitude with God must necessarily evoke from us a sense of awe, or the truth of prayer is itself in doubt. If our life in God is not grounded in awe, faith too easily becomes merely an upbeat form of ethical piety.

In 1926, Evelyn Underhill rightly warned that Western Christianity was effectively ignoring the necessity of adoration and awe. The result was a perilous drift toward "a religion which consciously or unconsciously keeps its eye on humanity rather than on Deity—which lays all the stress on service, and hardly any of the stress on awe. And that is a type of religion which in practice does not wear well." It is also a type of religion that will fail: as a sense of transcendence is diluted, so is faith.

In silence and in awe, we meet God. He Whom we cannot approach comes to us, even as He remains (in the graceful phrasing of Karl Rahner) "the incomprehensible mystery to be worshipped in silence." God addresses us not when we are babbling away about Him or even primarily to Him, but when we remain silent—not only when we refrain from speech, glances and gestures, but when we allow thoughts to become still and emotions calm. This kind of interior silence is real attentiveness—not heeding nothing, but being alert to the Presence that makes life and breath possible. Even in vocal or communal prayer, I must be rooted and grounded in a silent place with God. "It is by silence that the saints grew," according to a wise maxim.

Meditation and Contemplation

Can the mind be a part of this enterprise? Can we consciously effect an experience of God in silent awareness? That was certainly the stated belief of early Christians. "By settling the mind, I put myself in God's presence and act as though He were right there, looking at me," wrote Origen. "The thought of God—the God Who sees every stirring in our souls, even in the darkest parts of them—will certainly be beneficial." Just as thinking of a good person makes us want to imitate that person, so it is with God: "to think of Him will be more beneficial even than that, if we are convinced that He is present and hears us when we speak to Him." Meditation and contemplation are means to this end.

From the Middle Ages to the present, theologians, mystics,

saints and teachers have often differentiated various mental and spiritual conditions, classifying interior experiences, and categorizing and defining states of prayer. Today, however, many people understandably want to avoid the danger of this dry, academic systematizing of what cannot be subjected to technical examination in any case. In this regard, the West may benefit from the opposite approach of the East, which rejects anything like rational analysis and aims for transformation through the discipline of silence and withdrawal. But as is so often the case, a balance between the two may be in order.

The words "meditation" and "contemplation" are often used today without distinction. That said, there may be an advantage to maintaining the discrete particularities of each term.

Meditation involves the use of reason—thinking about the teachings of faith and about religious matters; reading and understanding Scripture or devotional books; or reflecting on God's action in history and in my life. In meditation, I make a great effort to assemble ideas and images, to gain fresh insights and to make resolutions based on my interior adherence to the meaning of teachings or prayers, hymns or creeds or texts. Both the Bible and the evolution of rabbinic thought indicate that meditation exercises a memory of the past, an understanding of the present and a will toward the future. As Jean Daniélou wrote, meditation is "a penetration into the meaning of things we already know—or rather things we think we know, but whose contents we are, in reality, far from having understood."

Meditation includes two forms or methods of prayer—vocal and mental. The first type uses traditional verbal formulas hallowed by time and general usage; the second type relies not on preexisting forms but finds words spontaneously. We might say that in vocal prayer, we try to mean what we say; in mental prayer, we try to say what we mean. Most people, perhaps, find that both methods are necessary: traditional prayers (the Psalms and the Lord's Prayer, for example) remind us of critical aspects of our life with God, and spontaneous personal prayers correspond to our own circumstances and to the specific ways God addresses us.

The Catholic devotion of the rosary is a good example of a form that combines both vocal and mental prayer. Based on the ancient monastic practice of repeating a prayer for a prescribed number of times, the rosary was devised in the 15th century for illiterate Christians who could not read the 150 Psalms—hence it took the form of reciting the well-known "Hail, Mary" 150 times, with intervals for the Lord's Prayer and a short verse of praise.* This was devised for much more than mere rote repetition, however: the recitation was intended to be combined with meditation on the principal events in the life of Jesus and his mother.

ॐ

There may come a time in a person's life, however, when meditation is no longer satisfying—or, indeed, a time when it becomes impossible. If this situation is not due to deliberate neglect or indifference—if, in fact, it accompanies a more profound yearning for God, then it is possible that one is summoned to contemplation. If meditation may be described as a turning from the things of the world in order to attend the things of God, then contemplation is a turning from the things of God to attend to God Himself.

That is the essential meaning of contemplation, in which the thinking and reasoning of meditation yield to a simple

*The rosary was developed by 15th-century Carthusian monks, whose piety influenced the Dominican friar Alain de la Roche. He died in 1475, after claiming that the devotion had been privately revealed to him by the founder of his Order, Saint Dominic (who died in 1221).

awareness of the presence of God, without depending on words or concepts, images or pious thoughts. Contemplation is not some rarefied psychological state I can either imagine, force or effect: it is the universal witness of all those who have known it that this awareness is a gift. The presence of God is not something I enter into or depart from at will—it is the very condition of my existence. In acknowledging that presence and turning to it, I realize it—that is, I make it real, living and effective. When that happens, nothing in life remains the same. All my perspective changes. I do not necessarily become good or better: it is simply a question of how I see, and how I permit myself to be seen.

"Be faithful about staying near God [and being] gently and quietly attentive to Him in your heart," Francis de Sales wrote to Jeanne de Chantal. "Be careful not to intellectualize, because this can be harmful—not only in general, but especially at prayer."

Francis knew his friend well, for Jeanne already had been moved to the simple, wordless prayer of contemplation. Whether or not we have fine thoughts or feelings matters little, she insisted: it is the slow action of God within us, unseen and unheard, that counts. She had known so much loss and grief in her life—the death of her husband, of children, the disruption of even her most devout plans—that she came to God completely empty and forlorn. And then she permitted Him to be her fullness. "Do nothing in God's presence," she advised a priest years later. "Be content simply to be there—yes, just sit there, convinced that this patience is itself a powerful prayer."

༄

Contemplation, then, is not a method of prayer we choose, as we can select various forms of meditation; contemplation is simple awareness, in stillness and silence, of God. In one respect, it is the abandonment of all ways; thus the desert of which the early mystics spoke and John of the Cross wrote is simply a metaphor describing the state of emptiness and openness we know when we give up reliance on ourselves and our formulas. In this aspect, contemplation has obvious parallels with the "nothingness" of Buddhist meditation.

The conviction of God becomes the presence of God; it is about receptivity of soul rather than activity of spirit. "For me, God is presence," said Karl Rahner. And so contemplation is a way of being, and as such it springs from the deepest levels of desire. Without it, religion and faith lose their essence, worship becomes empty formalism, meditation becomes only a comforting mental exercise and private prayer becomes mere babbling.

But it would be facile and even misleading to assert that contemplation is always wordless or imageless, or that once one experiences this state, one no longer needs meditation in the forms of vocal or mental prayer. An authentic spiritual life moves easily back and forth, up and down along the road, responsive to the divine activity, without deciding in advance just how and in what forms God will reveal Himself. People are nourished by different sorts of spiritual food: the important thing is to learn what nourishes *me*, what best harmonizes with *my* specific needs and spirit at this present moment, which is the present of God.

For this adventure, some degree of silence is necessary. That is the condition for us to be consoled by our contingency and delivered by our dependency: in silence, we know that we cannot heal our own wounds and supply our own needs—that for all our ideals and ambitions, we cannot provide ultimate meaning for our lives but only recognize it when it approaches us. In silence and darkness, we see and are seen. As the Bible insists from first page to last, we are where the Lord dwells. "The Lord is in His holy temple—let all the earth keep silence before Him."

Contemplation and meditation need each other. The former

can be volatile and requires ballast; the latter may become ponderous and self-referential. Along with the great primary witnesses to the events and experiences of the Judeo-Christian tradition, those most often cited in this book—Julian of Norwich and the author of *The Cloud of Unknowing*, Teresa of Ávila and John of the Cross, Lawrence of the Resurrection and Jean-Pierre de Caussade, Francis de Sales, Jeanne de Chantal and John Chapman—all agree that real prayer is always open, free, responsive, not directed or manipulated by the ego. God frees us from everything that is less than Himself—even from formulas, modes, methods and patterns of prayer. He will, in some way or other, have us for Himself, and will not permit anything, finally, to come between us and Him.

God in Our Everydayness

"We and our everydayness belong to Him," said Karl Rahner.

The story is told about a saint who was playing chess with a friend, while a group of companions were chatting nearby. The subject turned to what each would do if told he had to die within that very hour, and various statements were made: one would hurry home to his family; another would confirm that his property was in order; another would confess his sins; another would fall to his knees and pray devoutly.

When they turned to the saint for his reply, he said quite simply that he would continue his game of chess. There was a shocked silence until the holy man explained that he had built into his life moments when he played chess with great pleasure and gratitude to God for the leisure time. And so he could not imagine anything better than being called away to God in the midst of something God Himself had so graciously provided.

This is wisdom of a very high order. Prayer is as extensive as

life itself—it is indeed a habit of being, and it is not discontinu-
ous from anything in life that advances gratitude and furthers
the humanizing process. In his game, the saint was indeed serv-
ing God in the wit and tangle of his mind, and so he would go to
God as he had lived, wholly and in each moment as it was given.

The splendor of the collective experience of the Jewish and
Christian people is a long narrative in which God continually
penetrates the clouds of oblivion to embrace humanity in its
confusion, its frailty, its banality—its everydayness. Perhaps the
most shocking thing about this divine disclosure is that God has
taken with utmost seriousness the world as He has made it, and
that He loves and sustains it—and us with it.

The presence of God is, for many people, perhaps most evident not in moments of liturgical grandeur, nor even when people make great sacrifices for others—these seem rare in any case.
But something of God shines on our dimness when at last we see
the lovely small surprises of life for what they are: grace notes
enlivening the usual arrangement, little explosions of color in-
terrupting the prevalent gray. These revelations, these moments
when the Beyond seems for just a moment in the midst, often
occur when we least expect them—in the smile of a friend who
is happy to see us; in an unbidden act of simple human kindness; in a baby's absolute, unquestioning trust in a parent's embrace; in the sheer prodigality, the breathtaking abundance of
beauty in the world; in the vague but persistent intuition that
indeed our lives have purpose and are primed for meaning—that
life itself is not a swindle.

And then there is the emergence of goodness—the irrepress-
ible, unshakable goodness—of which people are so astonishingly capable, even in the worst circumstances. These are the
moments when human nature is vested in a little majesty at last.
These are the moments enabling us to endure the routines of
life without a smirking cynicism.

As a living, continuous process of connection to God, prayer expresses and clarifies our convictions about human life and destiny, and about our relationship with the world. Prayer interprets us to ourselves, for it comes from and returns to far deeper precincts than those of mere religion.

ॐ

"In prayer, we find our entire life over again," wrote a wise man.

The everydayness, the routines, the apparent treadmill that we may feel are our lot in life: so little seems to change that we may find ourselves wondering what good it might do to start praying in the first place.

But if we once start and then persevere, we sense that our hopes and hunches about the reality of God have been right, and a certain clarity at last breaks through the tedious, insistent fog. We know, having thrown ourselves into the arms of God, that we are so close to His heart that we cannot see His face. And then, despite everything and because of everything, we want to go on praying.

Notes

CHAPTER ONE: Of Time and Memory—
Some Historic Aspects of the Interior Life

1 **"Be still"**: Psalm 46, 10.
2 **"Many reasons"**: James, n.p.
4 **"It is certain"**: Albright, pp. 172–78.
4 **"It is difficult to imagine"**: Eliade, vol. 1, p. XIII. He is citing from the preface to his earlier work, *The Quest: History and Meaning in Religion* (1969).
5 **"Creator, Maker"**: Quoted in Appleton, p. 13.
5 **"My Shining One"**: The excerpts are drawn from Faulkner, plates 35 and 16 (the plates are unpaginated); from the chapters of the so-called Theban Recension of *The Book of Going Forth by Day* (which may be dated about 1250 B.C. and does not appear in *The Papyrus of Ani*; cf. Faulker, p. 129); also Heiler, p. 60.
6 **"O Lord, great are"**: Eliade, vol. 1, p. 69; on Cretan-Minoan religious life, see pp. 129–33.
6 **"I have prayed"**: Heiler, p. 59.
6 **"strip us of our"**: Cited in Appleton, p. 329.
6 **"my father, my mother"**: Ibid.
6 **"as a father and mother"**: Ibid.
6 **"You are a father and a mother to me"**: Trans. by DS from the French found in Vouaux, pp. 116 and 454.
8 **"I built your temple"**: *Iliad*, I, 35–42; Butler, trans. On ancient prayer, see, e.g., David E. Aune, "Prayer in the Greco-Roman World," in Longenecker, pp. 23–41, and his appended bibliography, pp. 41–42.
8 **"Great goddess Artemis"**: Butler (trans.), Homer, *The Odyssey* (slight alterations in the trans., by DS).
8 **"Without thee"**: *The Suppliants*, part XIII, antistrophe 3; see Morshead (the out-of-print text was obtained on the Web site *Greece.com*, hence n.p.).
8 **"all who possess"**: Jowett, trans., *The Dialogues of Plato: The Timaeus and The Critias*.

9 **On the various postures and gestures of Hebrew prayer:** King Solomon "knelt before the altar with hands outstretched toward heaven" (1 Kings 8, 54); see also Isaiah 1, 15, Jeremiah 4, 31 and Psalm 28, 2. This was still common as late as Tertullian (A.D. 196), who wrote in *De Oratione (On Prayer)* that Christians prayed "with our hands elevated temperately and becomingly" (see chapter XVII of *De Oratione* in CCEL: Ante-Nicene Fathers). Hannah stood for prayer (1 Samuel 1, 26), as did Jeremiah (18, 20). These various customs extended to the time of Jewish Christians and beyond: "We knelt down on the beach and prayed" (Acts of the Apostles 21, 5). Jesus referred to the custom of standing at prayer (Mark 11, 25).

9 **"Help me, Jupiter":** Veyne, pp. 210–11.

10 **"With outstretched arms":** Cited in Appleton, pp. 320–21.

10 **"You gave me":** *Encyclopædia Britannica 2002*, expanded edition DVD; see under *prayer—praise and thanksgiving*.

11 **"O God, you are my Lord":** This and other examples of primitive prayer are drawn from Heiler, pp. 1–64.

12 **On Confucius**, I have relied on Boorstin, pp. 9–18

13 **"Why do you ask":** Bradley, p. 147.

13 **"the Tao that can be told":** Johnston, p. 141.

CHAPTER TWO: Prayer as Dialogue (I)—
The Experience of Israel

15 **"Judaism" . . . "is unimaginable":** Posner et al., Foreword (n.p.).

15 **"Do not be frightened":** Joshua 1,9.

16 **"Now the Lord said to Abram":** Genesis 12, 1ff.

17 **"in a vision":** E.g., Genesis 15, 1 and 46, 2; Numbers 12, 6.

17 **"Do not be afraid":** Genesis 15, 1.

18 **"Here I am!":** Exodus 3, 4.

18 **"The Lord used to speak":** Exodus 33, 11. See also Numbers 12, 8: "With Moses," says the Lord, "I speak face to face—clearly, not in riddles."

18 **"Did I conceive":** Numbers 11, 12–14.

18 **"Is the Lord's power":** Ibid., 11, 23.

19 **"she was praying silently":** 1 Samuel 1, 13.

19 **"The Lord called":** 1 Samuel 31, 10.

19 **"grew up in the presence":** 1 Samuel 21, 21. On prayer in the OT in general, see Christopher R. Seitz, "Prayer in the Old Testament or Hebrew Bible," in Longenecker, pp. 3–22.

19 **"Here am I!":** Isaiah 6, 8.

20 **"Ah, Lord God!":** Jeremiah 1, 6.

20 **"I was like a gentle":** Jeremiah 11, 19–20.

20 **"Why do all who are treacherous":** Jeremiah 12, 1.

21 **"they can make":** Boulding, *The Coming of God*, p. 98.

21 **"Where can I go":** Psalm 139, 7–12.

21 **"You, O Lord":** Psalm 86, 5.15

21 **"The Lord is merciful":** Exodus 34, 6.

22 **"As a deer":** Psalm 42, 1–3.

22 **"O God, You are":** Psalm 63, 1.

22 **"the service that takes place":** Petuchowski, p. 17; see also Longenecker, pp. 203–227.

22 **"to love the Lord your God":** Deuteronomy 6, 5; this restates the
first of the Ten Commandments in positive form.

23 **"Christian guides":** "Hezekiah and the Power of Prayer," a sermon
delivered at Jesus College Chapel, Cambridge University, on April 29,
2001, by a leader of Beth-Shalom Reform Synagogue, Cambridge
(identified only as "DL").

25 **"It is absurd":** Peers, trans., *Interior Castle*, p. 53.

25 **"Prayer is encountering God":** Brock, trans., p. 171.

27 **"The Lord our God made a covenant":** Deuteronomy 5, 2–3.

29 **"Yet it is just":** Swenson and Swenson, p. 126.

CHAPTER THREE: Prayer as Dialogue (II)—
The Experience of Christianity and Islam

30 **"In the morning":** Mark 1, 35 and 6, 46; Matthew 14, 22–23; Luke 5,
16 and 6, 12. The so-called high priestly prayer of Jesus that comprises
John 17 is, like most of that gospel, an extended meditation on post-
Resurrection Christian faith. This does not, of course, mean that some
of the verses cannot be traced back through the oral traditions to Jesus
himself. But it has been axiomatic of biblical studies for almost a century that the gospels do not represent anything like journalistic re-
porting; they are documents of faith—composed not to convince or
convert but to reflect the belief of primal communities.

30 **"Beware of practicing":** Matthew 6, 1. 5–8. Regarding Jesus' reference to "the Father" (and occasionally to "my Father and your Father"), it is often maintained that Mark's inclusion of the original
Aramaic *abba* (14, 36), which is the only gospel occurrence of the
word, connotes Jesus' particularly intimate relationship—that in the
Garden of Gethsemane, he used a kind of diminutive or affection-
ate form, thus addressing God as "Daddy." But grammatically the

word, derived from *ab*, has a determinative form—that is, it simply
preserves the original meaning of the Greek word that follows it:
"Father." Sound Christology diminishes the likelihood that Jesus
would ever have dared to address God the Father as "Daddy"—for any
Jew, this would have been the height of irreverence. And to retroject
the later, theologically developed identification of Jesus with God (but
not with the Father) is unwarranted. More to the point, the occurrences of *abba* in Romans 8, 15 and Galatians 4, 6 indicate that the
word did not express Jesus' qualitatively different, exclusive relationship with God (also a claim that could be made only in light of later
Christology). The address—"*Abba!* Father!"—was in fact, for a time,
taken over into early Christian prayer. "The personal sense of the fatherhood of God was a typically Christian development of the Judaic
tradition, and this probably originated in a recollection of Jesus' teaching and of the example of his own prayer." Thus John Ashton, "Abba,"
in Freedman, vol. 1, pp. 7–8; also, see James Barr, " 'Abba' Isn't 'Daddy,' "
Journal of Theological Studies 39 (1988): 28–47.

31 **"We pray in our rooms":** Abba Isaac, cited by John Cassian (d. about
A.D. 435), in Luibheid, pp. 123–24.

31 **"who like to walk around":** Mark 12, 40. On the requirement of
forgiveness, see chapter 6.

32 **"I am as sure as I am alive":** Field, n.p.

32 **"Blessed be the God and Father":** 2 Corinthians 1, 3–4.

32 **"I remember you":** Romans 1, 9b–10.

33 **"I keep asking":** Ephesians 1, 16.

33 **"We have not stopped praying":** Colossians 1, 9.

33 **"pray without ceasing":** 1 Thessalonians 5, 17. The Greek is succinct:
ἀδιαλείπτως προσεύχεσθε—"Without ceasing, pray."

33 **"those who pray":** Origen, *De Oratione (On Prayer)*, 8; this is easily
available now, along with thirty-seven volumes of the writings of the
Early Church Fathers, on CD-ROM: *Christian Classics Ethereal Library*, version 4, from Calvin College (Grand Rapids). This valuable
disk also contains more than two hundred historic Christian documents and Bible study tools. See also Hamman, p. 259.

33 **"Prayer is not":** Ware, p. 80.

33 **On the so-called Jesus Prayer,** see, e.g., Bacovin.

34 **"though indeed":** Acts 17, 27–28. See, e.g., the commentary on Acts
by Carl R. Holladay, in Mays, p. 1103; and by Johnson, p. 316.

35 **"It is glory enough":** Cited in Appleton, p. 332.

35 **"is the hallmark":** Maqsood, p. 15.

36 **"any thought":** Ibid., p. 17.

36 **On the tale told by Rumi,** see Renard, *101 Questions and Answers on Islam*, pp. 67–68.

36 **"I exist in God":** Arberry, p. 42.

37 **"From God we come":** Colledge and Walsh, p. 283. I have slightly altered, for clarity, their translation from the Middle English.

37 **"My God, the stars":** Renard, *Windows*, pp. 92–94; see also the original sources, in Renard's notes, p. 395, notes 9 and 10.

37 **"So it is with":** Abhishiktananda, p. 11.

CHAPTER FOUR: Prayer as Dialogue (III)—
The Living God Speaks

39 **"came to believe":** On Ignatius and the discernment of spiritual intuitions, see William A. Barry, SJ, "How Do I Know It's God?" in *America*, May 20, 2002 (pp. 12–15).

41 **"Speak with God".** Kavanaugh and Rodriguez, *The Collected Works of St. Teresa of Avila*, vol. 2, p. 141.

43 **"through the conversations":** Teresa of Ávila, *Interior Castle*, in Peers, p. 47.

43 **"Since He is Lord":** Kavanaugh and Rodriguez, vol. 2, p. 144.

43 **"The fewer the words":** Cited in Heiler, p. 237.

43 **"That's all very well":** See Peers, *Interior Castle*, pp. 52–53.

45 **"Simple attentiveness":** Lawrence of the Resurrection, pp. 40, 69, etc.

47 **"We must hold it":** Farmer, vol. 1 (January), p. 167.

48 **"Well, I see":** Letter of Jeanne de Chantal from Annecy, August 14, 1634; see Thibert, p. 194.

49 **"Try to remain":** Letter of Jeanne de Chantal to Noël Brulart, in Thibert, pp. 198–99.

49 **"The uneasiness you feel":** Francis de Sales to a young woman, date uncertain; see Thibert, p. 100.

CHAPTER FIVE: Prayer as Petition

51 **On prayer as itself an act of petition,** see Augustine, *De Verbo Domini*; also, Thomas Aquinas, *Summa Theologica*, II–II, 83.

51 **"Your unfailing Providence":** From the Book of Common Prayer, the Daily Office: Rite Two, at Compline.

52 **"There's no time for doubt":** Griffin, *Doors into Prayer*, pp. 4–5.

52 **On prayer and magic,** see, e.g., Clark, pp. 311–15.

54 **The selection from the Socratic dialogue** *Euthyphro*, by Plato, is a combination of two translations—by Benjamin Jowett and by Harold

North Fowler—slightly modified by DS. (Both are available online, the first at *classics.mit.edu*; the second at *perseus.tufts.edu*.)

54 **"From you was our beginning":** Cited in Appleton, pp. 325–26; trans. ed. by DS.

55 **On Juvenal's Tenth Satire,** I am grateful to Bernard F. Dick for supplying me with a copy of his important essay (on which I here rely): "Seneca and Juvenal 10," *Harvard Studies in Classical Philology* 73 (1968): 237–46.

56 **"Be the canoe":** Ibid., p. 88.

56 **"Our Father":** Ibid., p. 348.

56 **"Lord, what a blessing":** Ibid., p. 100.

56 **"make the emperor's life":** This and the Japanese orations following are cited in Appleton, pp. 353–56.

57 **"a share in prosperity":** The Vedic hymns have been collected by, e.g., Pannikar.

57 **"O God . . . I pray":** Cited in Heiler, p. 252.

57 **"God our Lord":** Hadith al-Ruqya; see Appleton, p. 343, and Renard, *Responses to 101 Questions on Islam*, pp. 68–70.

58 **"Forgive us our shortcomings":** Maqsood, p. 317.

58 **"I do not know":** 1 Kings 3, 7–9. A longer form appears, written on the verge of the Christian era, in the Wisdom of Solomon 3, 1–18.

59 **"Before they call":** Isaiah 65, 24.

59 **"O Lord, answer me":** Psalm 86, 1–2, 6–7.

59 **"has a double effect":** Posner et al., p. 10.

59 **"O God, God":** Quoted in Heiler, pp. 293–94.

60 **"Bless me by enlarging":** 1 Chronicles 4, 10. True, the next verse admits that "God granted what he asked," but that simply records that Jabez indeed became wealthy; this is typical Semitic language, like "God sent rain."

60 **"When my enemy is tried":** Psalm 109, 7–12.

60 **On the Lord's Prayer,** the breadth of commentary and the depth of scholarship have been enormous over two millennia. In addition to sources cited in specific notes, see Cullmann, esp. pp. 37–69, and J. L. Houlden in Freedman, vol. 4, pp. 356–62; on the *Didache*, see Deiss, p. 16; on the Matthean version, see esp. the magnificent excursus in Schweizer, pp. 146–58. There are also brief reflections in DS, *The Hidden Jesus*, pp. 171–73.

61 **The dating of the *Didache*** has always been the subject of scholarly debate, but the consensus now favors the late first/early second century, with much of the material certainly reflecting Christian practices of the apostolic and subapostolic decades.

62 **"Teach us how to pray":** Luke 11, 1. The Lord's Prayer as we have it in the New Testament may be found in Matthew 6, 9–13; Luke 11, 2–4 represents a slightly different version of the oral tradition of sayings of Jesus utilized by him and Matthew. Behind Matthew and Luke is also Mark 11, 25, which records only the injunction to forgiveness: "When you stand praying, forgive, if you have anything against anyone; so that your Father also, Who is in heaven, may forgive you your trespasses." The Matthean version, it will be noted, has no such Lukan introductory request from the disciples: the context of the Lord's Prayer in the first gospel is rather a counterstatement to Jesus' injunction in the preceding verses not to heap up many empty phrases.

64 **"Hardly a clause":** H. Greeven, in Kittel and Friedrich, p. 285.

65 **On the background to God as Father,** see the note to chapter 3 on *abba*. There is no need to torture Jesus' references to "my Father and your Father" into a Christological assertion about an existential distinction between God's Fatherhood of Jesus and of us. The phrase simply clarifies the meaning of *"our* Father."

65 **"You are our Father":** Isaiah 63, 16.

65 **"I cried out":** Sirach 51, 10.

65 **"As a mother":** Isaiah 66, 13.

65 **"Wherever God is":** Teresa of Ávila, *The Way of Perfection,* in Kavanaugh and Rodriguez, vol. 2 (1980), pp. 140–41.

66 **"May His name":** I depend, with only slight modifications, on the Kaddish trans. by Schweizer, p. 151.

66 **"A name is a summary":** Origen, *De Oratione,* trans. William A. Curtis; from the CD-ROM, *Christian Classics Ethereal Library,* available from Calvin College (Grand Rapids, Michigan). The CD contains, in addition to much valuable ancillary material, the texts of thirty-seven volumes of Early Christian Fathers.

67 **"of this world":** John 18, 36.

69 **"is repeated daily by millions":** Huxley, p. 221.

70 **"You know what I want":** Colledge and Walsh, trans., p. 178.

70 **"My Father":** Matthew, 26, 39.

70 **"I asked for strength":** Cited, e.g., in Appleton, p. 119.

71 **"Give us this day our daily bread":** What is apparently the simplest and most direct phrase of the Prayer in fact contains the greatest linguistic difficulty: there has been a scholarly debate about the meaning of the word "daily" (επιούσιος—*epiousios,* in the Greek text) ever since Origen—the difficulty stemming from the fact that this is a neologism, the only occurrence of this Greek word in the Bible; in fact, it is doubtful that it exists elsewhere. The word *epiousios* was once

thought to have been in a Greek papyrus discovered in Egypt at the
end of the 19th century, but that was a damaged document—and
even that text is now lost. Without attempting to resolve what is perhaps forever destined to be a *crux interpretum*, I follow Cullmann,
Schweizer and others in seeing the petition as a good example of
metonymy: in the Prayer as in his ministry, the bread refers to all that
is needed for human sustenance.

71 **"Do not worry"**: Matthew 6, 25–32.

72 **"Do not worry about anything"**: Philippians 4, 6.

72 **"pray God for your welfare"**: Cited by Heiler, p. 252.

73 **"We beg You, O Lord"**: From Clement of Rome, writing to the
community at Corinth about the year A.D. 96; cited in Hamman,
pp. 25–28; see also Appleton, p. 212. The authenticity of this prayer has
never been disputed.

73 **"Keep watch"**: From Evening Prayer II, *Contemporary Office Book*,
p. 74.

CHAPTER SIX: Prayer as Forgiveness

81 **"Have mercy on me"**: Psalm 51, 1–3, 10.

82 **"He did what was evil"**: 2 Kings 21, 2.

82 **"he shed very much"**: 2 Kings 21, 16.

82 **"While he was in distress"**: 2 Chronicles 33, 12–13.

82 **"You are the Lord Most High"**: Prayer of Manasseh, found in some
manuscripts of the Hebrew Scriptures after the Psalter. It is a distinct
and distinctive short work (fifteen verses), but is considered a biblical
book by Jews, Catholics and Protestants. Most scholars date it in the
1st century B.C.

83 **"Christ was put to death"**: 1 Peter 3, 18–4,6. These verses were the
subject of the Ph.D. dissertation by DS; see Spoto, *Christ's Preaching
to the Dead.*

84 **"Teach me"**: Ambrose of Milan, *De Poenitentia*, 2, 8; 67, 73, cited in
Migne, 513B; trans. in Hamman, p. 198.

85 **"Forgive your neighbor"**: Sirach 28, 2–4. This book (also called Ec-
clesiasticus) comes from some time before 180 B.C.; the Hebrew original was translated into Greek some decades later.

85 **"Forgive us as we forgive"**: Matthew uses the Greek word for
"debts," Luke the word for "sins"—but behind both is the same Aramaic word, *hoba;* hence the connotation of the Greek is identical.

85 **"A king wished to settle accounts"**: Matthew 18, 23–25.

86 **"So my heavenly Father"**: Matthew 18, 35.

86 **"love your enemies"**: See, e.g., Matthew 5, 39–42, and Luke 6, 27–39.

86 **"Forgiveness . . . is a social":** Benedict T. Viviano, OP, "The Gospel According to Matthew," in Brown, Fitzmyer and Murphy, eds., p. 645.

87 **"Father, forgive them":** Luke 23, 34.

87 **"Lord, do not count":** Acts of the Apostles 7, 60.

87 **"God Most High":** Ruinart, pp. 416–20 (trans. in Hamman); see also Delehaye, p. 116.

87 **"Pray for your enemies":** Cited in Fleiss, p. 13.

87 **The selections from Buddhist, Hindu and Muslim traditions** are drawn from Jampolsky.

88 **"Those who refuse":** Renard, *Responses to 101 Questions on Islam*, p. 72.

88 **"If anyone continually asks":** Ibid.

88 **"O God, we remember":** Cited in Appleton, pp. 136–37.

89 **"Overcome evil with good":** Romans 12, 21.

92 **"Lord Jesus, for":** From the Book of Common Prayer (1979 revision).

93 **Forgiveness of others:** On this point and its expression, I am indebted to Cullmann, p. 57.

CHAPTER SEVEN: Prayer as Suffering

94 **"Have you not rejected":** E.g., Psalm 108, 11.

94 **"Remove the hardship":** Maqsood, p. 253.

94 **"Whatever you ask for":** Mark 11, 24; Luke 11, 9; Matthew 17, 20 and 21, 22.

95 **"Sometimes it seems":** Colledge and Walsh, p. 251 (from chapter 42 of Julian of Norwich, *Showings*).

96 **"My Father":** Luke 22, 41; see also Matthew 26, 39.

96 **"with loud cries and tears":** Hebrews 5, 7.

96 **"Prayer is warfare":** Attributed to Abbot Agathon, cited in Ward, *Sayings of the Desert Fathers*, p. 18.

97 **"There is no soundness":** From Psalms 38 and 55.

99 **On the crucifixion of Jesus,** I have drawn from *The Hidden Jesus*, pp. 225ff. All four gospels mention the presence of women at the death of Jesus, but the accounts are impossible to reconcile. Mark 15, 40 and Matthew 27, 55 mention (after recounting the death of Jesus) the nearby presence of women "looking on from a distance"—those who had served Jesus during his ministry. But they mention only Mary Magdalene, Mary the mother of James and Joseph (Mark: Joses) and (thus Matthew) the mother of the sons of Zebedee (possibly the same as Mark—Salome, who is not called the mother of the sons of Zebedee). Luke 23, 49 mentions only the presence "at a distance" of "acquaintances and women who had followed him." There is, then, no

mention of Jesus' mother, nor of any particular disciple, in the synoptic gospels. The only name that Matthew and Mark have in common with John 19, 25–27 is Mary Magdalene.

But for his own theological purposes, John goes further: "Standing near the cross of Jesus were his mother, and his mother's sister, Mary, the wife of Clopas, and Mary Magdalene." The syntax of this verse in the Greek is ambiguous, and I have deliberately preserved this ambiguity in the translation: are there four women or three? a named pair (Mary the wife of Clopas and Mary Magdalene) and an unnamed pair (Jesus' mother and his mother's sister)? or three women named Mary (with his mother's sister in opposition to "Mary, the wife of Clopas")?

"Identifications are easy to conjure but impossible to ascertain," as Barrett has tersely written (*The Gospel According to St. John*, p. 551). Against the idea of three women is the notion that Mary the wife of Clopas would not be "his mother's sister" because two sisters would not be named Mary—but of course John does not mention the name of Jesus' mother anywhere in his gospel. Her only other appearance occurs in 2, 1–11 (the wedding at Cana), but there, as in John 19, she is unnamed and addressed as "Woman." Serious Johannine scholarship rightly sees that the mother of Jesus is a richly symbolic figure in that gospel: if John had wished her two appearances in the narrative to refer to specific historic moments, why not mention her name, which everyone knew? As "Woman," however, she clearly assumes a theological significance reminiscent of the "Woman" Eve in Genesis, for whom Mary is obviously a counterstatement. The late John L. McKenzie is probably right in this regard: "The evangelists say clearly that all the disciples had fled and were absent at the death of Jesus; it is not strange that the sources of the gospels were ambiguous on who was actually present, but the synoptics are not ambiguous on the absence of Mary. *We must accept the words of Jesus to his mother and the beloved disciple as a theological construction of John* (italics his: see "The Mother of Jesus in the New Testament," *Concilium* 168 [1983] 8).

100 **"Lord, Lord, Lord":** These and the following two accounts of early martyrs are cited in Hamman, pp. 51–54.

101 **The dialogue by Shaw** occurs in *Androcles and the Lion,* act 2.

102 **"I believe in the sun":** Cited in Harris, *The Fire of Silence and Stillness,* p. 193.

102 **The life of prayer and faith** in the camps has been documented by Rosenbaum; see esp. p. 111.

103 **"Help me to pray":** Cited in Appleton, p. 163.

103 **the existence of evil:** On the problem of evil, see, e.g., Underhill, *The Spiritual Life*, pp. 84–87; Hick, esp. pp. 217–21; and Wright, pp. 62–66.

103 **"If I were to know Him":** Quoted by Küng, *Credo*, p. 90.

104 **"Often prayer consists":** Augustine, "Letter to Proba," in *Christian Classics Ethereal Library*, op. cit.

104 **"The little one I hold":** Cited in Appleton, p. 350.

105 **"Could the immortal God":** Hilary of Poitiers, *On the Trinity*, I, 1–7 and 10–12; see *The Nicene and Post-Nicene Library of the Fathers* (Grand Rapids: Eerdmans, 1983), vol. 9, pp. 40–43.

105 **"Why does anyone":** Thibert, p. 119.

105 **"Grant, when my hour comes":** Teilhard de Chardin, pp. 61–62. On suffering and God, see Küng, *Credo*, pp. 89–94. On yin/yang and on the Buddhist teachings on suffering, see especially Graham, pp. 36–42, and Dumoulin, pp. 4–27.

108 **"Many people feel":** John of the Cross, *Dark Night of the Soul*, II, 1–3.

109 **"Pray wholeheartedly":** Colledge and Walsh, trans., pp. 249–50.

109 **"bad humor":** The selections are from John of the Cross, *The Dark Night of the Soul*, Book I, chapters 9 and 10, in Kavanaugh and Rodriguez, *The Collected Works of St. John of the Cross*.

110 **On depression,** there is, of course, a vast literature. Relative to the life of prayer, I refer to Leech, pp. 162–64.

110 **"You have been":** Hudleston, ed., pp. 154–55.

111 **"The Lord will fight":** Exodus 14, 14.

111 **"is really a way to see things":** Renard, *101 Questions and Answers on Buddhism*, p. 49.

112 **"Prayer and love are":** Merton, *New Seeds of Contemplation*, pp. 221, 237–38.

113 **"I spent nearly twenty years":** Peers, trans., *The Life of Teresa of Jesus*; the citations here collected are from chapters VIII and IX, pp. 108–19.

113 **"an intimate sharing":** Kavanaugh and Rodriguez, *The Collected Works of St. Teresa of Ávila*, vol. 1, 2nd ed., p. 96.

113 **"I am sometimes":** Cited in Heiler, p. 235.

114 **"Set little store":** Peers, trans., *The Life of Teresa of Jesus*, pp. 131–35.

114 **"One must have passed through":** Hollings, ed., pp. 25 and 36.

114 **"God did not say":** Colledge and Walsh, trans., p. 165.

115 **"No matter how deep":** Widely cited—e.g., by Peter Kreeft, in "Shared Hells," included in Bruderhof Communities, pp. 156–61.

CHAPTER EIGHT: Prayer as Abandonment

117 **"Prayer is, at bottom":** Ruth Burrows, OCD, in Allen and Burrows, p. 12.

117 **"abandoning our own little ship":** Ibid., p. 101.

118 **On Zen,** see Swearer in Wakefield, pp. 399–400; also Dumoulin.

120 **"Those who want":** Luke, 17, 33.

121 **"The goal, in prayer":** Griffin, *Clinging*, p. 15.

122 **"a mighty interference":** Greenwell, p. 143.

123 **"You are my Father":** Cited in Heiler, p. 265.

124 **"Of what avail":** Appleton, p. 293.

124 **"the posture becomes":** Sara Regina Ryan, pp. 56–57.

124 **"With You I lack nothing":** See Psalms 16, 40, 56, 59, 73, 86.

125 **"Into Your hands":** Luke 23, 46.

125 **"What is needed":** Graham, p. 32.

126 **The prayer of Saint Ignatius** as he wrote it in Latin: *Suscipe, Domine, universam meam libertatem. Accipe memoriam, intellectum, atque voluntatem omnem. Quidquid habeo vel possideo mihi largitus es; id tibi totum restituo, ac tuae prorsus voluntati trado gubernandum. Amorem tui solum cum gratia tua mihi dones, et dives sum satis, nec aliud quidquam ultra posco.* See, e.g., Ganss.

126 **"I put myself in Your care":** Luther's Morning Prayer, from *Luther's Little Instruction Book* (aka *The Small Catechism of Martin Luther*), Appendix I: Devotions; trans. Robert E. Smith in 1994 for Project Wittenberg.

126 **"abandon ourselves":** Peers, trans., *Interior Castle*, p. 90.

127 **"even as the light of the sun":** Kavanaugh and Rodriguez, *The Collected Works of St. John of the Cross*—see *The Ascent of Mount Carmel*, Book II, iii. I have also drawn on a translation by E. Allison Peers.

127 **"In order to have pleasure":** Ibid., Book I, xiii.

128 **"Once and for all":** Lawrence of the Resurrection, p. 50.

128 **even our virtues:** "Yet she could see by their shocked and altered faces that even their virtues were being burned away." This memorable sentence occurs at the conclusion of Flannery O'Connor's short story "Revelation." See O'Connor, p. 508.

129 **"total dependence on God":** Thibert, pp. 68–69, 85; 51–52.

130 **"Come to my help":** Luibheid, trans., pp. 132–33.

130 **"a little word":** Walsh, trans., pp. 195–96. The simple, silent practice of the presence of God to which Cassian, *The Cloud of Unknowing* and Jeanne de Chantal refer is also at the basis of a modern method called

Centering Prayer—a method of contemplation according to which one simply attends to the divine presence at the center of one's being. To focus attention, a word or phrase or mantra is chosen and may be repeated. See Pennington and Keating (who originally devised the method with special attention to the needs of laypeople visiting the monastery where Pennington and Keating were then in residence as American Trappist monks). Centering Prayer shares the sense of simple contemplation with the method taught by the late English Benedictine John Main (1926–1982), q.v. These two modern methods of contemplative prayer owe very much to Cassian and to *The Cloud of Unknowing*, cited here, which urges attention to the presence of God by focusing on a single short word.

130 **"To wait with folded arms"**: Muggeridge, ed., "Letter 5, from Perpignan, 1741 [n.p.]."

131 **"we shall then act"**: Ibid.

131 **"We are often bored"**: de Caussade, pp. 20–22, 24–26, 27–29ff.

131 **"God's action"**: Ibid., p. 55.

132 **"This fortunate habit"**: To Sister Marie Thérèse de Vioménil, in Muggeridge, n.p.

132 **"The existence we have received"**: To Sister Marie-Anne-Thérèse de Rosen, dated 1724, ibid.

132 **On Caussade:** John Chapman is firmly in this tradition—see, e.g., pp. 143–145.

133 **"Why should I have any anxiety"**: Weil, p. 20.

133 **"I am no longer"**: Cited in Kendall and Kendall, p. 51.

134 **"The only thing"**: Hudleston, ed., pp. 149–52.

134 **"Mysteries are not truths"**: Marcel, p. 141.

CHAPTER NINE: Prayer as Serenity

136 **"Having committed oneself"**: Peers, trans., *Interior Castle*, p. 223.

138 **"the final goal"**: Dumoulin, p. 26; see also Kennedy, p. 17.

138 **"When a person pursues"**: Renard, *Responses to 101 Questions on Islam*, pp. 35–36.

138 **"I lie down"**: Psalm 3, 5–6. The Aaronic blessing is found in Numbers 6, 24–26.

140 **"God is closer"**: Colledge and Walsh, trans., pp. 288–89.

140 **"God is nearer to me"**: See C. F. Kelley (n.p.).

140 **"Madame, you are seeking"**: Cited in Underhill, *Mysticism*, p. 184. The original account may be found in Guyon, Part I, chapter 8.

140 **On Theophan,** see Kadloubovsky and Palmer, pp. 11–14.

141 **"Secure for yourself"**: Ibid., p. 254.
142 **"The principal thing"**: Ibid., p. 53.
142 **"The less one prays"**: Hudleston, p. 53.
142 **"transparency"**: Griffin, *Clinging*, p. 44.

CHAPTER TEN: Prayer as Loving

145 **"We succeed in prayer"**: Rahner, *The Need and the Blessing of Prayer*, pp. 25ff.
146 **"It is the nature of love"**: See Edwards, Sermon VIII, in *Works*, vol. 2.
146 **"I have loved you"**: Jeremiah 31, 3.
147 **"When Israel was a child"**: Hosea 11, 1.
147 **"love a woman"**: Hosea 3, 1.
147 **On the biblical notion of the love of God,** see William Klassen, "Love," in Freedman, ed., vol. 4, pp. 375–96.
147 **"in its highest form"**: Donin, p. 159.
148 **"God is love"**: 1 John 4, 8–21. The citations from 1 John that appear in these paragraphs are from this same chapter of that letter.
148 **"Faith means"**: Rivière, cited in Daniélou, p. 12; I have sought in vain the original locus of this quotation, which Daniélou does not supply.
149 **On the absolute claim of God on our adoration,** see, e.g., John Macquarrie, in Wakefield, pp. 307–8.
152 **"And if we are to love God"**: Houlden, p. 152.
152 **"Have you not heard"**: Tagore, 45.
153 **"was more united to God"**: Lawrence of the Resurrection, p. 47.
153 **"spontaneous prayer"**: Francis de Sales to Marie Bourgeois Brûlart (May 3, 1604); see Thibert, p. 103.
154 **"What I have been striving"**: Gandhi, *Pathway to God*, p. 4.
155 **"I do dimly perceive"**: Gandhi, *My God*, p. 4. This statement was drawn from a previous article, "On God" (1928). Gandhi also read this for a phonograph recording on October 20, 1931.
156 **"interpreted with poor intellects"**: B. R. Nanda, "Gandhi," *Encyclopædia Britannica 2002 Expanded DVD Version*. (Nanda is also the author of a Gandhi biography.)
156 **"Rather than personal fulfillment"**: On Buddhism and love, see, e.g., Les Kaye, in an essay submitted to the Washington, D.C., syndicate, Religion News Service, in 2003; this represents a talk he gave as spiritual director of the Kannon Do Zen Meditation Center in Mountain View, California, on August 4, 1999.
157 **"Even if"**: Renard, *101 Questions and Answers on Islam*, p. 69.

157 **"my ultimate desire":** Ibid., p. 70.

157 **"I love You":** Reprinted on the Web site www.sufimaster.org/Adawiyya.htm.

157 **"The madness of lust":** This and the following citations from Augustine are in *The Confessions*; see Ryan, pp. 66–67, 248, 254, 233–34.

159 **"loving conversation":** Migne, *Patrologia Graeca*, vol. 64, cols. 462–63, 466; trans. from *Christian Classics Ethereal Library*: Chrysostom, Homily 6, "On Prayer."

160 **"I have written":** Ward, trans., *The Prayers and Meditations of St. Anselm with the Proslogion*, pp. 239ff.

161 **"By love":** See Walsh, chapter 6; I have conflated the Wolters trans., pp. 59–60.

161 **"The important thing":** Peers, trans., *Interior Castle*, p. 76.

161 **"Whether we think of or speak to God":** Wesley, n.p.

162 **"I am accomplished":** Diary entry for March 9, 1941; see Hillesum, *An Interrupted Life*, p. 1.

162 **"Mortal fear":** Diary entry for November 10, 1941; see Hillesum, *An Interrupted Life*, p. 47.

163 **"What they are after":** Diary entry for July 3, 1942; ibid., p. 130.

164 **"She walked lightly":** Hillesum, *Letters from Westbork*, p. xvi.

164 **"I feel a growing need":** Diary entry for Sept. 15, 1942; Hillesum, *An Interrupted Life*, p. 168.

166 **The prayer or oath of Moses Maimonides** (cited in Appleton, p. 274) is today a matter of some dispute: some believe (perhaps because it was first printed in the West in 1793) that it should be attributed to the 18th-century German doctor Marcus Herz, a pupil of Immanuel Kant and a physician of high ethical principles, who composed it in honor of Maimonides.

166 **"O Lord, do not bring":** Exodus 32, 12.

167 **"Forgive the sin":** 1 Kings 8, 34.

167 **"While Peter was kept in prison":** Acts 12, 5.

167 **"Call for the elders":** James 5, 14.

167 **"ever living":** Hebrews 7, 25; see Romans 8, 34: "Christ Jesus died and was raised to the right hand of God—he it is who intercedes for us."

168 **"deliver the afflicted":** Clement of Rome, "The First Letter to the Corinthians," in Louth, p. 49.

168 **"Regarding the rest of mankind":** Ignatius of Antioch, "Letter to the Ephesians," ibid., p. 64.

168 **"More things":** From Tennyson, "The Passing of Arthur," in *The Idylls of the King*, lines 415–23.

169 **"O good and innocent"**: The Mende tribe of Sierra Leone; cited in Appleton, p. 351.

170 **"one mediator"**: 1 Timothy 2, 5.

171 **"Love is a direction"**: Weil, p. 93.

CHAPTER ELEVEN: Prayer as Transformation

173 **"Iron sharpens iron"**: Proverbs 27, 17. The text inspired a graceful sermon by Knox, pp. 112–18.

175 **"What is the point"**: Leech, p. 10.

175 **On the changes to be expected** from a habit of prayer, see, e.g., Gerald G. May, "To Bear the Beams of Love: Contemplation and Personal Growth," *The Way* supplement: "Contemplation and the Contemplative Life" 59 (Summer 1987): 24–34.

175 **"Don't waste time"**: Francis de Sales, letter of June 8, 1618: see Thibert, p. 167.

175 **On the absence of prayer** as such in Buddhism, and on its meditation techniques in general, see Kubose. On the practice of meditation, see Sogyal Rinpoche, esp. as interviewed by Ajay Ahuja in *Life Positive* (May 2000).

177 **"But what nourishes"**: Daniélou, p. 27.

177 **"Do not let me"**: Peers, *The Life of Teresa of Jesus*, chap. 30, p. 285; his translation has been conflated with that of Clifford in Capalbo, ed., p. 87.

177 **"The world is too much with us"**: Wordsworth, "The World Is Too Much With Us," written 1802–1804.

178 **"Repent"**: Matthew 3, 2.

178 **On *metanoiete* and the summons to a change of heart,** see the standard Greek dictionaries for the New Testament; see also Graham, pp. 121–23.

179 **"Take my yoke"**: Matthew 11, 29–30. For the etymological issues, see the OED under "yoga" and "yoke," and Kittel and Friedrich, pp. 301–2.

179 **"The great liberty"**: Forsyth, p. 62. See also Mursell, vol. 2, p. 401.

180 **"Not like"**: Houlden, p. 88.

180 **"Is it an easy thing"**: Newman, p. 781.

181 **"we shall see God"**: Ibid., p. 1537.

181 **"What do you do"**: Cited in Mursell, vol. 2, p. 457.

182 **"prayer as a whole"**: Bede, commentary on Mark, in the *Corpus Christianorum, Series Latina*, vol. 120 (Turnhout: Brepols, 1956), p. 550.

182 **"Prayer and meditation":** The citations from Baha'i faith were tran-
scribed from the BBC program "Religion and Ethics," broadcast De-
cember 24, 2002.

183 **Prayer as process:** For the remarks on the stages in the life of prayer,
I am indebted to some considerations expressed by Clark, pp. 322–27.

183 **"Our greatest protection":** Gregory of Nyssa, Homily 2 on the Song
of Solomon; see Migne, vol. 44, cols. 763–65.

185 **"He passes by me":** Job 9, 11.

185 **"Behold, Lord":** Cited in Appleton, p. 53.

186 **"What is the best thing":** Law, *A Serious Call to a Devout and Holy
Life*, in *Works*, vol. 4, p. 210.

186 **"let the whole world feel":** Bright, n.p.

186 **"the natural thing to do":** Hudleston, p. 184.

186 **"I wait":** Psalm 130, 5–6.

187 **"Who hopes":** Romans 8, 24–25.

187 **"Waiting means":** This and the following citations are from Tillich,
pp. 149–52.

CHAPTER TWELVE: Prayer as Silence

189 **On noise and speed,** see, e.g., Jean Leclercq, OSB, "Prayer and
Speed—Spirituality for the Man of Today," in Mooney, pp. 23–25.

190 **"the present state":** Quoted in Picard, p. 231; for several points in this
chapter, I am inspired by his book.

190 **"is not native":** Oates, p. 3.

191 **"Be still":** Psalm 46, 10.

191 **"For God alone":** Psalm 62, 1 and 5.

191 **"Be silent before":** Zephaniah 1, 7.

191 **"While gentle silence":** Wisdom of Solomon 18, 14.

191 **"Now there was a great wind":** 1 Kings 19, 11ff.

192 **"And it is only in silence":** Cited in Keating, *Intimacy with God*,
p. 153.

192 **"mysteries for shouting about":** Trans. from the Greek by DS. Ignatius of Antioch, *Epistle to the Ephesians*, in Louth, p. 66. The phrase,
notes Louth, is "a deliberately paradoxical expression. [The mysteries]
were prepared in the silence of God, in order to be proclaimed aloud to
the world" (n. 17, p. 68).

192 **"I hold firmly to stillness":** Lao-tzu, cited in Harris, *Frequently
Asked Questions*, p. 73.

192 **"One should be secretly":** Cited in Brock, p. 129.

192 **"prayer does not reach":** Ibid., pp. 191–94.

193 **"the conversation":** Ibid., pp. 250ff.; see also Merton, *Contemplative Prayer*, p. 29f. Regarding Hesychasm: there is a narrower sense of the word, which involved the practice of the so-called Jesus Prayer, which was to be accompanied by physical techniques involving breath control. See Kallistos Ware, in Wakefield, pp. 189–90 and (on "prayer of the heart"), p. 315.

193 **"silence of insight":** Ibid., p. 271.

193 **"Occupy yourself":** Cited in Renard, *Windows on the House of Islam*, p. 47.

193 **"To pray is to be attentive":** Main, *The Heart of Creation*, p. 100.

194 **"We have learned a great":** Cited in Collins, p. ix.

194 **"a religion which":** Underhill, *Concerning the Inner Life*, p. 15.

195 **"the incomprehensible mystery":** Rahner, *Foundations of Christian Faith*, p. 434.

195 **"It is by silence":** Attributed to Saint Ammonas, a 4th-century hermit; see Livingstone, p. 52.

195 **On meditation and contemplation,** see esp. Boulding, Hudleston, Daniélou, Downey, Johnston, Kennedy, Leech, McBrien, Mursell, Rahner, and Underhill (all titles). There is, of course, a vast literature on these topics, and these texts provide bibliographies.

195 **"By settling the mind":** Origen, "De Oratione," in Migne, vol. 11, col. 441-B.

196 **"a penetration into":** Daniélou, p. 21.

198 **"Be faithful about staying":** Francis de Sales to Jeanne de Chantal: January 16, 1610; see Thibert, p. 151.

198 **"Do nothing":** Jeanne de Chantal to a priest, 1640; ibid., p. 198.

199 **"For me, God is presence":** Quoted by Johnston, p. 92.

200 **"We and our everydayness":** Rahner, *The Need and Blessing of Prayer*, p. 42.

202 **"In prayer, we find":** Guardini, *The Spirit of the Liturgy*, p. 140.

Bibliography

Abhishiktananda (Henri Le Saux). *Prayer*. Delhi: ISPCK, 2001.

Adkins, Lesley, and Roy A. Adkins. *Handbook to Life in Ancient Rome*. New York: Oxford University Press, 1994.

Albright, William Foxwell. *From the Stone Age to Christianity*, 2nd ed. Garden City, NY: Doubleday Anchor, 1957.

Allen, Mark, and Ruth Burrows. *Letters on Prayer: An Exchange on Prayer and Faith*. London: Sheed and Ward, 1999.

Andrewes, Lancelot. *Pattern of Catechetical Doctrine*, in *Minor Works of Bishop Andrewes*. Oxford: Parker, 1846.

Appleton, George, ed. *The Oxford Book of Prayer*. New York and Oxford: The University Press, 1986.

Arberry, A. J. *Sufism: An Account of the Mystics of Islam*. London: George Allen & Unwin, 1950.

Bacovin, Helen (trans.). *The Way of a Pilgrim and the Pilgrim Continues His Way: A New Translation*. New York: Doubleday Image, 1978.

Barkway, Lumsden, and Lucy Menzies, eds. *Anthology of the Love of God from the Writings of Evelyn Underhill*. Wilton, CT and Toronto: Morehouse-Barlow, 1976.

Barrett, C.K. *The Gospel According to St. John*. London: SPCK, 1956.

Bloom, Archbishop Anthony. *Beginning to Pray*. New York: Paulist Press, 1970.

———. (as Metropolitan Anthony of Sourozh). *Living Prayer*. Springfield, IL: Templegate, 1966.

Boorstin, Daniel J. *The Creators: A History of Heroes of the Imagination*. New York: Random House, 1992.

Boulding, Maria. *The Coming of God*. Collegeville, MN: Liturgical Press, 1982.

———. *Prayer: Our Journey Home*. Ann Arbor: Servant Books, 1979.

Bradley, David G. *A Guide to the World's Religions*. Englewood Cliffs, NJ: Prentice-Hall, 1963.

Bretzke, James T. *Consecrated Phrases: A Latin Theological Dictionary*. Collegeville, MN: The Liturgical Press, 1998.

Bright, William. *Ancient Collects*. London: J. H. and James Parker, 1864.

Brock, Sebastian (trans.). *The Syriac Fathers on Prayer and the Spiritual Life*. Kalamazoo: Cistercian Publications, 1987.

Brown, Raymond E., SS, Joseph A. Fitzmyer, SJ, and Roland E. Murphy, OCarm. *The New Jerome Biblical Commentary*. Englewood Cliffs, NJ: Prentice Hall, 1990.

Bruderhof Communities (as compilers). *Bread and Wine: Readings for Lent and Easter*. Farmington, PA: Plough Publishing, 2003.

Burrows, Ruth. *Interior Castle Explored*. London: Sheed and Ward, 1981.

Butler, B. C. *Prayer in Practice*. Baltimore: Helicon, 1961.

Butler, Samuel (trans.). *Homer's Odyssey*. London: Cape, 1922 (orig. trans., 1900).

Capalbo, Battistina, ed. *Praying with Saint Teresa* (trans. Paula Clifford). London: SPCK/Triangle, 1988.

Chesterton, G. K. *What's Wrong with the World?* London: Cassell, 1910.

Christian Classics Ethereal Library, version 4. A CD-Rom marketed by Calvin College in Grand Rapids, MI. The CD contains 37 volumes of Early Church Fathers; Scripture translations and commentaries; and over 200 classic Christian works from antiquity to modern times.

Clark, Walter Houston. *The Psychology of Religion: An Introduction to Religious Experience and Behavior*. New York: Macmillan, 1958.

Colledge, Edmund, OSA, and James Walsh, SJ (trans.). *Julian of Norwich: Showings*. New York: Paulist Press, 1978.

Collins, Owed, ed. *Prayers and Readings for All Occasions*. London: Fount, 2002.

Contemporary Office Book: The Daily Office, Rite Two (includes the Book of Common Prayer). New York: Church Hymnal Corp., 1995.

Cullmann, Oscar (trans. John Bowden). *Prayer in the New Testament*. Minneapolis: Augsburg Fortress Press, 1995.

Daniélou, Jean (trans. David Louis Schindler, Jr.). *Prayer: The Mission of the Church*. Edinburgh: T&T Clark, 1996.

de Caussade, Jean-Pierre (trans. John Beevers). *Abandonment to Divine Providence*. Garden City: Doubleday Image, 1975.

Deiss, Lucien (trans. Benet Weatherhead). *Early Sources of the Liturgy*, 2nd ed. Collegeville, MN: Liturgical Press, 1975.

Delehaye, Hippolyte. *Les origines du culte des martyrs*. Brussels: Société des Bollandistes, 1933.

Donin, Rabbi Hayim Halevy. *To Be a Jew*. New York: Basic Books, 1972.

Downey, Michael, ed. *The New Dictionary of Catholic Spirituality*. Collegeville, MN: The Liturgical Press/Michael Glazier, 1993.

Dru, Alexander (trans.). *The Journals of Kierkegaard, 1834–1854*. London: Collins/Fontana, 1958.

Dumoulin, Heinrich (trans. Joseph S. O'Leary). *Understanding Buddhism: Key Themes.* New York: Weatherhill, 1994.

Edwards, Jonathan. *Works,* vol. 2. New Haven: Yale University Press, 1959.

Einstein, Albert. *Ideas and Opinions.* New York: Bonanza, 1988 (reprint of 1954 edition from Crown Publishers).

Eliade, Mircea (trans. Willard R. Trask). *A History of Religious Ideas,* 3 vols. Chicago: University of Chicago Press, 1978–1985.

Farmer, David Hugh, general consultant editor. *Butler's Lives of the Saints: New Full Edition,* 12 vols. (one for each month). Tunbridge Wells (UK): Burns & Oates, 1995; Collegeville, MN: The Liturgical Press, 1995.

Faulkner, Raymond O., trans. *The Egyptian Book of the Dead: The Book of Going Forth By Day,* 2nd ed., revised. San Francisco: Chronicle Books, 1998.

Feuerbach, Ludwig (trans. Marian [*sic*] Evans). *The Essence of Christianity.* London: John Chapman, 1854; reprint, New York: Harper & Row, 1957. Orig. publ.: *Das Wesen des Christenthums.* Leipzig: Otto Wigand, 1841.

Field, Claud (trans.). *Meister Eckhart's Sermons.* London: H. R. Allenson, 1909.

Fleiss, Hugh. *Essential Monastic Wisdom.* HarperSanFrancisco, 1999.

Forsyth, P. T. *The Soul of Prayer.* London: Independent Press, 1916.

Fowler, Harold North. *Plato in Twelve Volumes,* vol. 1. Cambridge, MA: Harvard University Press, 1966.

Freedman, David Noel, ed. *The Anchor Bible Dictionary,* 6 vols. New York: Doubleday, 1992.

Gandhi, M. K. *My God.* Ahmedabad (India): Navajivan Publishing House, 1962.

———. *Pathway to God* (compiled by M. S. Deshpande). Ahmedabad (India): Navajivan Publishing House, 1971.

Ganss, George E., ed. *Ignatius of Loyola: Spiritual Exercises and Selected Works.* Mahwah, NJ: Paulist Press, 1991.

Gordon, Matthew S. *Islam: Origins, Practices, Holy Texts, Sacred Persons, Sacred Places.* New York: Oxford University Press, 2002.

Gossen, Gary H., ed., in collaboration with Miguel León-Portilla. *South and Meso-American Native Spirituality: From the Cult of the Feathered Serpent to the Theology of Liberation* (volume 4 of *World Spirituality: An Encyclopedic History of the Religious Quest*). New York: Crossroad/Herder, 1997.

Graham, Dom Aelred. *Zen Catholicism.* New York: Crossroad, 1999 (orig. New York: Harcourt, Brace & World, 1963).

Greenwell, Dora. *Two Friends.* London: Gibbings, 1894.

Griffin, Emilie. *Clinging: The Experience of Prayer.* New York: McCracken Press, 1994.

————. *Doors into Prayer: An Invitation*. Brewster, MA: Paraclete Press, 2001.

Grou, Jean-Nicholas (trans. Joseph Dalby). *How to Pray*. Cambridge, UK: James Clarke & Co., 1995.

Guardini, Romano (trans. Elinor Castendyk Briefs). *The Lord*. Chicago: Henry Regnery, 1954.

Guardini, Romano (trans. Ada Lane). *The Spirit of the Liturgy*. New York: Sheed & Ward, 1935.

Guyon, Jeanne Marie Bouvier de la Mothe-Guyon, *La vie de madame J.M.B. de la Mothe-Guyon*. Paris: Elibron, 2001; orig. Paris: Les Librairies associés, 1792.

Hamman, Adalbert, OFM, ed. *Early Christian Prayers* (trans. Walter Mitchell). Chicago: Regnery, 1961.

Hammarskjöld, Dag. *A Room of Quiet: The United Nations Meditation Room*. New York: The United Nations, 1971.

Harris, Paul, ed. *The Fire of Silence and Stillness*. Springfield, IL: Templegate, 1996.

Harris, Paul T. *Frequently Asked Questions About Christian Meditation*. Toronto: Novalis, 2001.

Heiler, Friedrich (trans. Samuel McComb, "with the assistance of J. Edgar Park"). *Prayer: A Study in the History and Psychology of Prayer*. London and New York: Oxford University Press, 1932; reprint, Oxford: Oneworld, 1997. Orig. publ. *Das Gebet: Eine religionsgeschichtliche und religionspsychologische Untersuchung*. München: Ernst Reinhardt, 1921.

Hick, John. *Evil and the God of Love*. New York: Harper and Row, 1966.

Hillesum, Etty. *An Interrupted Life: The Diaries, 1941–1943* (trans. A. Pomerans). New York: Pantheon, 1984.

————. *Letters from Westbork*. New York: Pantheon, 1986.

Hollings, Michael, ed. *Daily Readings with St. Thérèse of Lisieux*. Springfield, IL: Templegate, 1987.

Houlden, J. L., ed. *Austin Farrer: The Essential Sermons*. London: SPCK, 1991.

Hudleston, Dom Roger, OSB, ed. *The Spiritual Letters of Dom John Chapman, OSB*, 2nd ed. London: Sheed and Ward, 1938.

Huxley, Aldous. *The Perennial Philosophy*. London: Chatto & Windus, 1946.

James, William. *The Varieties of Religious Experience* (The Gifford Lectures at Edinburgh University, 1902–1904). New York: Modern Library, 1994; reprint of the 1902 edition.

Jampolsky, Gerald G. *Forgiveness: The Greatest Healer of All*. Beyond Words, 1999.

————. *Good-bye to Guilt: Releasing Fear through Forgiveness*. New York: Bantam, 1988.

John XXIII, Pope. *Journal of a Soul* (trans. Dorothy White). New York: Doubleday, 1965; rev., 1980.

Johnson, Luke Timothy. *The Acts of the Apostles*, vol. 5 of the *Sacra Pagina* series (ed. Daniel J. Harrington, SJ). Collegeville, MN: Michael Glazier/Liturgical Press, 1992.

Johnston, William. *Arise, My Love: Mysticism for a New Era*. Maryknoll, NY: Orbis Books, 2000.

Jowett, Benjamin (trans.). *The Dialogues of Plato: The Euthyphro, Apology, Crito, Phaedo*. New York: Prometheus Books, 1988.

————. (trans.). *The Dialogues of Plato: The Timaeus and The Critias*. New York: Liberal Arts Press, 1949.

Kadloubovsky, E., and E. M. Palmer (trans.). *The Art of Prayer: An Orthodox Anthology*, compiled by Igumen Chariton of Valamo, rev. ed. London: Faber and Faber, 1997.

Kavanaugh, Kieran, and Otilio Rodriguez (trans.). *The Collected Works of St. John of the Cross*. Washington, D.C.: ICS Publications, 1974.

————. *The Collected Works of St. Teresa of Ávila*, 3 vols. Washington, D.C.: ICS Publications, 1976–85 (2nd ed. rev. of volume 1, 1987).

Keating, Thomas. *The Better Part: Stages of Contemplative Living*. New York: Continuum, 2000.

————. *Intimacy with God*. New York: Crossroad, 1994.

Kelley, C. F. (trans.). *The Book of the Poor in Spirit*. London: Longmans Green, 1954.

Kendall, Louise, and R. T. Kendall, eds. *Great Christian Prayers*. London: Hodder & Stoughton, 2000.

Kennedy, Robert E. *Zen Spirit, Christian Spirit*. New York: Continuum, 1997.

Kirzner, Rabbi Yitzchock, with Lisa Aiken, Ph.D. *The Art of Jewish Prayer*. Northvale, NJ: Jason Aronson, 1991.

Kittel, Gerhard, and Gerhard Friedrich, eds. *Theological Dictionary of the New Testament* (trans. and abridged in one vol. by Geoffrey W. Bromiley). Grand Rapids: Eerdmans, 2000. Orig. publ. in 9 German vols.: *Theologisches Wörterbuch zum Neuen Testament*. Stuttgart: Kohlhammer Verlag, 1933–1973; later in 9 unabridged English vols.: *Theological Dictionary of the New Testament* (also Eerdmans: 1964–1974).

Knox, Ronald. *The Window in the Wall*. New York: Sheed & Ward, 1956.

Komonchak, Joseph A., Mary Collins, Dermot A. Lane, eds. *The New Dictionary of Theology*. Wilmington, DE: Michael Glazier, 1987.

Kubose, Gyomay M. *The Center Within*. Compton, CA: Heian International, 1986.

Küng, Hans. *Credo: The Apostles' Creed Explained for Today* (trans. John Bowden). New York: Doubleday, 1993.

———. *On Being a Christian* (trans. Edward Quinn). Garden City, NY: Doubleday, 1974.

Law, William. *Works*, 9 vols. London: Richardson, 1792; reprinted London: G. B. Morgan, 1892–1893.

Lawrence of the Resurrection, Brother. *The Practice of the Presence of God* (trans. John J. Delaney). New York: Doubleday Image, 1977.

Leech, Kenneth. *True Prayer: An Introduction to Christian Spirituality*. London: Sheldon Press, 1980.

Lewis, C. S. *Prayer: Letters to Malcolm*. London: Collins/Fontana, 1983.

Liddon, Henry Parry. *Some Elements of Religion*, 6th ed. London: Longmans, Green, 1898.

Livingstone, E. A. *The Oxford Dictionary of the Christian Church*, 3rd ed. Oxford: The University Press, 1997.

Longenecker, Richard N., ed. *Into God's Presence: Prayer in the New Testament*. Grand Rapids: William B. Eerdmans, 2001.

Lonsdale, David, SJ. *Eyes to See, Ears to Hear*. London: Darton, Longman, Todd, 1990.

Louth, Andrew (trans.). *Early Christian Writings: The Apostolic Fathers*. New York: Penguin, 1987.

Luibheid, Colm (trans.). *John Cassian: Conferences*. New York: Paulist Press, 1985.

Main, John. *The Heart of Creation*. New York: Continuum, 1998.

———. *Word into Silence*. New York: Continuum, 1980.

Maqsood, Ruqaiyyah Waris. *The Muslim Prayer Encyclopedia: A Complete Guide to Prayers as Taught by the Prophet Muhammad*. New Delhi: Goodword Books, 1998.

Marcel, Gabriel (trans. Katharine Farrer). *Being and Having*. New York: Harper Torchbooks, 1965.

Mays, James L., ed. *Harper's Bible Commentary*. HarperSanFrancisco, 1988.

McBrien, Richard P. *Catholicism*, rev. ed. HarperSanFrancisco, 1994.

McGinn, Bernard. *The Mystical Thought of Meister Eckhart: The Man from Whom God Hid Nothing*. New York: Herder & Herder/Crossroad, 2002.

———, ed. *Meister Eckhart: Teacher and Preacher*. Mahwah, NJ: Paulist Press, 1986.

Menzies, Lucy, ed. *Collected Papers of Evelyn Underhill*. London: Longmans, Green, 1946.

Merton, Thomas. *Contemplative Prayer*. New York: Doubleday Image, 1971.

———. *New Seeds of Contemplation*. New York: New Directions, 1961.

Migne, J.-P. *Patrologia, Series Graeca*, vols. 11 and 64. Paris: Garnier, 1860.
————. *Patrologia, Series Latina*, vol. 16. Paris: Garnier, 1967.

Mooney, Christopher F., SJ, ed. *Prayer: The Problem of Dialogue with God* (Papers of the 1968 Bea Institute Symposium at Loyola College, Shrub Oak, New York). Paramus, NJ: Paulist Press, 1969.

Morshead, E.D.A. (trans.). *The Suppliants, by Aeschylus*. London: Macmillan, 1908.

Muggeridge, Kitty, ed. *Spiritual Letters of Jean-Pierre de Caussade*. London: Morehouse, 1988.

Mursell, Gordon. *English Spirituality*. 2 vols: *From Earliest Times to 1700* and *From 1700 to the Present Day*. Louisville: Westminster John Knox, 2001.

Newman, John Henry. *Parochial and Plain Sermons* (1891 ed.). San Francisco: Ignatius Press, 1997.

Oates, Wayne E. *Nurturing Silence in a Noisy Heart*. Minneapolis: Augsburg Fortress Press, 1996.

O'Connor, Flannery. *The Complete Stories*. New York: Farrar, Straus and Giroux, 1971.

Okumura, Augustine Ichiro, OCD. *Awakening to Prayer*. Washington, D.C.: Institute of Carmelite Studies, 1994.

Otto, Rudolf (trans. John W. Harvey). *The Idea of the Holy*. New York: Galaxy, 1958. Orig. publ. *Das Heilige*. Gotha: Klotz, 1917.

Pannikar, Raimundo, ed. and trans. *The Vedic Experience*. Berkeley: University of California Press, 1977.

Peers, E. Allison (trans.). *Interior Castle, by St. Teresa of Ávila*. New York: Doubleday Image, 1961.

————. *The Life of Teresa of Jesus*. New York: Doubleday Image, 1960.

Pennington, M. Basil. *Centering Prayer*. New York: Doubleday, 1980.

Pennington, M. Basil, Alan Jones, and Mark Booth. *The Living Testament: The Essential Writings of Christianity since the Bible*. San Francisco: Harper & Row, 1985.

Petuchowski, Jakob J. *Understanding Jewish Prayer*. New York: KTAV, 1972.

Philippe, Thomas (trans. Carmine Buonaiuto, ed. Edward D. O'Connor). *The Contemplative Life*. New York: Crossroad, 1990.

Picard, Max. *The World of Silence*. Chicago: Henry Regnery, 1952 (trans. Stanley Godman from *Die Welt des Schweigens*, Erlenbach-Zürich: Eugen Rentsch Verlag, 1948).

Posner, Raphael, Uri Kaploun, and Shalom Cohen, eds. *Jewish Liturgy: Prayer and Synagogue Service through the Ages*. New York: Leon Amiel, 1975.

Rahner, Karl (trans. William V. Dych). *Foundations of Christian Faith: An Introduction to the Idea of Christianity.* New York: Crossroad, 1996; orig., Freiburg im Breisgau: Herder Verlag, 1976.

Rahner, Karl (trans. Bruce W. Gillette). *The Need and the Blessing of Prayer.* Collegeville, MN: Liturgical Press, 1997.

Renard, John. *101 Questions and Answers on Islam.* New York: Paulist Press, 1998.

————, ed. *Windows on the House of Islam: Muslim Sources on Spirituality and the Religious Life.* Berkeley and Los Angeles: University of California Press, 1998.

Rosenbaum, I. J. *The Holocaust and Halakhah.* New York: Ktav Publishing, 1976.

Ruinart, Theodor. *Acta Martyrum: Opera ac studio collecta, selecta atque illustrata. Accedunt praeterea in hac editione acta ss. firmi et rustici ex optimis codicibus Veronensibus. Editio juxta exemplar Veronese novis curis quam emendatissime recusa.* Regensburg: Manz, 1950.

Ryan, John K. (trans.). *The Confessions of St. Augustine.* Garden City: Doubleday Image, 1960.

Ryan, Regina Sara. *Praying Dangerously: Radical Reliance on God.* Prescott, AZ: Hohm Press, 2001.

Sacks, David. *A Dictionary of the Ancient Greek World.* New York: Oxford University Press, 1995.

Schweizer, Eduard (trans. David E. Green). *The Good News According to Matthew.* Atlanta: John Knox Press, 1975.

Shaw, George Bernard. *Saint Joan, Major Barbara, Androcles and the Lion.* New York: Modern Library, 1956.

Sogyal Rinpoche. *The Spirit of Buddhism: The Future of Dharma in the West.* HarperSanFrancisco, 2003.

Spoto, Donald. *Christ's Preaching to the Dead: An Exegesis of I Peter 3, 19 and 4,6.* Dissertation for the degree of Doctor of Philosophy in the Department of Theology at Fordham University: New York, 1970. Also available through University Microfilms, Ann Arbor MI.

————. *The Hidden Jesus: A New Life.* New York: St. Martin's, 1998.

Swenson, David F., and Lillian Marvin Swenson. *Kierkegaard: Edifying Discourses.* Minneapolis: Augsburg Publishing, 1948.

Tagore, Rabindranath. *Gitanjali.* London: Macmillan, 1929.

Teilhard de Chardin, Pierre. *The Divine Milieu* (trans. Bernard Wall). New York: Harper & Row, 1960.

Thibert, Péronne Marie, V.H.M. (trans.). *Francis de Sales, Jane de Chantal: Letters of Spiritual Direction.* New York: Paulist Press, 1988.

Thomas Aquinas. *Summa Theologica,* 3 vols. (2nd rev. ed., 1920, trans. Dominican Fathers of the English Province). New York: Benziger, 1947.

Tillich, Paul. *The Shaking of the Foundations*. New York: Charles Scribner's Sons, 1948.

Ulanov, Ann, and Barry Ulanov. *Primary Speech: A Psychology of Prayer*. Atlanta: John Knox Press, 1982.

Ulanov, Barry. *The Prayers of St. Augustine*. Minneapolis: Seabury Press, 1983.

Underhill, Evelyn. *Concerning the Inner Life*. Oxford: Oneworld, 1995.

———. *The Essentials of Mysticism*. New York: Dutton, 1960.

———. *The Life of the Spirit and the Life of Today*. San Francisco: Harper & Row, 1986.

———. *Mysticism*. New York: Doubleday Image, 1990.

———. *The Mystics of the Church*. New York: Schocken Books, 1964.

———. *The Spiritual Life*. Oxford: Oneworld, 1999.

Veyne, Paul (trans. Arthur Goldhammer). *The Roman Empire*. Cambridge, MA: Belknap Press/Harvard, 1997.

von Balthasar, Hans Urs (trans. Graham Harrison). *Prayer*. San Francisco: Ignatius Press, 1986. Orig. publ. *Das Betrachtende Gebet*. Einsiedeln (Switzerland): Johannes Verlag, 1955.

Vouaux, L. *Les Actes de Pierre*. Paris: Letouzey, 1922.

Wakefield, Gordon S. *A Dictionary of Christian Spirituality*. London: SCM Press, 1983.

Walsh, James, SJ (trans.). *The Cloud of Unknowing*. Mahwah: Paulist Press, 1982.

Walshe, M. O'C. *Meister Eckhart: German Sermons and Treatises*, 2 vols. London and Dulverton: Watkins, 1979 and 1981.

Ward, Benedicta (trans.). *The Prayers and Meditations of St. Anselm with the Proslogion*. London: Penguin, 1973.

———. *Sayings of the Desert Fathers*. Oxford: Mowbray, 1975.

Ware, Kallistos. *The Philokalia*. London: Faber & Faber, 1983.

Weil, Simone (trans. Emma Craufurd). *Waiting on God*. London: Collins/Fontana, 1971.

Wesley, John. *A Plain Account of Christian Perfection*. London: G. Story, 1801.

Witner, Shohama Harris, and Jonathan Omer-Man. *Worlds of Jewish Prayer*. Northvale, NJ: Jason Aronson, 1993.

Wolters, Clifton (trans.). *The Cloud of Unknowing*. London: Penguin, 1961.

Wright, John H., SJ. *A Theology of Christian Prayer*. New York: Pueblo, 1987.

Index